Ka Ab Ba (Kabala)

Building The Lighted Temple
The Spiritual B-Ark

Metaphysical Keys to The Tree Of Life *& Oracle Keys to Dis-spelling Illusion*

The Ausarianization of Consciousness Tablet *Series 1 – A.C.T.S. 1*
The Spiritual Journey of Unfolding Consciousness

by
Dr. Terri Nelson
Nteri Renenet Elson

First Edition: 2000
Second Edition: 2003
Copyright © 2003 Dr Terri Nelson. Library of Congress Cataloging in Publication Data
All Rights Reserved. No part of this book maybe used or reproduced in any manner whatsoever without written permission except in the case of brief quotations embodied in critical articles and reviews. All inquiries may be forwarded to the address below.

ISBN: 0-9659600-9-9
Printed in the United States of America

Published by: The Academy of Kemetic Education, Right Relationship Maat, Inc.
53 Cedar St.
Mattapan, MA 02126

My deepest appreciation is given to S. R. D., one of the Initiates we are blessed to have in our midst, for her heartfelt steadfastness and labor in the editing phases of these Works.

The author is available for group lectures and individual consultations. For further information or to order additional copies contact:

АЖЕ

The Academy of Kemetic Education, Right Relationship Maat Inc.

The Academy for
Right Relationship and Right Knowledge

African Origin of The Ancient/Egyptian Wisdom

Awakening Consciousness   African Knowledge   Ausarian Enlightenment

The Knowledge & Education That Awakens 1st Eye Awareness into
The Metaphysics, Art & Science of Daily Living
Leading to Spiritual Transformation, Right Relationship, Soul Purpose Living, & Service
Classes Held At: 53 Cedar St., Mattapan, MA 02126

www.rrrk.net

(617) 296 - 7797

contact@rightrelationshiprightknowledge.net

<table>
<tr><td>

Metaphysical Key To:
Maa Kheru Symbol (front cover)

</td></tr>
</table>

When you have come toward the end of this book these symbols will be seen again and more deeply understood.

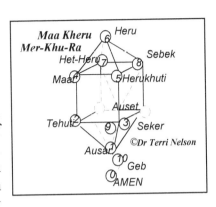

Maa Kheru Symbol:

There is no death. There is only the transmigration of the Soul from life into greater Life. Death is the seeming discontinuity of consciousness – a cutting into pieces of the ALL Consciousness. This is symbolized as the broken body of Ausar, cut into fourteen parts. At each 'death' the disciple appears again and again within the Hall of Amenta, that his heart may be weighed and thereby tested. Each time his heart has fallen short of being as light as the feather of Maat, he has to mount again the wheel of birth and death and fall back into the material realm. This cycle repeats itself as we undergo the Initiatory process. Higher states of consciousness are achieved – until the state of God Conscious is the stabilized Realization. The disciple, finally stands within the Hall of Amenta and is _found_ Maa Kheru. Thus, you are justified as living in truth, morally and in total equilibrium with the laws of God.

AUM

As Heru sphere 6 in the Tree of Life, you are the Word, that re-becomes THE WORD in your long pilgrimage to reconstruct the broken body of Ausar. Through the sounding of this powerful Hekau, (word of Power), the 'U' which saw duality, comes to see as One and affirms: 'I AM', the Divine marriage between Ausar-sphere 1 and Auset – sphere 9, Father/Mother, Spirit/Matter.

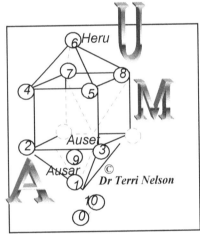

KaAbBa, MerKaBa, Chariot, Symbols:

If we dis-spell the word Chariot (see Metaphysical Keys to Dis-spelling Illusion) it reveals the 'Rota(ating) eye or 'I' of Hrakti 'O' (Herukti) that sees full circle. It is the eye of Heru on the double Hori(zon). Perched within the whole moving geometry within the mind of God:

1. You hold and see all within your Ab – heart.
2. You Mer (Mirror) the Image and Likeness of Father/Mother God – KaBa.
3. You become the Chariot of God.
4. You are now _impulsed from an effortless stream wherein the Will of God is known and_ your co-creative Son/Daughter Sun-Ship is made manifest – _The Lighted Temple is Built._

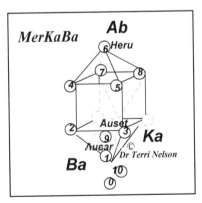

About The Author
Terri Nelson, PhD.E, L.I.C.S.W., M.S.W., M.S.E.P., Shækem RA АЖЕ (Reiki) Master
aka Queen Nteri Renenet Elson
The Neteru revealing Harvest to the Sons and Daughters of God

Dr. Terri Nelson is a Holistic Psychotherapist, Metaphysician, Priestess of Kemet and Teacher of the African origins of the Ancient wisdom. She is co-founder of, *The Academy of Kemetic Education, Right Relationship Right Knowledge, Maat, Inc.* where she teaches an African Centered Model for Psychological, Spiritual, and Character development which is underpinned by the History of Ancient Africa/Kemet (Egypt) and the Diaspora as a way of Self knowledge, healing and health. Her classes on the Application of the Ancient Wisdom in Modern Daily Living are helping others find solutions to life challenges. A specialty area that she brings penetrative insight to is, *The Spiritual and Psychological Journey of Unfolding Consciousness out of Africa.* Dr. Nteri is a gifted Wordsmith and Mtu Ntr Symbologist and has given important Keys for Dis-spelling Illusion in her books. She has a Bachelor of Science in Psychology (B.S); a Masters in Social Work (M.S.W); a Masters in the Science of Esoteric Psychology (M.S.E.P); and a Doctor of Esoteric Philosophy (PhD.E) with a concentration in Metaphysical and Kemetic/Egyptian Studies. She is an Independent researcher of the Ancient Wisdom teachings and was a member of The Black Knostic Study Group for several years under the late Dr. Alfred Ligon. She has had the honor of traveling to Kemet (Egypt) under the guidance of Elder Dr.Yosef ben-Jochannan and Dr. Clinton Crawford; and to Ghana under the guidance of Drs. Leonard and Rosalind Jeffries and Professor James Small. She is a Shækem Ra-АЖЕ Master. As teacher and eternal student of the Ancient wisdom her years of experience have made her a firsthand witness to that which both fetters and liberates the Soul in its Spiritual Journey. She has been garnering and distributing the wisdom and tools for Ausarian Spiritual Transformation and Resurrection or ASTR (STAR).

She has worked in the Behavioral/Mental Health field since 1980 and her training has included both traditional and alternative approaches to healing. Her working experience includes providing service within the Department of Mental Health and three Medical Associate Practices, which includes Harvard Vanguard Medical Associates where she worked as a Clinician in the Adult mental health department. She has worked many years providing psychotherapeutic services in the Massachusetts Correctional Institutions and in hospitals.

She has also had a private practice where she uses a variety of healing methods. She provides counseling and consultation to: individuals, couples, families, groups and agencies. Co-counseling together, she and her husband, Lester Nelson, Min., specialize in Relationship work with Couples, Individuals, Families and Groups.

Dr Terri Nelson is author of: *Ka Ab Ba Building The Lighted Temple; Secrets of Race and Consciousness; On The Way To Finding Your Soulmate; The Right Relationship Workbook and The Forgiveness Process Workbook.* She has given lectures nationally and internationally which includes: the Association for the Study of Classical African Civilization (ASCAC); Indigenous African Healers Conference; First World Alliance in New York; Institute for the Study of Race and Culture; The Melanin Conference; Sankofa; Mtw Ntr; etc.

Table of Contents

*Ka*Ba As Unity. What is the arising of the Number 1?

Ka and Ba as Duality. What is the arising of the Number 2?
What is the relationship between Ka and Ba?
How is Ka Spirit and Matter? What is this Double Nature?
What is BKA?
Ka Ab Ba As Trinity. What is the arising of the Number 3?
Metaphysical Key To: Number 1, 2 and 3. Three-Oneness KaAbBa. The
Divine Trinity. The 3 Aspects of Divinity. Ausar, Auset and Heru.
Three Aspects of Divinity. Spirit/Soul – Soul/Consciousness – Spirit/Matter
Continuum.
What are you as the Sun-Son/Daughter becoming fully conscious of?
Ka, Holy Ghost, Stool and Tool of God.

Metaphysical Key To: The Number 7. The 7 Planes of Consciousness. 7 Division
of The Solar Systemic Planes.
Metaphysical Key To: The Number 7. The 7 Souls of Ra. The 7 Soul Divisions
or 7 Divisions of Spirit. The Septentary Nature of Man and Creation. Understanding
the Ba, Khu, Sekhem, Ab, Sahu, Ka/Khaibit, and Khab Soul bodies.
Metaphysical Key To: Understanding the 7 Ra(y) Energies.
What is my Soul Ra(y) Energy or Soul Purpose?
If there are 7 Souls, why is Heru – sphere 6, or the Ab Soul, a key division
in my Spiritual Constitution that defines my Soul Ra(y) Purpose?
The Seven Principles of Kwanzaa.
The Seven Energy Centers/Chakras.

Metaphysical Key To: Affirming Lighted Temple Building – ASTR Daily Practice.
How are You Building The Lighted Temple?
How do you raise your vibration and…?
The Character or Personality/Temple is composed of three vehicles or bodies.
Ausarian Spiritual Transformation and Resurrection is transmuting the sub-stance of your
vehicles …
Metaphysical Key To: The 3 Soul bodies or Vehicles of Manifestation
Reascension Into Sacredness. *Song.*
Metaphysical Key To: Character dis-spelled is *Ka-Ra-Acter and Ka-Erect-er.*
What is Personality and Character?
What Are Some Of the 3rd Aspect Functions of The Ka-erecter or Ka-Ra-acter?
How is personal will used?
What happens when the Ka-erect-ter is brought under the Higher Ab and Ba Soul
program?
Metaphysical Key To: The 42 Admonitions. The Laws of Maat.
Metaphysical Key To: Understanding Ba - Ausar. Ba, Khu, Sekhem.

Metaphysical Key To: Understanding Ka -. Auset. Khab, Ka/Khaibit, Sahu.
Metaphysical Key To: Understanding Ab - Heru.   Ab.

What Is The Urgency For Making Rapid Preparation?

African Cosmology, African Centered Education
The Psychological and Spiriutal Journey of Unfolding Consciousness
Metaphysics and Mysteries

Kemet (also spelled Kmt, Kamit) is land within the Ancient Nile Vallcy Civilation in Africa and its people were called the Kemetians. This land and its people would later be re-named Egypt and Egyptians respectively, by the Greeks. These Kemites, our African Ancestors, used picture images or ideagraphs from nature all around them to communicate ideas, which is the language they called MTU NTR, MTW NTR, METU NETER or MEDU NETER. These symbols were later re-named Hieroglyphics by the Greeks. The Metu Neter, Ka Ab Ba, are pictured below.

Ka **Ab** **Ba**

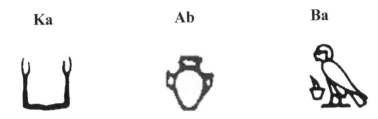

Our African Ancestors were Masters in the 'Science of the Soul' and 'Journey of the Soul'. They were Master Psychologists, Spiritual Practitoners, Metaphysicians or what may be called here, Kemeticians. They have given us these 3 primary Metu Neter for:
1. Understanding the Spiritual and Physical Anatomy of Man., Woman and Cosmos
2. Unlocking the Psychological and Spiritual Journey in Unfolding Consciousness
3. Unfettering the Soul from that which would threaten to impede it in its Journey

Why did our African Ancestors focus within these 3 Primary Metu Neter - *Ka Ab Ba*?
To answer this question the following analogy may best serve. When we 'click onto' an icon on our Windows computer screen, whole documents are opened up and a panorama of information is revealed to our poised and awaiting mind or mental field. By analology, the 3 primary Metu Neter are like these icons which were used by our Kemetic Ancestors. As we 'click' in turn onto the Metu Neter *Ka, Ab*, and *Ba*, the Psychological and Spiritual Journey in Unfolding Consciousness is revealed. These ideagraphs or pictures are the 'Divine idea and speech' which open our 1st eye and aid us to glimpse the Whole Moving Geometry within in the Mind of God. Thus, as the Journey unfolds, we are able to see the changing states in our consciousness which lead to changing states in our physical World.

On the Psycho/Spiritual Journey in Unfolding Consciousness what are you as the Sun-Son/Daughter becoming fully conscious of?
For the Kemetians Ka means Spirit. In the Metaphysical Keys that follow, you will see that, Ka – Spirit, takes of the substance of ITSELF to see ITSELF in form. Ka – Spirit, takes of the substance of ITSELF to have consciousness in form. Ka – Spirit, takes of the substance of ITSELF and begins to differentiate itself in/as Spirit-matter. This is one of the many Divine paradoxes. As much as Spirit is UNLIMITED and UNCONDITIONED it asserts its right to limit itself in form or matter in order to gain conscious experience of ITSELF. In various grades of

material form, IT – Ka, sees ITSELF. It is in *the seeing of ITSELF* that consciousness is born. Thus we are made Divine and human, Spiritual and material. For the Kemetians Ba means Soul and Soul is consciousness. We are told that Ka - Spirit precedes Ba Soul. This is expressed in the following accordingly: Alvin Boyd Kuhn, *The Lost Light*, p. 588.

"The Ba comes forth upon earth to do the will of its Ka.

This is derived from the Ritual Text of the *Prt Em Hru* which is expressed accordingly: E.A. Wallis Budge. *The Egyptian Book of the Dead*, p. 359.

The souls come forth to do the will of their Ka's and the soul of Ausar Ani cometh forth to do the will of his Ka.

The Soul-Ba comes forth upon the Earth to do the will of its Spirit-Ka. For the Kemetians Ab symbolizes the human heart. The heart is the seat of the Soul, the conscience and growing Self conscious identity. The Ab Soul is the conscious experience of how Spirit and Matter are relating. As man's consciousness develops he must also develop a 'conscience'. This is Heru or the Karest/Christ principle within you that guides you to be and act in accord with the Universal Law of Right Relationship. Through the relating aspect of Ab, the 'seeming' duality between Spirit-Matter with its myriad objective forms in play and display as Ba Ka are seen as ONE. Thus through Ab Soul consciousness the same One True Self is seen in every other Self.

This is expressed in the diagram at right. On our Psycho/Spiritual Journey in Unfolding Consciousness as Heru - sphere 6 in the Tree of Life, we make our descent into material life conditions. As Heru we are Sun-Son/Daughter. On our return journey, we make our hard, arduous climb of re-ascent Home again, into the Spiritual realms. You are becoming fully conscious of the perfect relationship between Father and Mother and Spirit and Matter. To become fully conscious is to live the

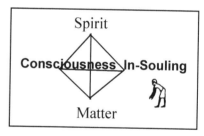

consciousness of Ausar Ba - that we are made in the Image and Likeness of God and All SELVES are but the ONE True Indivisible SELF.

By following and reclaiming their ways the Ancestors have taught me to be a Kemetc Psychologist and Spiritual Practitioner. Let us now peer within the wisdom of our African Ancestors.

Ka   **Ab**   **Ba**

Programs Offered By The Academy Of Kemetic Education Include:

Ka Ab Ba Building The Lighted Temple and Secrets of Race & Consciousness 1st, 2nd & 3rd Degree Certification Programs

The **Ka Ab Ba Building The Lighted Temple and Secrets of Race & Consciousness 1st, 2nd & 3rd Degree Certification Programs** are an African Centered Model for Psychological, Spiritual, and Character, development which is underpinned by the History of Ancient Africa/Egypt/Kemet, and the Diaspora as a way of Self knowledge, healing and health. Each Certification is a 9 month Academic year long Program offering advanced Training for Educators, Human Service Providers, African Conscious Practitioners, Clinicians, Counselors, and those who would like to deepen their Spiritual Journey. These Programs teach the application & practice of Ancient African Wisdom in Modern Daily Living. They impart understanding of how our African Ancestors were Masters in: a) the Science of Mind, Body and Soul b) developing Divine qualities which they called the Neter or Neteru and c) detailing the anatomy of the Soul, its Journey, and how to fulfill ones life purpose. They are based on the books authored by Dr Terri Nelson, 1) *Ka Ab Ba Building The Lighted Temple/Metaphysical Keys to the Tree of Life* and 2) *The Secrets of Race and Consciousness*. These Programs culminate with the opportunity for (students who are able) to summer travel to Africa for continued study and expansion in African consciousness.

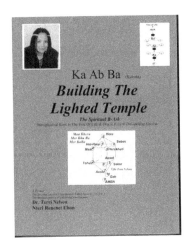

Our Programs/Services are offered both nationally and internationally and if you would like any of these offered in your City, State, Country, please contact, Dr Terri Nelson, **617-296-7797**.

This book is dedicated to –
•AMEN, Infinite Eternal All in All, Neter Neteru, Fount of All Possibility,
•Father/Mother Creator, Most High God/Goddess in Whom we live and move and have our being, Divined as AusarAuset,
•and to the Paut Neteru, the company of the Gods, guiding us into sacred space, imbruing us with all God qualities (Neteru), teaching us to live as Gods and Goddesses,
•and to the Ancestors who have gone before,
Those who have remained steady in the Light and
Those with hard won footsteps who have trodden their way back into the Light and
Those with heavy laden footsteps who are treading their way onto the path of Light
•In all praise and appreciation that you hear our prayers

KaAbBa   Building The Lighted Temple
The Spiritual B(ARK)

Introduction

The Spiritual journey of unfolding consciousness was well understood by our African/Kemetic Ancestors, and their Spiritual/Religious practices were of the highest development. George James expresses this accordingly: *Stolen Legacy*, p. 1.

> The ancient Egyptians [read here: Kemetians] had developed a very complex religious system, called the Mysteries, which was also the first system of salvation. As such, it regarded the human body as a prison house of the soul, which could be liberated from its bodily impediments through the disciplines of the Arts and Sciences, and advanced from the level of a mortal to that of a God. This was the notion of the summum bonum or greatest good, to which all men must aspire and it became the basis of all ethical concepts.

In some of the quotes that follow, you will at times see that language is used to esoterically 'veil' or hide meaning. In order to 'lift the veil' and reveal truer meaning, I have placed 'explanatory language' within brackets that looks like this [read here: …'explanatory language'] after the quote in question. This practice will occur throughout this text. The above theme is continued and expressed accordingly: H.P. Blavatsky. *The Veil of Isis [read here: - The Veil of Auset], V.I*, p. 2.

> A conviction, founded upon seventy thousand years of experience as they allege, has been entertained by hermetic [read here: - the Kemetic Teachings of Tehuti] philosophers of all periods that matter has in time become, through sin, more gross and dense than it was at man's first formation; that, at the beginning, the human body was of a half-ethereal nature; and that, before the fall, mankind communed freely with the now unseen universes. But since that time matter has become the formidable barrier between us and the world of spirits. The oldest esoteric traditions also teach that, before the mystic Adam, many races of human beings lived and died out, each giving place in its turn to another. Were these precedent types more perfect? Did any of them belong to the winged race of men mentioned by Plato in Phaedrus?

> As the cycle proceeded, man's eyes were more and more opened until he came to know "good and evil" as well as the Elohim themselves. Having reached its summit, the cycle began to go downward. When the arc attained a certain point which brought it parallel with the fixed line of our terrestrial plane, the man was furnished by nature with "coats of skin", and the Lord God "clothed them". This same belief in the pre-existence of a far more spiritual race than the one to which we now belong can be traced back to the earliest traditions of nearly every people.

In these collective works Titled, *The Ausarianization of Consciousness Tablet Series – The Metaphysical Keys to The Tree Of Life with Oracle Keys to Dis-spelling Illusion – ACTS,* I made the decision, to just try to tell *Our Story*, doing the best I could. Many have come before me in this same effort and many will come after me. As a Black Race, we are an Ancient people. As such, many stories are unfolding within Our Story. In my extensive research along with guidance from the Elders on the Inner realm, I have been guided not to go, 'head to head' or 'toe to toe' with the countless instances of misrepresentation, half-truths, distortions, white-washing, and racism in the reference materials. Such address and counter address would expend enormous energy as well as distract from the rhythm and flow of an already complex enough story – a story that ponders the 'seemingly' imponderable Spiritual Journey in Unfolding Human Consciousness.

Many of the Ancient wisdom teachings cited are from book references, which are themselves treasure chests containing the mysteries, yet requiring future research and investigation. However, let it be said at the outset that my research reveals (as amply noted by other researchers – John Jackson, Cheikh Anta Diop, et al) that there is a game that is being played. It is the game of:

1. *'saying'* and *unsaying'*, and
2. *'should have been saids'* and *'should not have been saids'*

In this game one must wade through a maze that has been set by authors who are skilled at both *'unsaying'*, then sometimes inadvertently *'saying'*, then *'unsaying'* again, that which is ultimately revealed as *the Greatness of Black Race People.* What is astonishing in this *'double speaking'* is how even in their attempts to *'unsay'*, they end up *'saying'* anyway. This is the game of discrediting, disappearing and degrading.

This work is an effort to retrieve and reclaim the image of the Black Race out of the throes and thralldom of the 'writer's pen' which has often been used as a hacksaw. As such, I focused my attention throughout this work in providing references which are the *'saying'* of the greatness of Black People while weeding through countless pages in the source material which are the *'unsayings'*, i.e., the degradation and disappearing of that greatness.

For example, one may say something to 'hold the story together' but then unsay it later. This is like a man who tries to sell a house which 'appears' structurally sound while the potential buyer is there, but who comes back later and removes supportive beams when the buyer is not looking. Ultimately, it boils down to the fact that Europeans cannot tell the story of the Spiritual journey of unfolding human consciousness with all the necessary inclusivity required, unless they are willing to tell the truth about the Greatness of the Black Race. One minute we are Sages, the next moment we are savages. What a conundrum!

The pages that follow give insight into this journey. You will hopefully see that *Sage and Savage* belong to 'no one race' but are inherent in the Spiritual Journey itself. There are already countless books whose sole objective is to *'unsay'*. Many quotes cited throughout this text will guide you in referring to them for your further research. You will find no shortage of demonstration of this game of 'doublespeak'; as for every numerous instance I caught them in *'unsaying'* they are likewise replete with instances of *'saying'*. Even though I give some limited example of this in this text, I leave this to your own researches as I have been guided not to engage in an endless game of ferreting these out. Instead, I have been guided to write a book that is:

1. *'Saying'* of the greatness of the Black Race

KaAbBa   Building The Lighted Temple
The Spiritual B(ARK)

2. A Guide for all Races in the *Unfolding Spiritual Journey of Human Consciousness*

I would like to express my deepest appreciation to numerous authors, many who are included in the Bibliography. They have contributed to deepen my understanding of the Kemetic (Egyptian) mysteries and Metaphysical Studies. Some of these authors such as George James, I regard as one of the *Chiefs* and Initiates in taking us back to the *source* of our Ancient Wisdom. He has played a major role in the retrieving and re-claim-ation process. This reconnection is our life blood. Others, like Gerald Massey, E. A. Wallis Budge, Albert Churchward and Manly P. Hall (to name a few) have demonstrated great courage in showing the undeniable root and link of Ancient Africa to all the religious systems that would develop worldwide. This is a reality that the Western World has been very challenged to acknowledge and accept. Still other authors, while having drawn extensively from The Ancient Wisdom, try to veil the source of this wisdom. In my years as an independent Metaphysical Investigator, I have sought to trace the wisdom back to the source. I have found that even the feeblest effort to uncover the truth readily ferrets out the undeniable – *It all goes back to Black.* Why is it that so many can not, will not, see the obvious? Why is it that so many can see, yet, will not say the obvious?

I leave these questions to be hotly debated by the now very long list of extremely competent, expert, eloquent and accomplished Black and other historians who have written extensively on this very subject. I am a seeker of truth. This seeking has led me to research within various fields – none of which I would consider myself 'expert' in. As a matter of fact, the more I learn the more dwarfed I feel by the magnitude of it all. What grows is not my sense of how much I know. What grows is my sense of how much there is to know. At the same time I do feel my work is suggestive for others to engage in deeper research. As a Metaphysical teacher, eternal student of the Ancient wisdom and Holistic Psychotherapist, my focus here is in garnering and distributing the wisdom and tools for Ausarian Spiritual Transformation and Resurrection or ASTR (STAR).

What is briefly noted here is that; the plunder and burning of the Royal Library of Alexandria, the killing and silencing of our Ancestors, and the closing of the Ancient Mystery Schools in Kemet (later called Egypt by the Greeks) contributed to a great splintering of the Ancient Wisdom. The edicts during the reigns of Emperors Constantine, Theodosius and Justinian (4th – 6th century A.C.E.) effectively declared and brutally enforced Christianity as the official religion. The closing of the mystery schools, wanton destruction of the Ancient wisdom and slaughter of our sages all set the so called 'New World' on a fast path into the Dark Ages. The tremendous work by our brother George James in his book, *Stolen Legacy,* first published in 1954, gives the broadest brushstrokes to the massive robbery of our history and Ancient mysteries, the magnitude of which is as yet unearthed. This, all done by an emerging World that would give little or no attribution to its source.

While we as African descendants sank deep into slavery, many would continue to crisscross the globe in an unrelenting robbery of the Ancient mysteries from the Tombs of our Ancestors. While we labored in chains many of these made themselves the next 'custodians' or 'caretakers' of the splintered wisdom of the Ancient Mystery Schools. Many of the books that have been

The Ausarianization of Consciousness Series 1
Metaphysical Keys To the Tree of Life & Oracle Keys to Dis-spelling Illusion
The Spiritual Journey in Unfolding Consciousness

4

'written' by the generations of custodians about the Ancient Wisdom are intended to both reveal and conceal, to both say then unsay, - the truth of the greatness of Black people. Mining and harvesting the *Treasured Blackness* within these great volumes has been a major part of my research.

In this regard, although highly veiled, I am deeply appreciative for the work of a long list of Metaphysicians and Esotericists including the Tibetan and H.P. Blavatksy, who were influential during the 1800 and 1900's when African descended people were still reeling from the impact of slavery and post slavery. Many of these works still require the labor of those serious students to anchor them back to their source.

I am deeply appreciative of my years of study with the late Dr. Alfred Ligon in Black Knostic studies, as a student in his group and Lodge member. Dr. Ligon guided my earliest toddling footsteps in trying to find my way through the maze of splintered Ancient Wisdom. I feel him guiding me now. I am likewise deeply appreciative of my years of study with Dr. Michael Robbins at The University of the Seven Rays who is author of, *The Tapestry of the Gods, V.I & II*, and *The Infinitization of Selfhood*. My Esoteric/Metaphysical studies here offered a profound Roadmap of the Spiritual journey of unfolding consciousness and the Constitution of Man and Woman, which is both human and Divine. They both cultivated within me the power of navigability and penetrative insight into the Ancient Wisdom teachings. I also am appreciative to Maharishi Mahesh Yogi for my studies in meditation and consciousness. I am deeply appreciative for the courage and wisdom of Dr Yosef ben-Jochannan. His careful tutelage as Elder and tour guide during a trip to Kemet further revealed the magnitude of the greatness of Black Race People, while pointing out the great lengths to which others have gone in attempt to steal our legacy.

The Tree of Life, The Kabala, The Paut Neteru
H. P. Blavatsky in her multiple volume works says the following about the power within the Kabala, The Tree of Life accordingly: *Isis Unveiled, V.I*, p. 14.

> The fundamental geometrical figure of the Kabala –[read here: Tree of Life, Paut Neteru] …contain…the key to the universal problem. This figure contains in itself all the others. For those who are able to master it, there is no need to exercise imagination. No earthly microscope can be compared with the keenness of the spiritual perception.

The words, *'this figure contains in itself all the others'*, reveals the power within the Tree of Life. In my own studies I have garnered knowledge in many areas: these include Astrology, Kemetic Neteru, Kabala, Rayology, stages of Initiation, Meditation, Traditional and Meta-physical Psycho-Spiritual practices, Numerology, Cosmology, Cosmogenesis, Consciousness, the 7 Cosmic Systemic Planes, Traditional and Esoteric Psychology, and so on. However, it is the cohering power within the Kabala or Paut Neteru that begins to pull numerous systems and ways of knowing together. The Tree of Life aids the development of the 1st eye in man and

5

KaAbBa Building The Lighted Temple
The Spiritual B(ARK)

woman. This eye is erroneously called the 3rd eye. It is the eye, which sees interiorly and confers innersightedness, revealing the whole moving geometry within the mind of God. Thus, do we see in wholeness. The 1st eye in man and woman has its correspondence with the eye of Ra. As Creation arises within the waters of space, called Nun by the Kemetians, it is the eye that *sees and knows*.

Although there are countless writers on the subject of the Tree of Life or the Kabala, I feel a deep appreciation for the works of Ra Un Nefer Amen in his two-volume work *Metu Neter*. Although the Jewish Kabalistic terminology of the sepiroh or spheres may be well known to any serious student of Metaphysical studies, his *overlay* of the Kemetic/Egyptian terminology for the Neteru or Paut Neteru upon this Divine Cosmogram takes us to the source. It acknowledges the contribution of Ancient Africa to the subsequent development of all Spiritual traditions world wide. His works have contributed to new depths in my own understanding and doors in consciousness have flung wide open, as suddenly the correct *vibration* has been sounded by the correct *Naming* of these Spheres. He is likewise a *Chief* and High Initiate and his work will be far reaching for generations to come. He is powerful in his 'saying' of the greatness of Black Race People without the extended need to 'read between the lines' as in the writings by other authors. He has reclaimed for us some of the major keys in Kemetic Spiritual teaching, Psycho-Spiritual practice, and transformation. He like other authors, will be quoted from time to time. However, the works of Ra Un Nefer Amen are Metaphysical Keys further revealing the syncretization power within the Tree of Life.

This cohering power of syncretization in the Tree of Life cannot be quoted; it can only be transmitted, as he and others have done in a *direct way,* while still others have done so in a *veiled way,* to keep the masses in ignorance. It is the syncretization power within the Tree of Life itself that:
1. Pulls all systems of thought together
2. Pulls all systems of thought back to Black – *the Source* – from which the World has – in the words of George James – *'stolen'.*

The works of H.P. Blavatsky, and the books of the Tibetan are likewise potent Metaphysical Keys in revealing the syncretization power within the Tree of Life. They are African ancestral (Lemurian, Atlantean) treasure chests, waiting to be mined and garnered. I have found the 24 Books of the Tibetan as revealing the voice of Tehuti, called Hermes by the Greeks. Even here, we can peer through the first of many veils when we look at the fact that these are called the 24 Books of the Tibetan. The number 24 read backwards or inverted is 42, as in the 42 Books of Tehuti. When carefully *read* – the hierarchical lineage is sensed and the Ashram of Tehuti is located. The books of the Tibetan provide detailed explanation of the Cosmic Planes and sub-planes revealing the subtlety and livingness of the Deities or Elohim and their qualities, called Neteru by the Ancient Kemetians.

Yet, as often as many books are forced to admit to the trained eye the obviousness of their Black and African source, they are equally as often remiss in doing so. Like so many others, these books are presented with an extended need to 'read between the lines'.

The Ausarianization of Consciousness Series 1
Metaphysical Keys To the Tree of Life & Oracle Keys to Dis-spelling Illusion
The Spiritual Journey in Unfolding Consciousness

6

Nevertheless, there is a tremendous need for investigators to do the work of harvesting, re-claim-ation, and syncretization. In this ongoing struggle, it is my hope that this re-claim-ation effort will be transmitted through my work. May it further reveal the contributions that the Black Race has and continues to make to:

1. Unfolding Human consciousness
2. Planetary consciousness
3. Solar consciousness and *Beyond*

Thus - may a more complete story of humanity in its Earthly journey, *be told.*

Firstly and Lastly, *My Greatest Teachers are The Neteru and Ancestral Sages Within.*

It was the vibration in the sounding of the trumpets that brought down the walls of Jericho. Metaphysically, if vibration can cause things to fall apart then vibration can likewise cause that which has been separate to cohere and come back together. When the Black Race comes back to the Ancient wisdom teachings, then we will be counted among the ranks of those sounding the harmonious sound that unites not only Black people but all people and therefore re-elevates the consciousness of the Human family into the Spiritual Kingdom.

KaAbBa   Building The Lighted Temple
The Spiritual B(ARK)

Chapter 1
The Tree Of Life   *The Divine Cosmogram*

In order to embark on a journey we need a map.
What are the two primary reasons for the choice of the Tree of Life as Map and guide for managing the Spiritual Journey in Unfolding Consciousness and the Spiritual Implications of The Perfect Storm – a time cycle in which we now live and must navigate?

1. The Paut Neteru is an Ancient symbol for understanding our Spiritual Faculty which is both human and Divine. It is therefore indispensable in our navigation efforts to Ausarian Resurrection.

2. The Tree of Life is a Divine Cosmogram and will be used in this Metaphysical course study.

A *Cosmogram* – is a structure or design that gives us a foundation upon which to append the dynamic movement of cosmic entities and events so that something of the Divine Plan may be revealed to our gradually unfolding consciousness. This Cosmogram is a magnetic template upon which formerly disparate concepts and systems may finally cohere and offer profound understanding to the disciple. Use of this Divine Cosmogram can empower the initiate or disciple to:

a. Experience a mental structuring or grid-work from which to maneuver and view the Divine organization and numberless correspondences that begin to emerge.
b. Open and receive the ever pregnant and potent Divine ideation ready to inflow the poised and awakened mind.
c. Manage a tremendous precipitation from the higher consciousness – the Ba and Ab aspects of our Spiritual faculty (which will be described later in detail.)
d. Meet the requirement that the Spiritual B-Ark or Lighted Temple that we are each building and navigating be rendered in fit condition and able to bear the Spiritual impress of the time in which we now live.

As African descendants many have not had access to the kind of education and training that strums the memory and structures the mind with templates that can organize human experience. In time may we all learn to use the Tree of Life with great ease swinging from vine to vine, limb to limb, plane to plane, maneuvering through the great jungle of illusion and to find our way back '*Home*'.

The many works by Budge, Massey, et al. have provided volumes on the Kemetic Neteru, giving revelation into the Ausarianization of Consciousness and the Neteru or qualities of Divinity. Likewise, countless books have been written on the Kabalah and Planes of Consciousness, as well as on Astrological and Rayological energies. All have provided us with volume upon volume of:

1. *Story*
2. *Template* to append a Story to
3. A *Sea of Divine Energies* (Neteru) to discern and wade through

The Ausarianization of Consciousness Series 1
Metaphysical Keys To the Tree of Life & Oracle Keys to Dis-spelling Illusion
The Spiritual Journey in Unfolding Consciousness

8

Yet these remained separate and disconnected for me until the phenomenal two Volume works entitled – *Metu Neter* by Ra Un Nefer Amen. He is foremost a pioneer in the re-claim-ation process by his Naming of the Spheres. • His work of *appending* the correct Kemetc Names for the 11 Neteru and the 7 Soul divisions versus the Kabalistic names to the Spheres in the Tree of Life has far reaching impact and revelation. The magnetic and attractive power of this one action alone has contributed to a major cohering together of the massive splintering within the Ancient wisdom by those who would see it divorced from its Black Source. For this I have much gratitude. The Tree of Life is pictured below with the Kemetic terminology as used by Ra Un Nefer Amen at left* and the Kabalistic terminology at right:

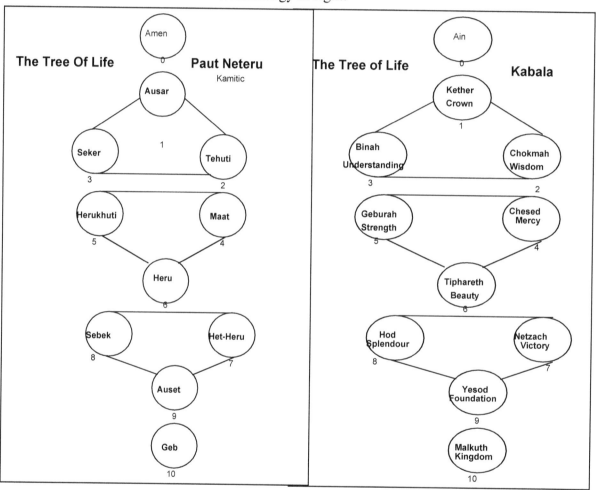

The chapters that follow bring the reader into a great expanse from which to view the Spiritual Journey of Unfolding Consciousness. Ausarianization of Consciousness is reconnecting with the

---

• See also Israel Regarde's work in naming of the spheres, *The Tree Of Life.*

KaAbBa   Building The Lighted Temple
The Spiritual B(ARK)

Metaphysical Keys in the Tree of Life which prepare the aspirant for Ausarian Spiritual Transformation and Resurrection ASTR (STAR).

What is the Destination? Where are we going?
The answer is simple. We are Re-ascending. Ausarian Spiritual Transformation and Resurrection begins with the Resurrection of the Heru or Karest principle within. This is later called the Christ Principle by the Christians. It is to be re-born into the Spiritual body. The challenges are great. Whatever tradition or terminology you choose to use, the considerations for humanity worldwide are still the same. Again these include:
1. Understanding our Spiritual Journey. Knowing our intention, course direction and destination
2. Knowing and cultivating a fit vessel for the Journey. Knowing your Spiritual faculty (or equipment)
3. Knowing the map and charting our course

You will see that contained within the Tree of Life, pictured on the following page, are all 3 components. Taken in total the Tree of Life is your Spiritual Economy, Faculty, Equipment, Make-up or Constitution. These terms are all synonymous and will be used interchangeably throughout this text. They describe the Tree of Life Map which is our Equipment, both Divine and Human. In its triple aspect it is your Map to chart your course by, Destination, and the Equipment in which you make your journey – *all in one*.

I have constructed two versions of the Tree of Life. Each contains numerous Metaphysical Key Overlays or Systems of Correspondence. My own Kabalistic, Kemetic, Esoteric, Ancient Mysteries research and Metaphysical studies have led me to offer these versions, as I find each lends great clarity to the process of Ausarian Spiritual Transformation and Resurrection. Both will be a continual reference source in our Metaphysical Studies. This will become evident as we begin to see the various Metaphysical Keys overlaid or appended onto and revealed within the Tree of Life or Paut Neteru.

See diagrams on following pages:

The Big Map

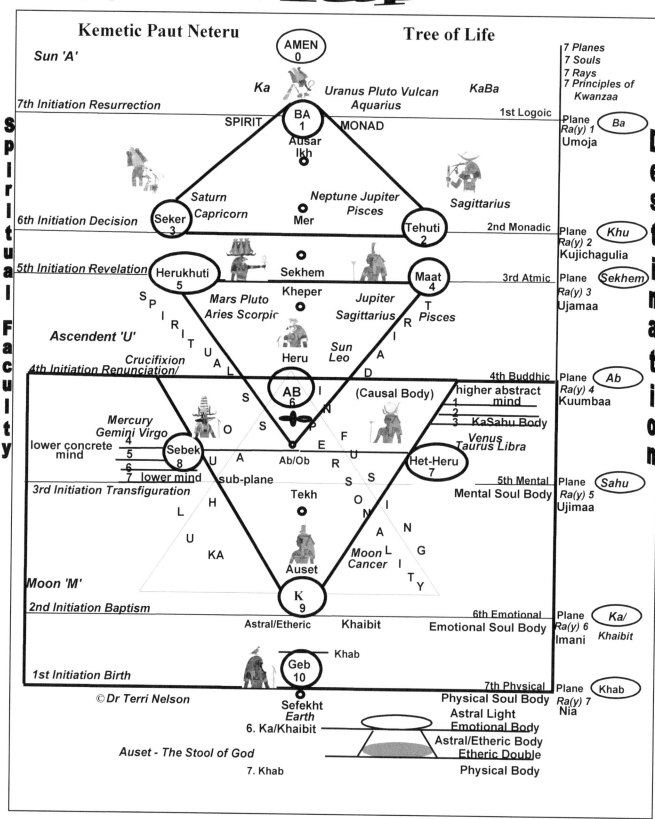

Kemetic Paut Neteru · Tree of Life

Sun 'A'

7 Planes
7 Souls
7 Rays
7 Principles of Kwanzaa

AMEN 0

Ka · KaBa

Uranus Pluto Vulcan Aquarius

7th Initiation Resurrection

1st Logoic · Plane Ra(y) 1 Umoja · *Ba*

SPIRIT · **BA 1** · MONAD

Ausar Ikh

Saturn Capricorn · Neptune Jupiter Pisces · Sagittarius

Mer

6th Initiation Decision · **Seker 3** · **Tehuti 2** · 2nd Monadic · Plane Ra(y) 2 Kujichagulia · *Khu*

5th Initiation Revelation · **Herukhuti 5** · Sekhem · **Maat 4** · 3rd Atmic · Plane Ra(y) 3 Ujamaa · *Sekhem*

Kheper

Mars Pluto Aries Scorpio · Jupiter Sagittarius Pisces

Sun Leo

Ascendent 'U'

Heru

Crucifixion

4th Initiation Renunciation/

4th Buddhic · Plane Ra(y) 4 Kuumbaa · *Ab*

SPIRITUALS · **AB 6** · (Causal Body) · higher abstract mind

1
2
3 · KaSahu Body

Mercury Gemini Virgo

lower concrete mind
4
5
6
7 lower mind

Sebek 8 · Ab/Ob · sub-plane · **Het-Heru 7** · Venus Taurus Libra

5th Mental · Plane Ra(y) 5 Ujimaa · *Sahu*

Mental Soul Body

3rd Initiation Transfiguration

PERSONALITY

Tekh

Moon Cancer

Auset

Moon 'M'

2nd Initiation Baptism · **K 9**

6th Emotional · Plane Ra(y) 6 Imani · *Ka/ Khaibit*

Emotional Soul Body

Astral/Etheric · Khaibit

Khab

1st Initiation Birth · **Geb 10**

7th Physical · Plane Ra(y) 7 Nia · *Khab*

Physical Soul Body

Sefekht Earth

6. Ka/Khaibit

Astral Light
Emotional Body
Astral/Etheric Body
Etheric Double
Physical Body

Auset - The Stool of God

7. Khab

Spiritual Faculty

Destination

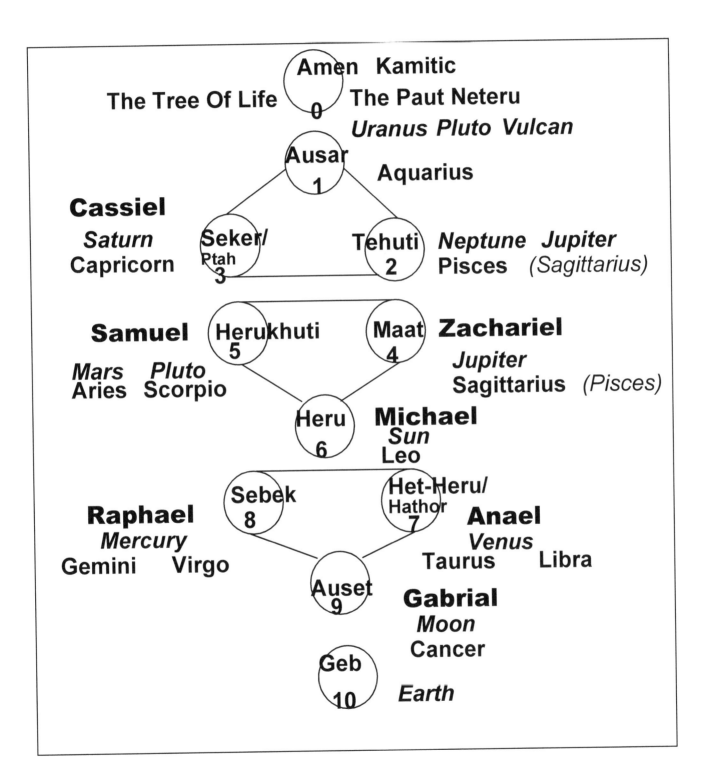

The Ausarianization of Consciousness Series 1
Metaphysical Keys To the Tree of Life & Oracle Keys to Dis-spelling Illusion
The Spiritual Journey in Unfolding Consciousness

12

We are an Ancient people and exhaustive Metaphysical research needs to be done to lift the veil on Our Story. This book is a meager attempt to shed light on: 1. Our Story as African and African Diaspora and 2. The way of Ausarian Spiritual Transformation and Resurrection which is our return '*Home*' in Unity, God, or ALL Consciousness.

As Our Story unfolds, Metaphysical Keys to the Tree of Life will be given to *Break The Spell of Illusion* and increase our ability to navigate the way Home. Four of these **Metaphysical Keys**, when absent from your consciousness, constitute **Major Impediments** to your Spiritual Awakening and Resurrection. If not overcome they can cause you to stumble at any time. These are listed here and explained in *The Ausarianization of Consciousness Tablet Series – The Metaphysical Keys to The Tree Of Life with Oracle Keys to Dis-spelling Illusion - ACTS -* They are:

---

4 Major Metaphysical Keys: 4 Major Impediments

1. Metaphysical Key To:
Know Thyself
Overcoming impediment # 1
Not Knowing our History
Not knowing your way Home and
Not taking responsibility for knowing, seeking, finding and
Being *all Spooked Up*

2. Metaphysical Key To:
Restoration of The 1st Eye
Overcoming impediment # 2
Blindness

3. Metaphysical Key To:
Knowing How to Tell Time
Overcoming impediment # 3
Loss of The Ability to Tell Time and
To Know What Time Is It

4. Metaphysical Key To:
The Law of Reincarnation (Rebirth) &
The Law of Cause and Effect -Karma
Overcoming Impediments # 4
Loss of the Laws to overcome death, fear of death and
conscious accountability for actions. Loss of the (ability to
have a Declaration of Innocence).

KaAbBa   Building The Lighted Temple
The Spiritual B(ARK)

Our story begins with the first Metaphysical Key:

> **Metaphysical Key To**:
> Know Thyself
> ***Overcoming impediment # 1***
> Not Knowing our History
> Not knowing our way Home and
> Not taking responsibility for
> knowing, seeking, finding and
> *Being all Spooked Up*

The words revealing this Metaphysical Key are well expressed accordingly: Gerald Massey. *Ancient Egypt The Light of The World, V. I,* p. 196-197.

> The soul of Neferuben … is the wise or instructed soul, one of the Khu-Akaru, is a master of the gnosis, a knower or knowing soul, and therefore not to be caught like an ignorant fish in the net. Knowledge is of the first importance. In all his journeyings and difficulties it is necessary for the deceased to know. It is by knowledge that he is lighted to find his way in the dark. Knowledge is his lamp of light and his compass; to possess knowledge is to be master of Divine powers and magical words. Ignorance would leave him a prey to all sorts of liers in wait and cunning enemies. He triumphs continually through his knowledge of the way, like a traveler with his chart and previous acquaintanceship with the local language; hence the need of the gnosis and of initiation in the mysteries. Those who knew the real name of the god were in possession of the word that represented power over the Divinity, therefore the word of power that would be efficacious if employed. Instead of calling on the name of god in prayer, they made use of the name as the word of god. And as these words and mysteries of magic were contained in the writings, it was necessary to know the writings in which the gnosis was religiously preserved to be in possession of the words of power. …

This brings us to the next Metaphysical Key:

> **Oracle Metaphysical Key to:**
> Dis-spelling Illusion

The Ancient wisdom tells us that Numbers and Letters are sacred and Divine Beings. Letters and Numbers are Oracles of God or Divine messages and messengers. These are the Ntr, Neter or Neteru (plural form) and known as qualities of God. Words are constructed by putting letters or neteru together that sound a vibration and convey quality. When we study the Kemetic Law of Vibration we understand that:
1. THE WORD that is with GOD at the beginning of Creation has a vibration
2. Every word that is derived from THE WORD, likewise has a vibration
This is also described in the major religious books.

The Ausarianization of Consciousness Series 1
Metaphysical Keys To the Tree of Life & Oracle Keys to Dis-spelling Illusion
The Spiritual Journey in Unfolding Consciousness

14

These same Letters also correspond to Numbers as shown in the following table. Letter A corresponds to the number 1, B to the number 2 and so on. When numbers are double digit you add these to reduce to a single digit (example: 16 = 1 + 6 = 7 = letter P).

		Neteru				Number and Letter		
1	2	3	4	5	6	7.	8	9
A	B	C	D	E	F	G	H	I
a	b	c	d	e	f	g	h	i
10	11	12	13	14	15	16	17	18
J	K	L	M	N	O	P.	Q.	R.
j	k	l	m	n	o	p	q	r
19	20	21	22	23	24	25	26	27
S	T	U	V	W	X	Y	Z	
s	t	u	v	w	x	y	z	0
1	2	3	4	5	6	7	8	9

Let's dispell the word Neferuben using the **Oracle Metaphysical Dis-spelling keys:**
 # 1. Oracle Metaphysical Dis-spelling Key:
Put letters of word or words together in a circle, like a serpent putting its tail in its mouth. Coming full Circle.

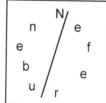

#2. Oracle Metaphysical Dis-spelling Key: Read letters, putting together words, going forwards, backwards and in zig-zag patterns.
#3. Oracle Metaphysical Dis-spelling Key: You may crossover in order to use a letter more than once. Place re-used letter in parenthesis ( ).
#4. Oracle Metaphysical Dis-spelling Key: You may add a letter to complete a word. Place added letter in parenthesis ( ).
#5. Oracle Metaphysical Dis-spelling Key: Letter substitution-you may substitute a letter. Place substituted letter in parenthesis ( ).
#6. Oracle Metaphysical Dis-spelling Key: Make a list of derived words. Try to make the longest continuous unbroken word or string of words.
Derived Word List:
Free - to be an unfettered Soul

Nu be(I)n(g) – a new being who emerges out of the waters of Nu or Nun. Nu, Nut or Nun is the Kemetic Goddess and symbolized the Spirit-Matter continuum or waters of space from which all creation arises.

Bennu –

#7. Oracle Metaphysical Dis-spelling Key: Look up definition (dictionary, glossary, reference texts, etc.)

Definition: In this instance the best story is the one told long ago by the Ancients in the following accordingly: E. A. Wallis Budge. *The Gods of The Egyptians, V.II,* p. 371.

Bennu – "The Bennu bird was worshipped by the Kemetians as the most sacred and was identified with the Phoenix. The Bennu not only typified the new birth of the sun each morning, but in the earliest period of dynastic history it became the symbol of the resurrection of mankind, for a man's spiritual body was believed to spring from the dead physical body, just as the living sun of today had its origin in the dead sun of yesterday. The Bennu sprang from the heart of Ausar and was, in consequence, a most holy bird…"

Ibid. p. 96, 97.

"According to the Kemetic mythos the renewed morning sun rose in the form of a Bennu, and this bird was the soul of Ra and also the living symbol of Ausar… According to *the Prt Em Ru, The Book of Coming Forth by Day,* " the deceased says, "I am the Bennu, the soul of Ra, and the guide of the gods in the Tuat; (xxixc 1); let it be so done unto me that I may enter in like a hawk, and that I may come forth like Bennu, the Morning Star" (cxxii. 6). "

#8. Oracle Metaphysical Dis-spelling Key: Meaning. See the relationship and oracle or story of the Neteru – Put word list together to tell a story.

Meaning:

To be a Neferuben is Ausarian resurrection. It is the return in consciousness to your Eternal Home now as a Free Bennu, a free soul, a Nu (New) Being.

In using the **Oracle Metaphysical Dis-spelling Keys,** along with many other **Metaphysical Keys** to the Tree of Life, we will attempt to break the 'spell of illusion' in our re-ascent up the Tree of Life.

The Spiritual Journey Continues…
The Story of Humanity's Spiritual Journey in Unfolding Consciousness is Revealed Within the Tree of Life.

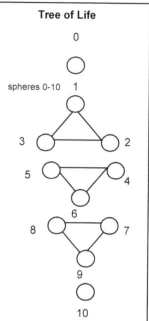

What is the Tree of Life?
As stated in the Introduction, the Tree of Life is a Divine Cosmogram to which Our Story may be appended. It acts as a template upon which the many pieces may find coherence and the dynamic movement of our Divinity may be revealed.

The Tree of Life or Paut Neteru guides us in our re-ascent into Ausarian consciousness and thereby resurrection. It is our map and roadwork – back to the source – our Eternal Home. Your work in Metaphysical studies is to re-awaken to the Image and Likeness of God that 'is' and that 'you are' and have 'always been' from the beginingless beginning. You re-ascend by climbing up the Tree of Life. Each sphere on the Tree of Life is like a huge limb that you must gain firm footing upon before you can stretch up to the next limb in your climb. Firm footing is gained by your conscious experience within each sphere.

What is Ausarian Resurrection and Ascension?
Man/Woman grows 'down' the Tree of Life in his long involutionary descent into matter. Man/Woman grows 'up' the Tree of Life in his evolutionary re-ascent back to the *source*. The climb both – down and up – the Tree of Life, is the story of how man and woman both forget and then remember that which they have always been – Sons and Daughters of God. Through your study of the Tree you will learn the Metaphysical Keys to begin to *break the spell of illusion*. It is the process whereby you raise your consciousness from a lower, material, coarse vibration to a higher, Spiritually refined vibration. You ascend by transmuting the lower substance in your own nature. You will learn more about the effort and the cultivation of the will that is involved in this process.

The Tree of Life Cosmogram is pictured above but is not filled in fully. We will fill it in as we go along. In opening this story we begin with the basic structure of the Tree of Life. A brief description, which will serve our purpose for now, is as follows: The first division in the Tree of Life is to see that it is made up of spheres numbered 0 – 10. Each sphere is properly called a *Sephira,* the plural of which is Sephiroth. Sephira means emanation. We will refer to each sephira as a 'sphere'. The Tree of Life is built with these spheres. Using these spheres we start by recognizing how the Tree of Life is constructed and that:
1. We can make different sets of divisions within our constitution of which the Tree of Life is a symbol

KaAbBa Building The Lighted Temple
The Spiritual B(ARK)

2. Each division set gives us a different view and thus a variety of ways to gain a deeper understanding of the workings within our Spiritual faculty

3. The divisions in the Tree of Life that we will examine in this and subsequent chapters are as follows:

a. Division into 11 spheres (spheres 0 – 10) – The Neteru or qualities of the 11 Kemetic Neteru

b. Division into 3 primary triangles – KaAbBa or BaAbKa

c. Division into 7 Planes of Consciousness, 7 Divisions of Soul-Spirit – 7 Primordial Energies

As we examine each division, we will overlay onto the Tree of Life various systems or Metaphysical Keys of understanding. This will allow us to look at the various correspondences between systems. Ultimately, the Tree of Life will 'fill in' with greater detail as we go along in our Metaphysical Studies. It is important to understand that the process of 'overlaying' is used to sequentially reveal the various correspondences that are *organic* within the Tree of Life.

This will bring understanding of the dynamic movement in the Spiritual Journey of unfolding human consciousness. Thus we gain innersight into:

1. How man and woman have made their descent 'down' the Tree of Life

2. How man and woman will make their re-ascent 'up' the Tree of Life

3. The experience of Ausarian Resurrection

Many passes will be made down and up the Tree of Life throughout these chapters. As we make these passes, overlays of various Metaphysical Keys will be appended to the Tree of Life, which will deepen understanding.

The Ausarianization of Consciousness Series 1
Metaphysical Keys To the Tree of Life & Oracle Keys to Dis-spelling Illusion
The Spiritual Journey in Unfolding Consciousness

18

Chapter 2
The Division Into The 11 – The Neteru Or Qualities Of Deity
The Nature Of The 11 Spheres At Work In Man And Woman

This pass down the Tree of Life will be to look within the Numbers or Neter 0 – 10 giving rise to 11 Spheres that form the Tree of Life and are the realms of the Kemetic Neteru. This is why the Tree of Life is called the Paut Neteru or the Company of the Gods (See E.A.Wallis Budge). Each Neter expresses qualities of Divinity within us. Attuning to the Divine qualities within our Spiritual make up helps us to express the higher aspect of these Divine energies in our life. This brings us to the next

---

Metaphysical Key To:
Understanding Energy
Energy is Energy
Energy may be used:
1. Positively at a higher turn of the spiral in its strength, Spiritually optimal and Divine level of expression or
2. Negatively at a lower turn of the spiral in its weakness, despiritualized and debased level of expression

---

The Neter are qualities of Energy. This Metaphysical Key informs us that Energy may be used positively as a strength at its Spiritually optimal and Divine level of expression, or negatively in its weakness at its despiritualized and debased level of expression. The choice is ours to cultivate 'the Will' so that the Spiritual qualities of the Neter are reflected and radiated through our Temple without the distortions which weaken reflection. This brings us to the next

---

Meditation Key To:
The Kemetic Neter Within Each Sphere
The 0 zero as Divine cipher and the 10 Spheres forming
the 11 Spheres within The Tree of life

In making the first of many passes down and up, and up and down, the Tree of Life, we begin with meditation upon and within each Kemetic Neter. In order to experience the movement within each Sphere and throughout the Tree of Life or Paut Neteru:
1. Begin each Meditation by taking some deep breaths. *With each in-breath* breathe in a sense of peace and ease and calm. *With each out-breath* breathe out any stress or tension and really create a space within you and around you and throughout the room
2. Read through and ponder upon the Meditation to each Kemetic Neter
3. Close your eyes and Meditate upon the movement and energy *within* each sphere before moving to the next
4. Meditate upon the movement and energy *between* the spheres in the Tree of Life

KaAbBa   Building The Lighted Temple
The Spiritual B(ARK)

> **Metaphysical Key:**
> Sphere 0 AMEN Meditation

Kemetic Name: Amen – See re-claim-ation in Kemetic naming of Sphere 0 *Amen*
by Ra Un Nefer Amen, *Metu Neter,V.I & II* **vs.**
Kabalistic Name –Ain

In Meditation deep:

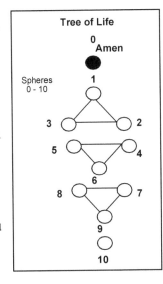

- Within your inner eye, the 1st eye located between your eyebrows, imagine a great flash of Light.
- See this as a brilliantly radiant and radiating Light.
- This Light is so bright that it is blinding. *(hold)*.
- Be within this Light. Become one with this Light.
- Now, moving within this Light begin to trace it back to its Source.
- See this Light converge and become an ever narrowing beam as you in consciousness continue to trace it to its Source.
- Continue to trace it back to its Source.
- Back to its Source.
- Back to its Source.
- As you near the end of this narrowing beam become aware that you are now totally submerged in DARKNESS.
- The AMEN.
- This is the ABSOLUTE, the ALL IN ALL, NETER NETERU.
- Be within this DARKNESS, BLACKNESS
- This is the BEGININGLESS BEGINNING, THE FOUNT OF ALL POSSIBILITY, THE SUPREME BE-NESS, THE ROOT CAUSELESS CAUSE, THE INFINITE, THE ETERNAL. THAT WITHOUT POINT OR CIRCUMFERENCE, THE BOUNDLESS ALL, THE EVERYTHING AND NO-THING. LIMITLESS POTENTIAL,
- Sphere 0 is known by many names: THE NAMELESS, THE ALL, GOD, SPIRIT, AIN, are just a few names for the ABSOLUTE REALITY.
- Within this awareness of ABSOULUTE BE-NESS feel your access to all potential, all power, all wisdom, all creativity.
- Experience unlimited Be-ness. Experience your unboundedness.
- Here, without lack or limitation. Here resting within all potential. Feel your freedom and infinite expanse.

The Ausarianization of Consciousness Series 1
Metaphysical Keys To the Tree of Life & Oracle Keys to Dis-spelling Illusion
The Spiritual Journey in Unfolding Consciousness

20

Metaphysical Key:
Sphere 1 Ausar Meditation

Kemetic Name: Amen – See re-claim-ation in Kemetic naming of Sphere 1 *Ausar*
by Ra Un Nefer Amen, *Metu Neter, V.I & II*
Kabalistic Name – Kether – Crown

In Meditation deep:

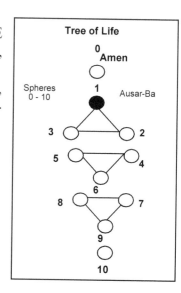

•Within The AMEN, ALL IN ALL, NETER NETERU, SUPREME BE-NESS, THE FOUNT OF ALL POSSIBILITIES, THE INFINITE, THE ABSOLUTE REALITY – *Creation Stirs.*
•There is a raying forth of Light and the One as BE-NESS (Sphere 0, AMEN) becomes the One as Creator Ausar – Sphere 1, the Be-coming One.
•Moving your awareness now from the DARK of the Unmanifest
•Light appears as a bright blaze.
•This is Ausar and we now enter within sphere 1.
•This is when God the INFINITE is reflected forth in God the Creator.
•The Divine archetypal design and creative substance is rayed forth and complete within Ausar.
•Thus a Universe, a World, man and woman, all multiplicity is created. Divinized as Ausar, God is reflected in all that is created and man and woman are made in the Image and Likeness of God.
•God transcendent becomes God indwelling. Therefore, Ausar as man, Ausar as woman has all the Divine qualities of God which express as Omnipotence, Omnipresence and Omniscience.

Silently Affirm the following:
•When I am living my Ausarian consciousness I am fully expressing the God that dwells within me.
•I may express all of the Divine qualities of the One Reality, The Supreme Being.
•I may know full Godhood and Self realization.
•I know unity of Spirit and I know the underlying unity within and between all created Beings.
•Unity of Spirit is full consciousness of the whole of the Tree of Life.
•As I identify within my Ausarian consciousness – my One True Self Realized Being – my entire Spirit is unified.
•I transcend the fragmentation that occurs in my consciousness when I falsely identify with selves that are less than the fullness of the One True Self.
•**But where in man's Spirit, is this registered?**

KaAbBa Building The Lighted Temple
The Spiritual B(ARK)

Metaphysical Key:
Sphere 2 Tehuti Meditation

Kemetic Name: Tehuti – See re-claim-ation in Kemetic naming of Sphere 2 *Tehuti*
by Ra Un Nefer Amen, *Metu Neter, V.I & II*
Kabalistic Name – Chokmah-Wisdom

In Meditation deep:

•We now enter within Sphere 2, Tehuti.

•This is Divine wisdom and Divine mind.
•This is Divine love.

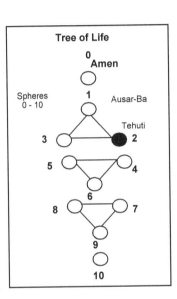

•Listen and attune to the voice of Tehuti, the inner wisdom and
 guiding aspect of your Spirit.
•Residing within Tehuti is the Divinely intended design for your life,
 your to-be created World.
•The Divine archetype and design, pure and perfect without distortion
 or flaw resides here.
•Here is the blueprint of how the God indwelling in us will ultimately
 become God manifest who walks upon the Earth.
•It is within this aspect of your Spirit that you must attune in order to
 glimpse what in unity is the perfect idea and ideation in the mind of
 God.

•Tehuti is like the Puzzle Box Cover of a multitudinous piece puzzle.
•It is the inner oracle that speaks within you – what the Christians call the 'Still Small Voice'.
•By listening to this aspect within your Spirit you may glimpse the Divinely intended design and
 intuit the way to manifest and arrange these pieces as you co-creatively build your life,
 environment, and the World.
•Align now with Divine mind.
•Seek the voice of Tehuiti for Divine wisdom and instruction in accord with the law of right
 relationship (Maat – sphere 4) for building with order, truth, beauty, and unity.
•**But how is the Divine design to be expressed?**

The Ausarianization of Consciousness Series 1
Metaphysical Keys To the Tree of Life & Oracle Keys to Dis-spelling Illusion
The Spiritual Journey in Unfolding Consciousness

22

| **Metaphysical Key:** |
| Sphere 3 Seker Meditation |

Kemetic Name: Seker – See re-claim-ation in Kemetic naming of Sphere 3 *Seker*
by Ra Un Nefer Amen, *Metu Neter, V. I & II*
Kabalistic Name – Binah – Understanding

In Meditation deep:

• We now enter within Sphere 3, Seker.

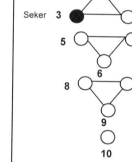

• The Divine archetypal design for the to-be created Universe is
issued forth from Tehuti and registers as vibration within Seker.
• Through Seker Divine Purpose is to be realized within 'a ring pass
not' of expression.
• Here is the vibrational boundary in which Divine purpose is to be
structured.
• The full archetypal design is sounded forth and vibrates within the
'ring pass not' of its space and time boundaried field.
• Seker is creative intelligence.
• It is the structure and co-measured power for the fullest
achievement of God's intended design.

• Affirm:
• May I vibrate and manifest the *total sound* of the grand archetypal design of my being.
• May the limiting 'ring pass nots' of identification with the lesser selves be shed.
• May the full purpose of the Divinely intended design be achieved and actualized in me.
• May my attunement with the Tehuti and Seker aspect of my Spirit enable me to achieve the
Divinely-intended- informed-purposed-expression of God's Divine Plan.
• May full Self Realization of the One True Self be my Crowning Glory.

KaAbBa Building The Lighted Temple
The Spiritual B(ARK)

Metaphysical Key:
Sphere 4 Maat Meditation

Kemetic Name: Maat – See re-claim-ation in Kemetic naming of Sphere 4 *Maat*
by Ra Un Nefer Amen, *Metu Neter, V.I & II*
Kabalistic Name – Chesed – Mercy

In Meditation deep:

•We now enter within Sphere 4, Maat.

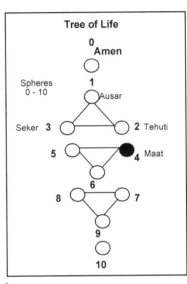

•Maat is our access to the Universal Laws which govern right
relationship.
•They assure the right of every being to achieve its purpose of
Self expression to the fullest.
•Without violating the rights of others and while allowing others
to achieve this same right of Self expression.
•These laws allow each entity its time and space for full Self
realization.
•They guide man and woman in acting accordingly.
•As the initiate within The Hall Of Amenta
•You will stand before – The Lord of the World – Divinized as
Lord Ausar – God indwelling.
•Your heart will be weighed upon a scale against the feather of Maat.
•This is the symbol of truth, righteousness, justice, World order, correctness, harmony and peace.
•Here you will respond to the 42 Negative Confessions (described later) – Declarations of
Innocence regarding how you have conducted yourself in or out of accord with Divine Law.
•If you are found out of harmony and balance, your Soul will seek circumstance again and again
upon the wheel of birth and death.
•This will allow you to make corrections which bring your life in accord with Divine Law.
•The essence of the lessons learnt in each lifetime will be garnered within the treasure house of
your Soul (Heru – sphere 6).
• The Initiatory process goes forth.
•This cycle repeats itself over and over until higher states of consciousness are achieved
•You appear before the scales and *at last* the scale is held in balance.
• Finally as a disciple, you stand within the Hall of Amenta and are found *Maa Kheru.*
•Thus you are *justified* in truth, living morally and in total equilibrium with the law of God.
•The One state of God Conscious Realization – Ausar, has been achieved.
•Bring your awareness into alignment with the Universal laws that govern all relationships in
God's created Universe.
•See yourself as working and living in accord with these laws.

The Ausarianization of Consciousness Series 1
Metaphysical Keys To the Tree of Life & Oracle Keys to Dis-spelling Illusion
The Spiritual Journey in Unfolding Consciousness

24

> **Metaphysical Key:**
> Sphere 5 Herukhuti Meditation

Kemetic Name: Herukhuti See re-claim-ation in Kemetic naming of Sphere 5 *Herukhuti* by Ra Un Nefer Amen, *Metu Neter, V.I & II*
Kabalistic Name – Geborah – Strength

In Meditation deep:

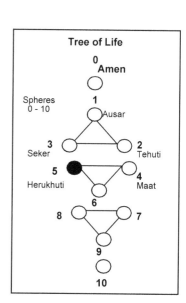

•We now enter within Sphere 5, Herukhuti.

•Imagine the might required to assert yourself to your fullest potential.
•Vibrating and manifesting the total sound of the grand archetypal design of your being.
•Imagine the strength and power needed to assert the *Divinely-intended design in your life expression.*
•Imagine being moved forward to assert all potential within the boundaried field of existence that Seker confers.
•At the same time imagine the power needed to honor the right of all to express the fullest potential – the Self, which is the *same* Self in you and in all.

•Herukhuti is the admonition to Live
•Maat is the admonition to Let live
•The delicate balance must be maintained between War and Peace, Might and Right, Mars and Jupiter, self-centeredness and Altruism, selfishness and Benevolence.

Ask yourself:
•Have I asserted myself to my fullest potential?
•Have I wisely and justly managed the transgressions of the law by others without becoming transgressor myself?
•Have I aggressed against the right of others to assert this same right of full Self expression?

KaAbBa   Building The Lighted Temple
The Spiritual B(ARK)

Kemetic Name: Heru- See re-claim-ation in Kemetic naming of Sphere 6 *Heru*
by Ra Un Nefer Amen, *Metu Neter, V.I & II*
Kabalistic Name – Tepereth – Beauty

In Meditation deep:

•We now enter within Sphere 6, Heru.

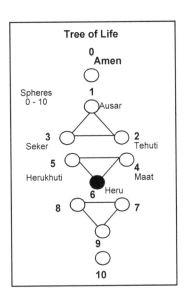

•Heru is the will. It is the use of the will to choose whether to live a
life in accord with Divine will or not.
•You may choose to build askew or in alignment with *the Divinely
intended design for your life.*
•You incur the Karma of both good and bad deeds.
•The will governs the heart.
•The heart is the seat of the Soul.
•Heru is the guidance of your Soul, the accumulated wisdom of many
lifetimes.
•You have had many incarnations upon the wheel of birth and death.
•Therefore Heru is the wisdom – the Spiritual essence that has been
garnered in your long pilgrimage to Ausarian consciousness, your
One True Self.

Affirm:
•It is through Heru that I am becoming fully conscious of the perfect blending of Spirit and
Matter within me.
•When my will is aligned with the Divine will and purpose my heart is made light and purified.
•Building out of accord with the Divinely intended design leads to the accumulation of regret,
remorse, anger, etc. which weighs the heart so that it is heavier than the feather of Maat.
•What will free me from the wheel of birth and death is to conform my mental, emotional and
physical vehicles or bodies into one-pointed aspiration to serve as instrument for the Higher
Soul Program within my Spiritual equipment.
•Through the bending of my personal will into alignment with Divine will, I express *co-creator-
ship* in the Great Divine Plan.
Thus, as Heru I am the 'I' that comes forth to affirm, 'I and my Father (Ausar) are One'.

The Ausarianization of Consciousness Series 1
Metaphysical Keys To the Tree of Life & Oracle Keys to Dis-spelling Illusion
The Spiritual Journey in Unfolding Consciousness

26

Metaphysical Key:
Sphere 7 Het-Heru Meditation

Kemetic Name: Het-Heru- See re-claimation in Kemetic naming of Sphere 7 *Het-Heru*
by Ra Un Nefer Amen, *Metu Neter, V. I & II*
Kabalistic Name — Netzach – Victory

In Meditation deep:

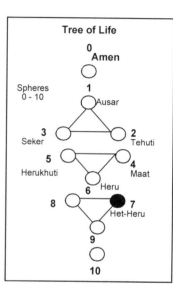

Tree of Life

0
Amen

Spheres
0 - 10

1
Ausar

3
Seker

2
Tehuti

5
Herukhuti

4
Maat

6 Heru

8

7
Het-Heru

9

10

•We now enter Sphere 7, Het-Heru.

•As man and woman you have the faculties of higher abstract mind
(sphere 7) and lower concrete mind (sphere 8).
•Through the power of the imagination and abstract mind of Het-
Heru you are attuned to the archetypal plane.

•The magnetic and attractive power of Het-Heru confers the power
to draw forth from Tehuti – sphere 2, that glimpse of the Divinely
intended design that may be understood and incorporated by higher
and lower mind.
•Through the cohering power of the imagination you may glimpse
and draw forth that aspect of the Divine plan that may be currently
expressed and implemented.
•Through the cohering power of love and aspiration you are able to
draw the fragments of segmented living into intelligent wholes so that the Divinely-intended
design for your life may be approximately realized.

•Attune now to the power of Het-Heru and use the magnetic, attractive power to see your life
cohering into a greater sense of wholeness and joy.

KaAbBa   Building The Lighted Temple
The Spiritual B(ARK)

Kemetic Name: Sebek – See re-claim-ation in Kemetic naming of Sphere 8 *Sebek*
by Ra Un Nefer Amen, *Metu Neter, V.I & II*
Kabalistic Name – Hod – Splendour

In Meditation deep:

•We now enter within Sphere 8, Sebek.

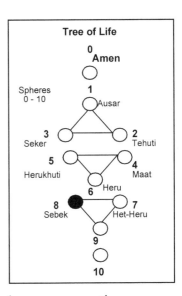

•This is the thought-form making part of our equipment.
• It is how Divine ideation is clothed in a garment called a thought –
form.
•Here, the Divine ideation or archetypal lives within Tehuti – sphere
2, called the Khus by the Kemetians may become tangible as
concrete thoughts.
•Through the mind, experience the power of clothing Divine
ideation in thought –form.
•Sebek is the power to think, plan, reason, analyze, discern,
discriminate, categorize, differentiate and separate.
•Experience the potency that allows you to have in-form-ation about
the World around you and to communicate ideas.

•Yet in our Sebekian mind we may grasp in part and our thoughts can become separative.
•We may come to believe that the part we examine in the mind represents the whole.
•We come to identify with the limited and fragmented contents of the mind that can only be
refreshed and have livingness through contact with Divine mind –Tehuti – sphere 2.
•We come to believe in our own sense of lack and limitation.
•Moreover we come to believe we ourselves are separate from everyone and everything else.
•Our actions are then guided by this illusory 'sense of self and others' leading us to create a
World unspiritualized and unreflective of our Ausarian consciousness.

•When the lower mind of Sebek is held steady in the higher Ab and Ba Soul light, the underlying
unity in all the seeming diversity in God's creation is beheld and made manifest.
•It is through the clarity of perceived thought – Sebek – sphere 8, and the aspiration for a wider
truth of being – Het-Heru – sphere 7,
•That you can use your will – Heru – sphere 6, to impress the creative building substance of your
receptive, unconscious nature – Auset – sphere 9,
•So that *the Divinely-intended- design for your life may be realized.*

Metaphysical Key:
Sphere 9 Auset Meditation

Kemetic Name: Auset See re-claim-ation in Kemetic naming of Sphere 9 *Auset*
by Ra Un Nefer Amen, *Metu Neter, V. I & II*
Kabalistic Name – Yesod – Foundation

In Meditation deep:

•We now enter Sphere 9, Auset.

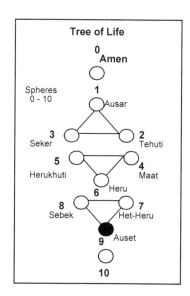

•In the waters of the Mother deep the Father/Ausar is reflected.
•The Father has impregnated the waters with the fullness of his
 effulgent glory.
•She is the beholder of the Divine archetypes and the receiver of
 higher creative impressions. She is the womb of the One True Self.
•Upon her still clear waters the luminous-mirror reflection of God is
 seen.

•Yet long ages of fog, forgetfulness, fragmentation, false desire and
 mire of illusion distort the true reflection of the Father within
 Mother/matter.
•However, she is ceaseless and persevering devotion to re-gather the
 broken body of Ausar which is the brokeness in consciousness
•Bring your awareness to Auset or the emotional/astral body in your Spiritual make-up.
•Invoke erasure of long accumulated maya, glamour and illusion from her by the use of your
 Ausarian power of Spirit.
•Experience the calming of the tempest tossed emotional seas within.
•Experience her cleansing, clearing and purification.

•Become aware of the Mother's re-newed reflective clarity and receptivity to the Father
 upon the clear, limpid surface of the waters within.
•Experience the unification of the MotherFather- AusetAusar.
•This is Divine Marriage within as the mother now in her clarity and stillness reflects the One
 True Self Realized Being-ness.
•Hotep –Peace –Nirvana.

KaAbBa   Building The Lighted Temple
The Spiritual B(ARK)

> **Metaphysical Key:**
> Sphere 10 Geb Meditation

Kemetic Name: Geb – See re-claim-ation in Kemetic naming of Sphere 10 *Geb*
by Ra Un Nefer Amen, *Metu Neter,V.I & II*
Kabalistic Name – Malkuth – Kingdom

In Meditation deep:

•We enter within Sphere 10, Geb.

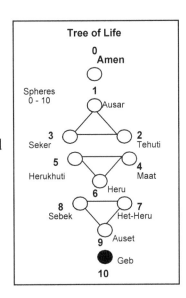

Affirmation:
•This is my tangible physical reality that I co-create for myself.
•This is my Khab or physical body and the etheric vital body.
•My degree of awakening directs the plane of consciousness that
this vital energy will be drawn from for the building and
maintenance of my Temple.
•This is the physical body, the environment, the World itself.
•This is where I bear witness to my *co-creatorship* in building true to
the Divinely intended design.

•Bring your awareness to your physical body.
•Meditate upon how you have been building this vehicle in your
Lighted Temple.
•Are you building a Spirit-filled and Light-filled body, environment and Planet Earth –Geb?

For description of The Kemetic Neteru see E. A. Wallis Budge, *The Gods of the Egyptians, V.I & II,* Gerald Massey, *Ancient Egypt The Light of The World, V.I & II,* and Ra Un Nefer Amen, *Metu Neter, V.I & II.* Also see, *The Ausarianization of Consciousness Tablet Series 2 – The Metaphysical Keys to The Tree Of Life with Oracle Keys to Dis-spelling Illusion.*

Going forward, our focus now within this study will be the Spiritual Journey of unfolding consciousness within the 3 Primary Triangles of Ka Ab Ba and the 7 Soul Divisions.

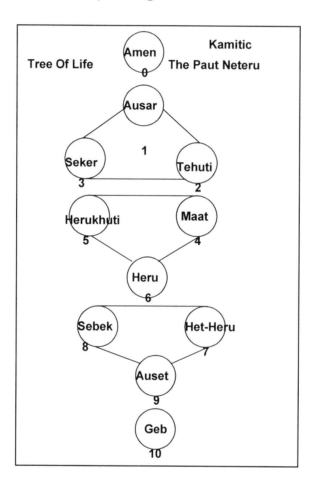

Chapter: **3**
The Eldest Race On The Planet Is The Black Race

Our Story Continues…
We are all one human family. Yet, the Races within the human family do not emerge or make their appearance all at once during this 4th Round or World period in which we now live. The eldest Race on the Planet is the Black Race. In time other Races gradually unfolded on the Planet. This brings us to the next

Metaphysical Key To: The Root Races

There has been extensive (Esoteric) veiling of the Ancient Wisdom regarding the Races. This has contributed to much confusion and has served to hinder our ability to properly view the Spiritual Journey of Unfolding Consciousness within the human family. Presently, the consciousness of our Earth humanity is an admixture of African, Semitic and Aryan/European Races. Esoterically, these are also called the 3rd, 4th and 5th Root Races, with the 3rd being Ancient and elder and the 5th being recent and younger.[*] The 3 Root Races now overlapping combine to form a consciousness admixture that I am describing in this text as:

3-4-5   AfricanSemiticAryan - Konsciousness Admixture - ASA-KA

Even though the 3rd, 4th, and 5th Root races have certain physiological characteristics our focus is more about particular states of consciousness and how these are blending together at this time in our Earth History. Taken together they influence this World period. The Planetary *blending of consciousness* is what we confront as a Humanity in our next evolutionary steps. Our collective Spiritual Journey leads us now to:
1. Move from a state of separativeness and materialization in consciousness – which now dominates our planet Earth – to that which is unitive, synthesizes and re-Spiritualizes.
2. Understand the cycle of time in which we now live and the qualitative backdrop of energies available to lift us into the Ausarianization of Consciousness and the re-Spiritualization of our Planet.

Eons ago our Ancestors lived in *cycles of time* when the Earth was in a Spiritualized state. The human, animal, plant and mineral kingdoms were more in balance and man and woman partook nurturance from the Earth, according to their need. *Man and woman's consciousness was*

---

[*]This Name and Numbering is described in greater detail in, *The Ausarianization of Consciousness Series 2*. The letter K has been substituted for the letter C in the word Consciousness. See *Metaphysical Keys to The Tree Of Life with Oracle Keys to Dis-spelling Illusion* in the Appendix for explanation.

unbroken. In other words, they did not see themselves as a 'self' separated from other 'selves.' The spark of 'separative consciousness' had yet to be fanned to a flame. Instead, they saw themselves as intricately interdependent and at one with all creation. This was a state of Unity, God, All or Omniscient consciousness. It is Ausarian consciousness in the Kemetic Spiritual tradition (See Ra Un Nefer Amen, Massey, Budge).

Man and woman were in deepest communion with the Divinity in all and with the Spiritual Kingdom of Celestial beings or Neteru. This Spiritual Hierarchy are those helping agencies that are guiding Earth humanity into a greater measure of Spiritual Light. Known by many names which include: Neteru, Paut Neteru, Deities, Elohim, God Kings, Kabiri, Annunaqi, Manasa-devas, Sons of Maat, Lords of the Flame, Solar Ancestors, Agniswatas, Solar Angels, Celestial Beings, Holy Ones, Angels, Orisha and so on (See *The Gods of the Egyptians; Ancient Egypt the Light of the World; Let's Set the Record Straight; Secret Doctrine;* 24 Tibetan Books [*A Treatise on Cosmic Fire, Initiation Human & Solar,* etc.]; *The Divine Plan; The Rosicrucian Cosmo-Conception; Lemurian Scrolls; Lost Keys of Enoch;* et. al.). These seeded and guided early humanity both from the inner Spiritual plane or invisible realm and upon the outer physical plane or visible realm as they walked among man and woman as God Kings. In a much later cycle, of time the Greek philosopher Hesiod (eighth century B.C) would write about this state of consciousness. According to: Robert Lawlor, *Voices of the First Day,* p. 69-70.

> A golden race of mortal men was created at the beginning of time. The golden race lived like God, pain and suffering were unknown to them, death arrived like a self-induced dream, and the earth was fruitful without human toil. Food was plentiful, no wars or strife marred the happiness of human beings.

As an Ancient people, our story extends into the night of time.
•It is *Exoterically* known (more commonly) that Africa is the cradle and birthplace of humanity some estimated 4 – 7 million years ago
•It is *Esoterically* known (more veiled/hidden) that events in African (Lemurian) consciousness were unfolding 18 million years ago (See *Secret Doctrine; Rosicrucian Cosmo Conception; Tibetan Books; Origin and Evolution of The Human Race).*

This suggests that:
•If we are made in the Image and Likeness of God and that
•We are no less than we have always been from the beginingless beginning and endless ending
•Then we knew Unity or God Consciousness and then *fell* from this awareness

Much in the literature says, then unsays this. To say it would mean that a more Ancient people knew, and walked upon Earth in the state of God Consciousness. A consciousness that so-called, present day, advanced, 'modern man' is trying to 'get back to'. Why would we be trying to get back a state of being we never had, and cannot remember? What are people who sit and meditate really trying to achieve anyway? The Bible tells us that, 'There is nothing new under the Sun'.

KaAbBa   Building The Lighted Temple
The Spiritual B(ARK)

We are still trying to unearth the greatness of the Ancient World. What was known then dwarfs the so-called 'advances of the modern World' of today. Accordingly: *Isis Unveiled, V.I* p. 526.

> Whenever, in the pride of some new discovery, we throw a look into the past, we find, to our dismay, certain vestiges which indicate the possibility, if not certainty, that the alleged discovery was not totally unknown to the ancients.

Nirvana which is a state of God Consciousness was not first experienced by Buddha in 600 B.C.E, but thousands of years ago (Exoterically) and millions of years ago (Esoterically) by our Ancient African Ancestors. Exoterically this state of return in God Consciousness was called Seket-Aarnru, Hetepu or Hotep, which means – *Peace.*

There is a *genocidal arrogance* in some of the literature that says that the 'remnant' of the Ancient tribal people of the World will die out, become extinct. Racial hatreds and tensions have led one racial group to try to destroy another. What we must come to terms with is the fact that each Root Race has its respective part to play in the Divine plan. God consciousness indwells within skins ranging in hues that are black, brown, red, yellow and white. Accordingly: Max Heindel, *Rosicrucian Cosmo Conception,* p. 311- 312.

> Races are but an evanescent feature of evolution… Races are simply steps in evolution which must be taken, otherwise there will be no progress for the spirits reborn in them.

It is after all, a journey in consciousness and *what goes around comes around*, full cycle – that *now is then* and *then is now* and the *serpent will put its tail in its mouth.* Today, as one human family, we are gathering 'closer together' due to technological advances in communication and travel which make the Earth which is called Geb – sphere 10, in the Tree of Life – seem smaller. Our future depends upon what we now choose to do in our *closer proximity.* We must now offer up the sum total of the 'parts' we have played as ONE whole humanity. In the sum total of our collective consciousness we must now work in lifting our Earth into sacredization and Spiritualization. Accordingly: *The Veil of Isis, [read here: Auset] V.I,* v. preface.

> Yet we do not hesitate to accept the assertion of Biffe, that "the essential is forever the same. Whether we cut away the marble inward that hides the statue in the block, or pile, stone upon stone outward till the temple is completed, our New result is only an *old idea.* The latest of all the eternities will find its destined other half-soul in the earliest.

And Likewise: Ibid. p. 4.

> Max Muller states accordingly: Many things are still unintelligible to us, and the hieroglyphic language [read here: Metu Neter] of antiquity records but half of the mind's unconscious intentions. Yet more and more the image of man, in whatever clime we meet him, rises before us, noble and pure from the very beginning; even his errors we learn to understand, even his dreams we begin to interpret. As far as we can trace back the footsteps of man, even on the lowest strata of history, we see the Divine gift of a sound and sober intellect belonging to him from the very first, and the idea of a humanity emerging slowly from the depths of an animal brutality can never be maintained again.

The Ausarianization of Consciousness Series 1
Metaphysical Keys To the Tree of Life & Oracle Keys to Dis-spelling Illusion
The Spiritual Journey in Unfolding Consciousness

34

Division into the 3 - The Nature Of The Trinity At Work In Man And Woman – The Story of Ausar, Auset and Heru

As the Eldest Race Our story is an Ancient story. Furthermore, within Our story other stories have been enfolded and encoded and have evolved over time. Thus Our Story is *story, within story, within story*. The story of **Ausar, Auset and Heru** is one such story. This brings us to the next

Metaphysical Key To:
The Number 3
The Divine Trinity
The Trinity/Triune Nature of Man/Woman and Creation
Ausar, Heru, Auset
BaAbKa or KaAbBa

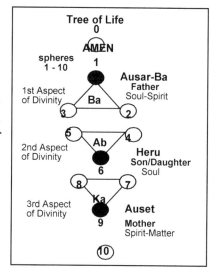

This pass down the Tree of Life will be to look within the Number or Neter 3 – the 3 Primary Triangles that form the Tree of Life and the Divine Trinity or the 1st, 2nd and 3rd Aspects of Divinity. This brings us to the next

Metaphysical Key To:
The Overlay of The Divine Trinity
Within The Tree of Life

In the diagram at right, we see the overlay of the Divine Trinity revealed within the Tree of Life. The story of the Divine Trinity pre-dates Christianity by what is exoterically known as thousands of years (and what is esoterically known as millions of years).[1] Ausar, Auset and Heru are later called Osiris, Isis, and Horus, respectively by the Greeks.

In this story Ausar and Auset harmoniously rule their kingdom as king and queen of Kemet. Egypt is the name later given to Kemet by the Greeks. The Greeks and others re-named much of our story. To the Kemetians, Numbers and Letters were called Ntr or Neter, which are qualities of God or Neter. Quality is vibration. Our story gives us an important archetype and geometrical design revealed in Number. Neter or Number provides the vehicle through which the Neteru or qualities of God speak. The Trinity is one such numerological vehicle or template upon which the events of unfolding consciousness are taking place and expressing Divinity. The divisioning of the nature of creation and man/woman into 3 discrete qualities of energy is the story of the Divine Trinity. These 3 powers qualify and guide our Spiritual journey of unfolding

---

[1] See *Secret Doctrine. 24 Tibetan Books* under the name Asauras, Kumaras, Sanat Kumara.

consciousness. In the diagram we see the division of the Tree of Life into 3 primary triangles called KaAbBa or BaAbKa depending upon which direction up or down the Tree of Life we move in. Here we see that:

•The Ba Triangle is the 1st Aspect of Divinity and is comprised of spheres 1, 2 and 3.

•The Ab Triangle is the 2nd Aspect of Divinity and is comprised of spheres 4, 5 and 6.

•The Ka Triangle is the 3rd Aspect of Divinity and is comprised of spheres 7, 8 and 9, with sphere 10 completing the square or quartenary, described later.

This Divine Trinity is shown in the 3 colored spheres. Ausar and his wife Auset are pictured as sphere 1 and sphere 9 and their Son/Daughter Heru as sphere 6, respectively. These are the 3 aspects of Divinity within our Spiritual make-up or equipment which are Father (Spirit-Soul), Son/Daughter (Soul) and Mother (Spirit-Matter).

We begin with these 3 divisions because they show us where we are going, how and why. These three terms represent our straight line of re-ascent. Thus our intent, direction and destination are immediately defined. In *The Ausarianization of Consciousness Tablet Series 1 – The Metaphysical Keys to The Tree Of Life with Oracle Keys to Dis-spelling Illusion,* we will look at how the Ancients arrived at these three terms – KaAbBa. For our purposes now the question is:

How does the Story of Ausar, Auset and Heru contribute in telling *Our story* about the Spiritual Journey of Unfolding Consciousness in man and woman?

We are told by the Ancient wisdom in the story of Ausar, Auset and Heru, that:

1.   Ausar and Auset harmoniously rule their kingdom as King and Queen.
2.   Heru is the son of Ausar and Auset.
3.   Ausar is slain by his jealous brother Set.
4.   A fierce battle ensues between Heru and Set in which Heru must avenge his Father's death and be restored as the rightful heir to the throne. This symbolizes the re-establishing of the Kingdom of God on Earth.

The Ausarianization of Consciousness Series 1
Metaphysical Keys To the Tree of Life & Oracle Keys to Dis-spelling Illusion
The Spiritual Journey in Unfolding Consciousness

36

Chapter 4
So how did we move from a state of paradise where, *'the Earth was fruitful without human toil, food was plentiful, no wars or strife marred the happiness of human beings?'* What changed in consciousness?

What is Ba?
To begin to respond to this question we move to the emanation of Spirit in the creative process and briefly describe Sphere 0 and Sphere 1. They will be described in greater detail later.

Our story begins with
Sphere 0 and the Arising of Sphere 1
1st Aspect of Divinity Triangle

In DARKNESS within THE ABSOLUTE, THE ALL, NETER NETERU, AMEN, AMEN-NU, THE SUPREME BE-NESS, THE FOUNT OF ALL POSSIBILTIES, THE INFINITE, just a few names for the ABSOLUTE REALITY – *CREATION* Stirs.

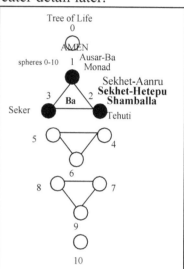

From this stirring within AMEN, THE ALL, there is a raying forth of Light and The One as Creator issues forth from the ABSOLUTE ALL – AMEN –sphere 0. This is Ausar, or sphere 1. Sphere 1 is known by various names and is symbolized here as Ba and Ausar in the Kemetic system (See Ra Un Nefer Amen) and will be referred to in this text as Ausar Ba.

```
Metaphysical Key To:
Understanding Ba
```

Ausar Ba
1st Aspect of Divinity Triangle
The Eternal Knower
Spirit –Soul
Ba Triangle – composed of
Spheres 1, 2 and 3.

Division 1 – Ba Triangle in the Tree of Life
The first triangle is called Ba. It is what the Esotericists call Monad or Logos. Ba means Soul and Soul is consciousness. It is sphere 1 in the Tree of Life. Spheres 1, 2, and 3 comprise the Ba Triangle or 1st Aspect of Divinity. When our awareness resides within the Ba triangle, then we

are experiencing what is called Ausarian consciousness by the Kemetians and Monadic consciousness by the Esotericists. Here, God the INFINITE is reflected as God the Creator. Hence, Universe is created with all its multiplicity of Super Cosmic Galaxies, Suns, Planets, Worlds, Humans and so on. God transcendent becomes God indwelling. God is reflected in all that is created and man and woman are made in the Image and Likeness of God. Therefore, man and woman have all the Divine qualities of God. These Divine qualities are called Neter or Neteru (plural).

When we bring our consciousness to the Ba triangle within our Spiritual equipment, we are entering that center of peace, which has its correspondence in the etheric Planetary Center called *Sekhet Aanru* and *Sekhet Hetepu* by the Kemetians, and Shamballa by later day Esotericists. In this 'place' we gather as One with/as the Gods and Goddesses. It is the center where the *Will of God is Known.* As the *seeker* who returns and resides within this abode you are THE WORD MADE TRUTH, having sounded the fullest sound of the power of Seker – sphere 3.

Who is Ausar Ba?
You are Ausar Ba.
Ausar Ba is The One True Self Realized Being-ness and Identification of man and woman. Within the raying forth from AMEN – sphere 0, Ausar – sphere 1, comes into subjective being with the Divine archetypal designs and creative substance rayed forth and complete within him or her to become, The Self Realized Being-ness that he or she already is. With the emanation of Spirit into the One, we now make a descent down the Tree of Life:

The *stirring* within AMEN, THE ABSOLUTE, gives rise to Ausar Ba who 'seemingly' leaves his ETERNAL *Home* and begins a journey. The Pilgrim called Ausar Ba, sets out on the Spiritual Journey.

In our Eternal Home we know peace – called Hotep by the Kemetians. Peace comes from the Realization that we are made in the Image and Likeness of God. This is our One True Self Identification. As Ausar Ba we 'seemingly' leave our Eternal Home and begin a journey that we never really went on – except in appearance. This appearance, though *unreal* and called *illusion,* would eventually cause us to forget the *Real.*

Yes, this seeming appearance of leaving our Eternal Home and setting out on a journey that we never really went on would cause us to forget the *One True Self* that we are and have always been from the beginingless beginning. As we begin our Spiritual journey in unfolding consciousness our awareness is still AT-ONE with the Higher Spiritual realm and the full remembrance of the Supernal Light of our Eternal Home is our consciousness.

We are Ausar Ba, The One True Self Realized Being-ness. The Drawer from the Fount of All Possibility. Unlimited – we are The Drawer of All Power, All Wisdom, and All Pervading Presence. As we continue along the Spiritual Journey, we gradually descend into the more material realms below and become more and more submerged in matter. From the first and highest plane, we descend as if taking an elevator through the seven planes of consciousness.

The idea as we make our descent is to *remain* polarized within the higher realms. However, we endure many impacts along the way. Impact after impact we forget the Higher planes of our birth and we come to experience a 'self' that is *less than* our One True Self. In time, we come to believe that we *are* the impacts of physical, emotional, sexual abuse, dis-ease, poverty, loss of self esteem (Self estimation), victimization, enslavement, death, and all manner of love-less conditions. Along our descent into the utmost limits of matter and material consciousness – we come to feel diminished and begin to take the illusion of these conditions as our *reality.* With continual descent, through each successive plane and *seeming* disconnection from the higher planes, our consciousness grows successively more material, dense and dark.

So we move from our full identification as Spirit Beings into an identification with the coarse matter of our physical bodies struggling in the World for material existence. As we reach the lowest point in our descent – the 7th plane – memory of our Image and Likeness of/as God, our All in all-ness – *fades.* Our Light obscures, awareness dims. Thus we undergo a seeming obscuration or blotting out of – The One True Self.

- At last, the illusion of the Spiritual journey in which we:
- Seemingly leave our Eternal home,
- Descend into increasingly darkening material conditions and
- Experience self diminishing impacts along the way –
- *Becomes real.*
- Our One True Spiritual Identity becomes -
- *The unreal.*
- Yet in essence:
- We are no less than the Image and Likeness of God
- No less than the fullness of the One True Self
- That we have always been
- From the beginingless beginning.

Man/Woman grows 'down' the Tree of Life in his long involutionary descent into matter. Man/Woman grows 'up' the Tree of Life in his evolutionary re-ascent back to the source. His climb both down and up The Tree of Life is the story of how man and woman both forget and then re-member that which they have always been – Sons and Daughters of God. To understand the involutionary and evolutionary cycle we must understand – The Kemetic Law of Vibration. The Spiritual Journey brings us to the next

KaAbBa Building The Lighted Temple
The Spiritual B(ARK)

Metaphysical Key:
The Law of Vibration

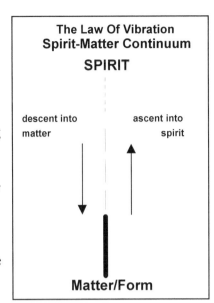

The Ancients knew that:
1. All is Spirit and that
2. Spirit periodically seeks to know ITSELF by reflecting itself into its dual aspect of Spirit-Matter
3. Spirit is matter at its lowest level of vibration and
4. Matter is Spirit at its highest level of vibration. (See *The Kybalion; Secret Doctrine*)
5. All in Universe is vibration
6. Spirit vibrates at the highest, fastest most refined level
7. Matter vibrates at a lower, slower more coarse or dense level

We see in the diagram at right that, Spirit-Matter is a continuum and can not be separated. Any 'seeming' separation is just an appearance in our changing consciousness. Ultimately:
1. As Spirit vibrates at a lower, slower rate we have the arising of a more coarse dense substance which is more material. We call this matter or form.
2. As Spirit vibrates at a faster level, we have the arising of a more refined subtle substance which is more Spiritual.
3. All is Spirit and
4. All resolves in Spirit
5. This Law of vibration is reflected in the 7 Planes of Consciousness later described.

The Law of Vibration is seen operative along the Spirit-Matter continuum in what is called the involutionary and evolutionary cycles of human consciousness. This brings us to our next

Metaphysical Key To:
Involutionary and Evolutionary Cycles
The Spiritualization and Materialization in Consciousness

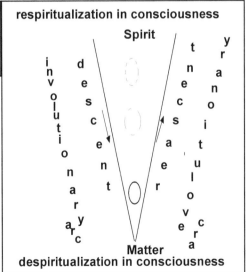

Pictured in the diagram at right is the: **Involutionary and Evolutionary Cycles**

On the involutionary arc, consciousness makes its descent becoming more materialized. The vertex in the 'V' illustrates how Spirit has made its deepest descent into matter.

On the evolutionary arc, consciousness is making its return ascent and becomes re-spiritualized. Taken together this is the involutionary and evolutionary cycle of human consciousness.

This brings us to our next

> **Metaphysical Key To:**
> Combining the Metaphysical Keys
> To reveal various Correspondences

By merely putting these 2 diagrams side by side we start to see the power in combining the
Metaphysical Keys in the following:
1. The Law of Vibration and/as The Spirit-Matter Continuum
2. The Involutionary and Evolutionary Cycles – revealing
3. The Spiritualization and Materialization in Consciousness

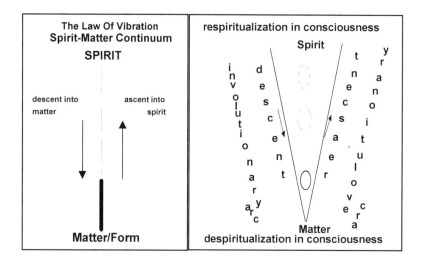

In our unbroken Ausarian consciousness, we knew the underlying unity guiding the seamless
relationship between all beings in creation. In our broken consciousness, we began to honor the
'part' more than the whole. *Hard at play* in the game of *particularization* where interconnection
is not seen and upheld - man has killed, enslaved one another, destroyed and polluted the
environment and violated his own nature, health and well being - Geb - sphere 10. In a World of
separativeness and particularization of consciousness, humanity is starting to glean the need and
the higher aspiration to now be *hard at work* trying to make all the pieces fit back together again.

KaAbBa Building The Lighted Temple
The Spiritual B(ARK)

What has happened for man and woman in the Spiritual Journey of Unfolding Consciousness over cycles of time?

Our story continues...
•The cycles of time would lead man and woman into an Involutionary descent
•In time a despiritualization in consciousness would occur
•The 'ways' of innate knowingness and wholeness
•Would become the veiled and concealed 'secrets'
•Withheld from the masses of humanity
•Leaving them to *grope* in the dark
•Trying to find their way back 'Home'
•We are the prodigal Son/Daughter who has 'seemingly' left home and has
•*Gone out* on a journey as Heru
•We are likewise Son/Daughter who stayed Home - Ausar
•Yes, paradoxically, we are both Ausar and Son/Daughter called Heru
•Our I-dentification as/with both is the 'two made One' and
•The journey towards Ausarian, Unity or God consciousness
•This return journey in consciousness is Kemetically expressed as
•*"Nuk Ausar, I am Ausar"*
•This return journey in consciousness is biblically expressed as
•*"My Father and I are ONE"*

We seemingly leave our Eternal Home and begin this journey down the Tree of Life, traveling through the 7 Planes of Consciousness (described later), from the invisible to the visible realm, with many impacts along the way. The idea of course, as we make our descent is *to remain* in Ausarian Consciousness, All Consciousness - The highest plane of consciousness, Ba sphere 1. In a state of Ausarian consciousness we are in alignment with Divine Mind as we manifest our work in the World – Geb – sphere 10, and the lowest plane of consciousness. We have the use of personal 'will' to choose to do otherwise.

In the Metaphysical Keys that follow, you will see that Spirit takes of itself and begins to differentiate itself in/as Spirit-matter. This is one of the many Divine paradoxes. As much as Spirit is unlimited and unconditioned it asserts its right to limit itself in form or matter to gain conscious experience of ITSELF. In various grades of material form, IT sees ITSELF. It 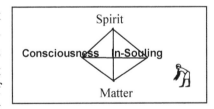 is in *the seeing of ITSELF* that consciousness is born. Thus you are made human and Divine, material and Spiritual. This is expressed in the diagram at right.

On our Spiritual journey in unfolding consciousness as Heru – sphere 6, we make our descent into material life conditions. On our return journey, we make our hard, arduous climb of re-ascent Home again, into the Spiritual realms.

•As the *returning one* in your ascending journey Home you will meet *the Eternal One* who is yourself, who never left. The *Eternal One* greets you with a sound incessantly sounding since the beginingless beginning which affirms, *'I K-N-O-W'.*

•As the *returning one* – you greet the *Eternal One* which is yourself with a sound now garnered by your re-mem-bering. It is the putting back together again, the brokeness in consciousness through a multitude of lifetimes lived in time-space bound quantums of existences until you at last affirm, *' I K-N-O-W THAT I K-N-O-W'.*

•Remembering is transcending the particularization of thought which affirms, *'I Think I Know'.*

We might ask:

Why this Spiritual journey in unfolding consciousness?

Why did you need to *Go Out* from a state of *K-n-o-w-I-n-g* on a journey – only to return to say, 'I KNOW THAT I KNOW?'

This same question has its higher reflection when we ask,
Why Did the ABSOLUTE create?' If the ABSOLUTE is INFINITE ALL and ALL KNOWING (OMNISCIENCE) why did it need to ex-ternalize a part of itself in order to see itself reflected as Spirit-in-form to *K-n-o-w ITSELF?*

· Perhaps when you make your return ascent in
  your journey Home
· And meet The Eternal One face to face
· Which is you who never left home
· You will know more about the *Stirring* within
  the ABSOLUTE
· Which is reflected in your stirring and leaving
  Home
· Like the babe that stirs and leaves the womb
· On your seeming Spiritual Journey in unfolding
  consciousness
· That you never really went on
· Except in illusion
· Thus in your return do you see that:
· You are truly made in the Image and Likeness of God
· Thus do you become as God.
· In the Wordless *K-N-O-W-ING*
· When the imponderable, unanswerable, Wordless *W-h-y*
· Is at last, at rest
· Within the Deep, DARK, Silence as yet –
· *Unstirred.*

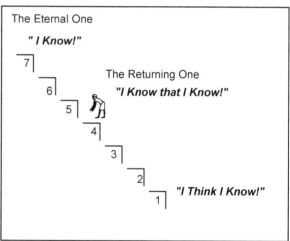

Chapter 5
The Story Of Ausar, Auset and Heru – The Divine Trinity Continued…

Metaphysical Key To:
The Story of
Ausar, Auset and Heru
The Divine Trinity

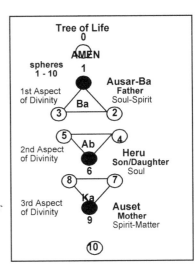

We now continue Our Story of: The Divine Trinity Ausar, Auset and Heru

A fuller version of the story is found in various texts. Excerpts from this story will be given as Our story continues (See also, Budge, *The Book of Coming Forth by Day, Prt Em Hru,* (Egyptian Book of the Dead); *Osiris The Egyptian Religion of Resurrection;* Dr. Muata Ashby, *Ausarian Resurrection*). An abbreviated version is as follows:

Ausar is the Divine King who ruled Kemet with his very abled wife Auset at his side. Ausar had established peace and harmony in the land of Kemet, which was governed under the Universal laws of Tehuti – sphere 2, and Maat – sphere 4. The Kemetic Laws of Tehuti are later referred to by the Greeks as the Hermetic Laws of Thoth, or Hermes Trismegistus (See also G.R.S Mead, *Thrice Greatest Hermes;* William Wynn Westcott, *Collectanea Hermetica;* Three Initiates, *Kyballion;* The Tibetan, *The 24 Tibetan Books)*. People lived in accord with Divine will and purpose in building and maintaining a Kingdom. This brings us to the next

Metaphysical Key To:
Restoration of The 1st Eye
Overcoming impediment # 2
Blindness

Their 1st eye was active and enabled them to see the Divine architectural design for living in harmony with nature. There was no need for an external force within the Kingdom when all vibrated in accord with Divine will and law. The people prospered and lived in peace known as Hotep. Ausar would travel to far off lands to establish God's kingdom. In his absence, his wife Auset was unwavering in her devotion to the Divine rulership of Ausar.

All the while, their jealous brother Set was plotting to overthrow the Kingdom of Ausar. At last, Set found his opportunity which was occasioned by a banquet held for Ausar. Set, along with 72 of his confederates secretly plotted and devised a scheme in which they got the measurements of Ausar. They then had a royally jeweled sarcophagus made to his exact size. The coffin was just one of a myriad of sacred symbols used by the Kemetians to express the Spiritual journey of the Soul in the afterlife. These sacred symbols, the Ritual and all that was required for success in the journey in this life and the afterlife were central in their unfolding consciousness. So eagerly, guests at the banquet each took a turn at trying to fit the coffin - but without success. Finally, Ausar's time to try it out for size had come. Naturally, since the coffin was specially designed for him, the King fit *exactly*. Immediately, the coffin was seized upon by Set and his evil doers who nailed it shut, cast it into the Nile – thereby drowning Ausar. At last, Ausar is slain by his jealous brother Set.

Upon learning about her husband's death, Auset wept violently and cut off a lock of her hair. She donned her mourning wear and began a long and ceaseless search for her beloved husband. Upon finding him she transformed herself into a swallow-hawk and caused the life force to be raised up from him, and by taking his seed into her body, she conceived their son, Heru. As you can see, this is the story of the *Immaculate Conception* which would later be incorporated into Christianity. She hid herself and the child. Later, Set came upon the body of Ausar. In an angry rage, he cut it into fourteen (14) pieces – one for each night of the waning Moon – and dispersed these about. Here we see the number 7 doubled into the number 14. The Number 7 reveals the Septenary of man/woman and Creation. This Metaphysical Key is later described.

When are we in Ausarian consciousness and what changed over time?
You are in Ausarian consciousness when you are King upon the throne in rulership of your Spiritual equipment. Thus, do you walk as God and Goddess upon Earth, and Heaven and Earth are made One. When Auset discovered what Set had done she again, with ceaseless devotion, went about re-gathering the broken body of her husband, burying and making a shrine to each piece as she went about her work. Later, Heru, the son of Ausar and Auset, eventually comes to maturity. A fierce battle ensues between Heru and Set in which Heru must avenge his Father's death and be restored as the rightful heir to the throne as King.

What is the brokenness of the body of Ausar?
1. The brokeness of the body of Ausar is a key, symbolizing the brokenness in man and woman's consciousness of the Divinity within.
2. It is likewise a symbol of the brokenness, separation and part-I-cularization in consciousness of the Divinity within the human family.
3. It is the result of the descent down the Tree of Life and the converging cycle(s) of time, which make up *The Perfect Storm,* in which we now live.

What causes the brokenness, separativeness and particularization in consciousness?
This separativeness, or particularization in consciousness occurs when we come to identify with selves that are less than the fullness of our True Identification as Ausar Ba – sphere 1. It is when we use the personal will to fashion a World that is based on a limited and limiting sense of a 'self' now seen in *part* and not in *wholeness*. We are the Tree of Life. It is our Spiritual Faculty both Divine and human.

KaAbBa Building The Lighted Temple
The Spiritual B(ARK)

In Ausarian Resurrection, you are trying to put back together the broken consciousness within yourself and within the human family. In the involutionary descent, the process of 'death sets in' as man and woman exercise use of their personal will to freely choose right or wrong action. As man's consciousness develops he must also develop a 'conscience'. This is known as Ab by the Kemetians. It is the 2nd Aspect of Divinity and is symbolized by the human heart. This is Heru or the Karest/Christ principle within the 6th sphere in the Tree of Life. Conscience guides you to be and act in accord with the Universal Law of Right Relationship. Your obedience to these laws is what increases your Soul light and insures escape from death. Conscience is the internal Self correction, which attunes you to the deific qualities or Neters which keep you on course. You are connected with the qualities of the Neter through the:

1. The 11 spheres in the Tree of Life grouped within
2. The 3 primary triangles of KaAbBa or BaAbKa and channeling through the
3. The 7 Division into 7 Planes of Consciousness, 7 Divisions of Soul-Spirit – 7 Primordial Energies

Chapter 6
From Where Have We Come
Why Were Our Ancestors Able To Build With Greatness?

This question brings us to the next

> **Metaphysical Key To**:
> Knowing How to Tell Time
> *Overcoming impediment # 3*
> Loss of The Ability to Tell Time and
> To Know - What Time It Is

Anchoring the past, our ancestors stood in the full glory of the light of day. They had lived against the backdrop of Supernal Light and beheld it with reverence. They awoke each morning with the fullness of the drenching Spiritual light that poured forth all around and imbued every waking moment. The Sun – called Ra – was a visible symbol of the invisible Presence of the 'All in all' and the 'all in All' everywhere called by the name – AMEN – sphere 0, in the Tree of Life.

The Ancestors guided by the Inner Spiritual Council of Neteru – the Elohim – read and understood large cycles of time and could foretell the great outlines of coming events. They knew that the Planet was to undergo her deepest descent into darkest and densest materialization in consciousness. Life on earth would become de-spiritualized and more material. They knew of the cycles to come and that each cycle would run its course over time, eons long. Once the Ancients had the ability to know certain cycles they had the ability to be at play with time clocks, telling time backwards and forwards in increments of thousands and millions of years.

They built when consciousness was more Spiritualized. The Earth itself and the sub-stance which comprised the bodies of man and woman were more etherialized or less coarse, dense and materialized. All vibrated at a higher Spiritual level in the great Spirit-Matter continuum. Their backdrop in consciousness was upon the landscape of Supernal light. Through the use of the 1st eye the African ancestors saw interiorly the greatness within the Divine architectural design and plan. This greatness was manifested exteriorly in the outer World they built. All that has been built since in the so-called 'modern World' is *dwarfed* under the magnitude of their greatness. This brings us to the next

> **Metaphysical Key To:**
> Impersonality of The Cycles of Time

KaAbBa Building The Lighted Temple
The Spiritual B(ARK)

In our Metaphysical studies we seek to understand the *impersonality of the cycles* of time that *rise and fall*. It is important to see that whenever we look upon an event in human history we must simultaneously look at it upon the backdrop of time in which the event is occurring. It is the backdrop of the cycle of time that makes certain qualities (neters) of energy available that qualify the event.

The use of an analogy will serve as example to illustrate:
Imagine two men who go out to sculpture a tree. One goes out by day and works in the light. The other goes out by night and must work in darkness. What would each produce? You might well imagine the man working by day and guided by sight would sculpt that which is more beautiful than the man who is blinded and working by night.

By analogy, in the early cycle of time, man was sent out to build and sculpture in the light of Spiritual day. In *an unbroken consciousness* and *unity of the whole* the Divine design is more easily revealed. Thus he builds with truth, beauty and in accord with the Great Divine Plan as evidenced by the Pyramids and all the monuments left by the Ancients all over the World.
•In a latter cycle of time man is sent forth to build and sculpture in the darkness of material night.
•Furthermore he is given the *full weight* of self consciousness
•And the exercise of personal will in making his choices of
•How and what he builds
•In a World of *separativeness and particularization of consciousness*
•Out of accord with the Divine Plan
•Man is hard at work trying to make the pieces all fit together
•He experiences great pain, agony, and travail in the quarries of life
•As he fashions a New World upon the prior World
•In this cycle – in the Material darkness of night – man builds that which is grotesque and hideous
•Until he painstakingly re-ascends into the light of unbroken consciousness or Omniscient consciousness again where
•The *Divinely Intended Archetypal Design and Universal Law of Right Relationship are again revealed.*
•Today, within the human family
•Each of the Root Races –
•African, Semitic and Aryan/European has whatever pieces they have to work with
•With whatever their remembrance of the Divine design is
•With whatever Spiritual practices they still posses to aid their *sight*

Our great Kemetic Neter of wisdom called Tehuti – sphere 2, in the Tree of Life has long ago warned us of this day in the following accordingly: The Ancient text entitled, *The Virgin of The World, The Sacred Books of Tehuti* (See Mead, *Thrice Greatest Hermes;* Ashby, *Ausarian Resurrection*).

"…your mind shall lose its sight so as to think the contrary of what is true…."

The Ausarianization of Consciousness Series 1   48
Metaphysical Keys To the Tree of Life & Oracle Keys to Dis-spelling Illusion
The Spiritual Journey in Unfolding Consciousness

The following nursery rhyme reflects the brokeness, separation and part-icularization in consciousness operative within man and woman and between the human family on our Planet today. It is the result of the descent down the Tree of Life and becoming forgetful of our Image and Likeness of God – symbolized by Ausar – The One True Self – sphere 1.

"Humpty Dumpty
Sat on a wall
Humpty Dumpty
Had a Great Fall
All the King's horses and all the King's men
Couldn't put Humpty together again"

Humpty is the World Egg, the Universal Ba, the Grand design of Kosmos that we in Unity, God or Ausarian consciousness seek to re-construct. It is the Kosmic Soul. In the chapter on: *What Time Is It* we will look at cycles of time that are qualifying our Earth experience now. We will tell time. But not by using the clock on your wall that ticks off a mere 24 hours and truncates your view of who you are in the Universe. We will use larger time clocks that restore our relationship with Kosmos.

Man and woman are in the process of trying to:
1. Reconstruct the Trinity (Divinity) within which relates the 3 in 1 and the 3 made 1 that we are of Spirit/(Life) – Soul/Consciousness – in Spirit/Matter-Form.

Man and woman are likewise in the process of trying to:
2. Reconstruct the Septenary (seven divisions) which relates to the 7 in 1 and the 7 made 1 – that we are

Ausarian resurrection is the putting back together:
1. The 10 spheres of consciousness
2. The 7 divisions in Spirit or 7 Souls and Planes of Consciousness
3. The 3 aspects of Divinity
4. The 2 of Father-Mother into
5. The 1 of Ba and finally
6. The abstraction into the '0', zero of Amen from which all arises

For now it is important to take note that it is the focusing of consciousness in the Ba, the highest division of the Spirit, that enables you to realize:
1. The Self As One and the same as that dwelling in all things
2. The Self As being One with God
3. One then becomes as Ausar

KaAbBa Building The Lighted Temple
The Spiritual B(ARK)

This is expressed in the following accordingly: Ra Un Nefer Amen. *Metu Neter V.I,* p. 122.

> Once we understand the true nature of man's spirit-that it is made up of seven divisions – it will be plain to see that a true religion can only be a system that aims at raising Man's focus of consciousness to the higher divisions of his spirit to allow him to function in a God-like manner.

What is Initiation and how do these Metaphysical Keys apply?

Initiation is your growing awareness within *each* of the 3 triangles, 7 planes and 10 spheres of consciousness as you make your 'conscious re-ascent' up the Tree of Life. Initiation by initiation you ascend the *rungs of the ladder* up the Tree of Life. With each rung upward you are sounding a higher Spiritual vibration, a higher appeal. Initiation is the process whereby you undergo successive expansions in consciousness. It is through these stages of initiation that so-called 'secrets' of the Ancient Wisdom are again revealed whereby man *re-members* how to put his 'broken consciousness' back together again – thus realizing, Unity of Spirit and return to the inner-sightedness of the whole.

Man and woman are confined to the womb and the tomb upon the Wheel of Birth and Death until the 4th initiation. At the 4th Initiation you are able to get off of the wheel and thus freely come and go between the Heavenly and Earthly realms. This brings us back to a previous

> **Metaphysical Key To:**
> Right of Ascent and Descent of Spirit

1. Spirit has the right to make its deepest descent into matter without abstraction (withdrawal from form) and likewise
2. Spirit has the right to make its greatest ascent (while) in matter (form) without abstraction
3. It is the Law of Vibration in action

We stand as witnesses to a Spiritual law. If we could just bear to see and realize that it has been expressing itself before our very eyes.

What does this mean?

Man is both Divine and human. Man has even appeared animal like and inhuman. It is the Law of Vibration in action. An example will serve to illustrate. Our example takes us aboard a slave ship where we may look at the condition of both slave and captain upon the slave ship. To see the demonstration of the law that Spirit reaches its lowest descent into matter without abstraction – we view first the condition of the slave.

The slave lay with shackled hands and feet for weeks now in the darkened hull of the slave ship. His muscles are abraded down to bone which is now exposed. His wounds are raw and infested. Death and human despair are all around him. The stench of vomit, human waste and rotting corpses assaults his senses. Appalled as we may be by this sight, we see that from behind the eyes of this man is *Spirit* – and that – Spirit has the right to find its way into the lowliest material

condition without abstraction or death of the form of this man. Even though he cries out to death for release from his agony and suffering, he is living through these conditions.
Next –

We likewise view the captain above upon deck of the slave ship. The sun is upon the captain's face. Yet he is obsessed and consumed by thoughts of greed and lust. He murders with little or no provocation anyone who thwarts his mission, whether slave or crewman. He passes long days on the ship with the sport of slave torture and humiliation. At night he comforts himself with the degradation and rape of slave women. Again we see in this man also that *Spirit* has the right of descent into matter without abstraction. Death does not come just because Spirit indwells in the vilest of mental, emotional and physical conditions. Even though in gloating arrogance he taunts death itself, he is living through these conditions.

The Ages of Light followed by the Ages of Dark must be seen as impersonal as the light of day that is followed by the dark cover of night. These cycles contribute to the rise and the fall of great civilizations in the ongoing Spiritual journey of man and woman. The optimal, supernal heights are followed by the most debased cycles of debauchery. This is a hard saying. In man's inhumanity to man there has been great injustice. In combining Metaphysical Keys in the following overlays we see the Law of Vibration revealed in the Tree of Life:

Metaphysical Key To:
The Overlay of The Law of Vibration and
The Respiritualization and Despiritualization cycle
Within The Tree of Life

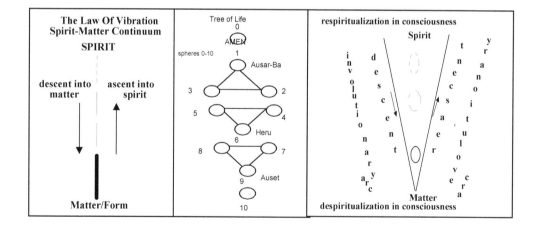

KaAbBa Building The Lighted Temple
The Spiritual B(ARK)

This brings us to the next

Metaphysical Key To:
1. The Kemetic Law of Rhythm
2. The Kemetic Law of Neutralization
3. The Kemetic Law of Compensation

This is expressed accordingly: Three Initiates, *The Kybalion,* p. 159.

> Everything flows out and in; everything has its tides; all things rise and fall; the pendulum-swing manifests in everything; the measure of the swing to the right, is the measure of the swing to the left; rhythm compensates.

We are told by the Kemetic Ancient Wisdom that even though the Law of Rhythm is invariable that the Law of Neutralization is used by the Kemetic Masters to keep the consciousness poised within the Higher Ego which are the Ba and Ab Triangles. This is the raising of the consciousness above the negative swing of the pendulum enabling the Kemetic Master to watch as it passes beneath. This is expressed accordingly: Ibid.

> The Kemetic Master, or advanced student, polarizes himself at the desired pole, and by a process akin to "refusing" to participate in the backward swing, or, if you prefer, a "denial" of its influence over him, he stands firm in his polarized position, and allows the mental pendulum to swing back along the unconscious plane.

This brings us to the next

Metaphysical Key To:
1. The Kemetic Law of Rebirth/Reincarnation -Birth, Death and Transformation
2. Kemetic Law of Cause and Effect, Consequence - Karma
   Overcoming Impediments # 4
   Loss of the Laws to overcome death, fear of death and conscious accountability for actions.
   Loss of the (ability to have a) Declaration of Innocence.

This is expressed accordingly: Ibid.

> The Kemetians regard the chain of lives as continuous, and as forming a part of one life of the individual, so that in consequence the rhythmic swing is understood in this way, while it would be without meaning unless the truth of reincarnation is admitted...

> There is always an action and reaction; an advance and a retreat; a rising and a sinking; manifested in all of the airs and phenomena of the Universe. Suns, worlds, men, animals, plants, minerals, forces, energy, mind and matter, yes even Spirit, manifests this Principle. The Principle manifests in the creation and destruction of worlds; in the rise and fall of nations; in the life history of all things; and finally in the mental states of Man....Thus it is with all living things; they are born, grow, and die-and then are reborn.

The Ausarianization of Consciousness Series 1
Metaphysical Keys To the Tree of Life & Oracle Keys to Dis-spelling Illusion
The Spiritual Journey in Unfolding Consciousness

52

It is only through this truth of reincarnation that we can hold an awareness of the unfolding Spiritual Journey in consciousness of the Root Races. Our failure to reclaim the Metaphysical Key to Reincarnation is a major Impediment (#4) in the Spiritual Journey of Unfolding Consciousness. It is our ability to move within the 1st eye and see the bigger picture and know that there is no 'death'. If you have not thought much about the loss of this Metaphysical Key in your Spiritual Journey, the following reveals that those who have access to the 'stuff of our story' did in fact, give it some thought. This is expressed accordingly: *Rosicrucian Cosmo-Conception* p.167.

> But it was necessary that he should become thoroughly awake to the great importance of this concrete existence, so that he might learn from it all that could be learned. So long as he felt that he was a citizen of the higher Worlds and knew for a certainty that physical life is but a small part of real existence he did not take it seriously enough. He did not apply himself to the cultivation of the opportunities for growth which are found only in the present phase of existence. He dallied his time away without developing the resources of the world, as do the people of India today, for the same reason.
>
> The only way in which an appreciation of concrete physical existence could be aroused in man was by depriving him of the memory of his higher, spiritual existence for a few lives. Thus, during his Earth life, he came to hold no positive knowledge of any other than the one present physical life, and was in this way impelled to earnestly apply himself to living it. **There had been religions previous to Christianity which had taught Rebirth and the law of Consequence, but the time had now come when it was no longer conducive to man's advancement that he should know this doctrine, and ignorance concerning it came to be regarded as a sign of progress.** This one single life was to be made paramount. Therefore we find that the Christian Religion, as publicly taught, does not embody the laws of **Consequence and Rebirth.** Nevertheless, as Christianity is the religion of the most advanced Race, it must be the most advanced Religion, and because of the elimination of this doctrine from its public teachings, the conquest of the world of matter is being made by the Anglo-Saxon and Teutonic races, in which this phase has been carried furthest.

Let's take for further examination the words, 'There had been religions previous to Christianity which had taught Rebirth and the Law of Consequence, *but the time had now come* when it was no longer conducive to man's advancement that he should know this doctrine, and ignorance concerning it came to be regarded as a sign of progress'. The reference to 'these early religions' and to 'he' must *certainly* be to the elder 3rd Root Race of the African/Negro.

Who did this elimination and of what right? What degree of destruction, murder, secrecy would achieve the Law of Rebirth being expunged from our Spiritual practice and memory!
We are overcoming the impediment of the loss of the Law of Rebirth/Reincarnation from our Spiritual practice. We are also overcoming the impediment of not knowing what time it is. The above quote bears witness that 'Someone' is keeping tract of time even though *Christian*

believers have been warned **not** to be "Observers of Time" – see *Deuteronomy*. Clearly, keeping tract of time has been used by one Race of people to gain advantage over another.

The African Doctrine of Last Things
Our Story of Immortality?
Within the book entitled, *Osiris [read here: Ausar] The Egyptian [read here: Kemetc] Religion of Resurrection* by E. A. Wallis Budge, there is a chapter with the title, *"The African Doctrine of Last Things-Immortality"*. It guides us in understanding, Immortality and the journey of unfolding consciousness, expressing through the 7 Soul divisions in our Spiritual equipment. The concept of immortality is expressed in the following accordingly: The Chapter XlX. p. 116-117.

> The offerings found in the pre-dynastic tombs of Kemet prove that the indigenous inhabitants of the country believed in existence after death, and the persistent allusions to "everlasting life" and immortality which are found in the texts of all periods show that the belief in a resurrection was general. Two or three passages are sufficient to prove how definite this belief was, and it is unnecessary to quote more than the following: To Unas, a king of the Vl dynasty, it is said, "hail Unas! Assuredly thou hast not gone as one dead, but as one living to sit upon the throne of Ausar (Osiris)." Again, the same king is declared to be the son of the god Temu, the Father-god and Creator, and it is said: "He (i.e., Temu) liveth, this Unas liveth; he dieth not, this Unas dieth not." That this life beyond the grave was everlasting is proved by the words of Thoth [read here: Tehuti], who said to the deceased: "Thou shalt exist for millions of years, [thy] period of life shall be millions of years." The deceased says that his soul is both God and eternity, therefore God is eternal and His servant partakes of the attributes of the Neter and lives forever with Him.

As African people we are 'millions of years old'.

What is Continuity of Consciousness where no death is experienced?
1. Imagine laying in bed at night, hitting the rewind button on your day and processing the day's events. Here you are, the eternal Knower and Observer, who stands in back of the drama of life witnessing and extracting the essence of each daily lesson that one day of living brings.
2. Now imagine laying in bed and closing your physical eyes for a final time as you move through the portal of life to afterlife. Again, as the eternal Knower and Observer, imagine having this same awakened consciousness that now hits the rewind button on your *entire* lifetime, extracting the essence from the life's lessons which have been garnered.
3. As the eternal Knower and Observer awakened in *continuity of consciousness* you become aware of the succession of lifetimes that you have lived, as well as the spaces in between these lifetimes.
4. Each lifetime is like a quantum packet of mortality in an unbroken stream of immortality. (See *On The Way To Finding Your Soulmate,* Dr. Terri Nelson)
5. You are able to witness your immortality.
6. Rather than isolate your awareness within any particular lifetime or quantum packet of mortality you can bring your awareness to the continuous, unbroken, uninterrupted, eternal stream and connection with *Spirit/Life.*

•So, as we have stood as witnesses to the low in the descent
•So we will stand in witness to the greatness of re-ascent.

Marcus Garvey expresses this according to: Dr. Tony Martin, *The Ideological and Organizational Struggles of Marcus Garvey.*

> Garveyism decreed that the attainment of its ultimate goals was inevitable, the goals in this case being the resurgence of the Black Race: "In the cycle of things he lost his position, but the same cycle will take him back to where he was once.

•We will walk once again upon the Earth as Gods
•When Spirit asserts its right to its highest ascent in woman and man
•After much rehearsal in the 7 planes of consciousness along its descent down
•Through the planes of the Tree of Life
•Thus does each Prodigal Sun – Son/Daughter
•Ultimately return Home
•Having gained the entire
•Conscious experience of Spirit
•At every level of its immersion into matter and
•Matter in its re-ascent into pure Spirit
•Every vile and glorious station
•Back to Omniscient consciousness, Ausarian Consciousness
•The Spiritual Journey is from God to God
•As you bring your consciousness back
•Into the awareness of the All
•The Amen in The Tree of Life
•You are set back to Ground '0'
•This re-absorption takes place through meditation
•And living in accord
•With the Universal Laws of Maat
•Man finds himself once again
•Polarized in the ONE
•The first sphere of the Tree of Life
•A King upon the throne
•As the One of Ausar Ba
•You are able to draw from The Fount Of All Possibility
•All that is needed to work co-creatively
•In the great Divine Plan.
•This Soul awareness attunes you to the source
•Of Omnipotence, Omnipresence, and Omniscience

KaAbBa   Building The Lighted Temple
The Spiritual B(ARK)

As The Spiritual Journey Continues...
The Ancestors watched the shade steadily go down, gradually blotting out the Spiritual light of day as we passed through the Golden, Silver, Copper and Iron ages. With each passing cycle light dimmed and darkness grew. Now well seeded among us, these Elder Guides, Teachers, and God Kings gradually retreated to the inner plane leaving man to work his way back into the Spiritual Kingdom – a *Coming Forth by Day* after his long night of descent. They continue to guide and await man's re-ascension into sacredness. *The Prt Em Heru – The Book of Coming Forth by Day* – is the Book of Life that has been left to us by our great Ancestors. It has been improperly called *The Egyptian Book of the Dead.*

The Ancestors tried to keep the 'circle' in consciousness unbroken and practice the ways of wholeness, but separativeness in consciousness began to grow. The tenders and keepers of the Planet were forced to put away their healing ways. Gradually, healing ways were not respected in a world where man, animal, plant, nature and God are seen as separate. Disunity prevailed. To safeguard the future of the Earth they buried the wisdom deep within her so that the power of the Ancient Wisdom would not fall into the hands of those who would now come.

Everywhere *conquering and acquisition* on the physical plane would take the place of *ceaseless Spiritual contemplation.* Reverence for the Divine in all creation would be forgotten except in the consciousness of the healers and timekeepers who *know and await.*

•In the beginingless beginning
•Before we 'seemingly' left our Eternal Home and
•Began a journey that we never really went on
•We knew the simultaneous Every-thing-ness and No-thing-ness of All-at-once-ness.
•As we became self – conscious beings
•Who gradually fell into the illusion of subject-object
•We began to experience a One-at-a-time-ness.
•This one-at-a-time-ness gave us the power
•To 'mentally' dissect God's creation
•Hard at play we became steeped
•In the game of discriminating *this* as separate, distinct and different from *that*
•This is mind, called Manes by the Kemetians
•In our deepest 'fall'
•One-at-a-time-ness just plain came to mean
•'Me'-ness and
•*Isolation grew*

Separative consciousness would run rampant in the later cycles of time to come. The battlefield and battle lines between the forces of darkness and forces of light would be drawn in the Semitic 4th Root Race. The 5th Root Race of men – the Aryan/Europeans – would emerge against the backdrop of ever darkening night in the Kali Yuga Cycle (This is described in, *ACTS 2,* chapter: *Cycles of Time).* Those of the African 3rd and Semitc 4th Root Races would see their domination by the Aryan 5th Root Race consciousness. The older inhabitants and caregivers of the Earth would undergo great suffering. Countless numbers were killed. Many of the Ancient wisdom teachings were burnt and destroyed. Still other Ancient Wisdom Teachings were splintered and carried off to build the newly emerging 'World'. Accordingly: The Tibetan, *Esoteric Psychology V. 1*, p. 346.

> In the fourth race (the Atlantean) [read here: Semitic Race] the conflict was begun, and consciousness was born. In the fifth race (the Aryan) the crisis of the battle will be seen…

The Ancestors would await to see what would be built by the prevailing consciousness of the newly emerging race. They would be both awed and aghast at what would be revealed. According to Vera Stanley Adler, *Initiation of The World*, p.140:

> Civilization moved westward once more. Those branches of the Aryan sub-races who were to perform the great feat of taking the deepest, most blinding dip into matter, there to wrestle for its mastery on its own level (without the aid of spiritual insight) were being collected together in the ordained lands-France, Germany, Britain and many of their neighbors. It is now time for the lowest depths of the material world to be sounded, and having been mastered fairly, upon its own level, to be raised and fused with the highest possible spiritual level.*

And likewise expressed in the following accordingly:

Anderson Thompson, *African World History Project*, p. 17.

> White supremacy began thousands of years ago with the invasions of the Indus and Nile Valleys by nomadic Aryans. Along with conquering and controlling the land (space), Europeans have also taken control of time. For example, the strategy of Western History is to focus all eyes on the important dates pertaining to the late arrival to civilization of Aryans who attempted to make sense of the Ancient African Civilizations they had desecrated…. Regarding time, Western Historiography is a set of facts systematically contrived to rationalize and explain European world dominion in the context of a fabricated sequence. It celebrates four thousand years of violent, murderous, Babaryan, migratory, tribal conquests of Africa….Aryans battered their way into every corner of Africa, ravishing and destroying land, resources, and people. Their present-day museums and art centers from Berlin to Baghdad are arrogant exhibits of this four thousand years of world Barbaryan plunder and theft.

---

* In her book, *The Initiation of The World*, p.140, Vera Stanley Adler is describing a smaller Kali Yuga cycle (4,320, 43,200) within the greater Kali Yuga of 432,000 . Nevertheless her description for the smaller cycle is aptly reflected in the larger cycle.

KaAbBa Building The Lighted Temple
The Spiritual B(ARK)

As the fifth Root Race emerged upon the Earth globe, those most possessed by a separative consciousness easily, wantonly and viciously wounded, destroyed, killed, and polluted without regard. After all, how can what is separate from the self be regarded? No aspect of Divine creation has been spared. No man, woman, child, animal, plant or mineral. Our water, air and earth have all been defiled. The sacred fire of Ra (Kundalini), the sexual and co-creative power has been degraded and dissipated. As we made our deepest descent in the downspiraling cycle of time a consciousness possessed by the most vilest and coarsest materialism would have its rule on the planet. Finally, the shade had been fully drawn down and darkness prevailed upon earth.

Unspeakable horrors happened in the darkness!

Chapter 7
What Is darkness and DARKNESS?

As one human family we make up the collective consciousness of our Earth that has been evolving over eons of time. On a higher turn of the spiral, the collective consciousness in the human family may be expressing itself at its Spiritually optimal and Divine level. On a lower turn of the spiral, the collective consciousness in the human family may be expressing itself at its most, materially debased and despiritualized level. Our personal and collective will, thought, desire, choice and action is either working in or out of accord with the Divine Will, Love, Intelligence, and Law that is guiding our Earth into a greater measure of light. Our choices determine how *and* if we are manifesting the Kingdom of God on Earth. We are the evolving Planetary Mind.

No matter what Root Race one 'belongs to' this collective consciousness, which now pervades our Planetary consciousness, is the province in which all humanity must work to re-Spiritualize, clear and cleanse of its accumulated darkness. This brings us to the next

| **Metaphysical Key To:** |
| darkness and DARKNESS |

There are those who fear DARKNESS and this fear acts as an impediment in the Spiritual journey. Humanity has only to fear the darkness of its own making. We would not fear true DARKNESS which is sphere 0 – in the Tree of Life. Let's discern the difference between *darkness* and *DARKNESS*.

What is darkness?

The darkness of which I speak here is humanity's darkness in consciousness as a Planetary family. This humanly created darkness is born out of our accumulated wrong thought, word and deed. It is the veil of illusion, maya and glamour that has created its long darkening shadow upon the Earth. It is constructed out of desire-tinged thought-forms that pollute the ethers of our Earth. These desire-tinged thought-forms cause us to react out of negative emotion and mental patterning. If not dealt with, they suffocate our reach in consciousness to touch the Divine archetypal ideation and design that would guide our way Home. Like sitting in a stuffy room circulating the same stale air, we circulate the same overworked and outworn thought-forms around our Planet that are devitalized, devitalizing and vamporous to our life.

Now, to use such a term as vampire-like or vamporous, has some of you spooked up already. You are afraid to look, to see and to know the metaphysics of your own oppression. By analogy, we can ask the following:

a. Does humanity think that it could have the thick, black smoke from our industrialized lifestyle darkening the sky and polluting our bodies on the physical plane and *be exempt from*

KaAbBa Building The Lighted Temple
The Spiritual B(ARK)

b. The same black and dark accumulation in the Earth's aura around us from the poor quality of our thoughts and desires on the mental and emotional planes?

What is the Planetary accumulation in need of clearing and cleansing?
Although the quote that follows uses language that Esoterically tries to veil its meaning, the relevant point is made accordingly: Tibetan, *Glamour A World Problem*, p. 33.

> … in Lemurian days [read here: African/Negro consciousness], glamour and illusion were relatively unknown from the human standpoint. There were no mental reactions and but little emotional response to environment…. Glamour began to be found in Atlantean days, [read here: Semitic consciousness] and since that time has steadily precipitated, until today when the Hierarchy [read here: Governing Deities] looks at humanity it appears to be walking in a deep and constantly changing density of currents which hide and distort, and which swirl around the sons of men and prevent their seeing the LIGHT as it is. … In our race, the Aryan [read here: European consciousness], the world illusion is gathering weight and slowly emerging into recognition in the human consciousness and this is a real point gained, for that which is recognised can then be intelligently handled, if the will to do so exists. Today illusion is so potent, that few people whose minds are in any way developed but are controlled by these vast illusory thoughtforms, which have their roots and draw their life from the lower personality life and desire nature of the masses of men.
>
> It is interesting to remember also in connection with our Aryan race that these thought-forms draw their vitality also from the realm of ideas, but of ideas wrongly intuited and grasped and forced to serve the selfish purposes of men. Their forms have been brought into activity by the **steadily growing creative power of mankind** [read here: misuse of manes/mind], and have been subordinated to the wishes of men, through the use of language with its power to limit and distort. The illusion is also precipitated more potently than would otherwise be the case by the effort of many devoted idealistic men **to impose these distorted thought-forms upon the mental bodies of the masses….**

We locate a significant event in unfolding consciousness by relating the words in the above quote to the quote which follows. In the story of Ausar, Auset and Heru we now turn to a discourse that is occurring between Auset and her son Heru. In it she teaches him how to come into maturity, so that he may avenge his Father's death, and come into his rightful inheritance of the throne of his/her Kingdom. She speaks about this *spark of mind* or power *'to know'* and use the mind accordingly: *Virgin of the World, The Sacred Books of Tehuti* (See Mead, *Thrice Greatest Hermes;* Ashby, *Ausarian Resurrection*).

> O Heru…Souls have the power to create due to their ability to know and use the mind….O Heru, this power became the source of pride and conceit.

Glamour and illusion may be defined as our over self-identification with the *substance of* and *belief that* we are our thoughts, emotions and physical bodies. Thus we see the 'other' in the same self-limiting way. Thought forms are part of the collective conscious. These desire-tinged thought-forms tug at your energy field even when you are unaware or unsuspecting. Their heaviness veils the Planet which obstructs and obscures right relationship between the Races (particularly black and white), between men and women, and between one religion and another. They meet you at the 'door' as you try to access that which is needed in the World. In each instance, the negative energy of these thoughtforms contribute to disharmonious relationships, strain, violence and death.

What may we do to dispell Planetary illusion and glamour and infuse the ethers of our Planet with the livingness of Divine ideation?

Just as we must be conscious to shield and protect ourselves from a polluted environment, we must likewise be conscious to shield and protect ourselves from an accumulation of negative and distorted thoughtforms that fill the World with life draining fear, violence and rampant desire that serve to benefit those who would keep the World the same. The key is in examining the use of images and *'the use of language with its power to limit and distort'*.

Another Chief among us, named Minister Louis Farrakhan, struck a blow in rending the veil when he spearheaded the Million Man and Million Woman March. These are best described as the MMM – The Million Master Marchers. The ideation of bringing people together who have long been apart, was a major Planetary event of the last century in recharging the ethers with higher vibration, design and intent. Anytime one among the human family acts with great courage to rend the veil and bring in greater light, it is like opening the Planetary window so that the inhabitants of Earth might be imbued with a *breath of fresh air*.

Likewise, the work of another Chief among us, Nelson Mandela, was key in dismantling the system of Apartheid in South Africa and averting human atrocity of great proportion. This system sanctioned racial segregation and political and economic discrimination against nonwhites. If you dispell the word Apartheid you see that it reveals the word Apart 'I'e d. If you see with a part "I" or eye, you know the Self in part. If you see the Self in part, you see the 'other' in part also. The eye that knows the One True Self sees the *same* One True Self *everywhere*. Humanity is the organ used by the Spiritual being ensouling our Planet to express consciousness.

Humanity is the repository of its most exalted and most depraved thought-forms. By glimpsing the collective mind of the human family one has a read on the progress of our Planetary consciousness.

KaAbBa   Building The Lighted Temple
The Spiritual B(ARK)

What is DARKNESS?
The DARKNESS of which I speak here is the DARKNESS of the womb, the Earth, the night sky, deep space, eyes closed in meditation, silence, BLACKNESS, - The ABSOLUTE AMEN, THE ALL.

What might we do to attune to this DARKNESS?
Meditation as a practice for the Ausaranization in consciousness will be emphasized throughout this text. Yet, a simple and sacred ritual is given by another Chief among us – named Dr. Maulana Karenga – in the re-claim-ation of the 7 principle powers – The Nguzo Saba through the celebration of Kwanzaa. This celebration teaches us to light the central Black candle as a symbol of Unity – Umoja.

This is to invoke memory within consciousness of BLACKNESS, DARKNESS – the unity from which we arise, and to which we return. The SOURCE of all Creation. If you are spooked up and confused you cannot discern between darkness and DARKNESS and you may have difficulty performing the simple ritual of lighting a BLACK candle. When we reflect on all the negative associations of black and dark, it is no wonder that we have felt a loss of ability to contact and *hold* within the BLACK AND DARKNESS of our Divinity. After all, for 2000 thousand years, you have been taught that God is a figure in the form of a Man who is depicted to look nothing like Black, Dark, or African people. As a consequence we have lost sight of how to navigate the BLACK Ocean, The DARKNESS, The DEEP. We are like the whale –

• The Whale swims as a Master of great cycles of time upon the vast ocean expanse.
• Yet, like the Whale, we have spun out
• We have Beached ourselves.
• Whales come to warn us
• Turn back toward *Home*
• Time to turn our *'outgoing'* footsteps around.
• Like the Whale, we are trapped within the little eddy of time
• No longer attuned to the vast ocean expanse and vast cycles of time
• We are spinning our wheels
• Caught in the ever tightening coil
• In the downward spiral of material consciousness.
• We have lost our bearings.
• We have lost sight of how to navigate the BLACK Ocean
• The DARKNESS, The DEEP –

When the 1 is superimposed upon the zero or Divine cipher it gives us the symbols of indivisible unity. It also gives us our first view of Two-in-one or Two-Oneness as indicated in the following diagrams:

The Ausarianization of Consciousness Series 1   62
Metaphysical Keys To the Tree of Life & Oracle Keys to Dis-spelling Illusion
The Spiritual Journey in Unfolding Consciousness

1. The vertical line on the cross of Spirit-Matter forming a left and right half of the circle

2. The horizontal line on the cross of Manifestation forming an upper and lower circle

It is the indivisible unity that arises within this symbol or '0' that our story now moves to. As we shall see, reconstructing the broken body or consciousness of Ausar into the indivisible unity that *it is* and has *always been* is an ongoing theme in our story. Many lifetimes are spent perched or polarized in the lower divisions of your Spiritual equipment feeling cut off before your conscious awareness extends to reach the Divine guidance within the higher divisions. Let's return now to the indivisible unity and how it arises. In order to look at the arising of Ba we must return to sphere 0 in the Tree of Life.

KaAbBa   Building The Lighted Temple
The Spiritual B(ARK)

What Is this DARKNESS?
Our story continues…

This brings us to the next

+--+
| **Metaphysical Key To:** |
| Sphere 0 |
| |
+--+

Sphere 0, AMEN

Sphere 0 is shown by the colored sphere in the Tree of Life diagram at right.
Kemetic Name: Amen – See re-claim-ation in Kemetic naming of the Sphere 0, AMEN
by Ra Un Nefer Amen, *Metu Neter V.I & II* **vs.**
Kabalistic Name –Ain

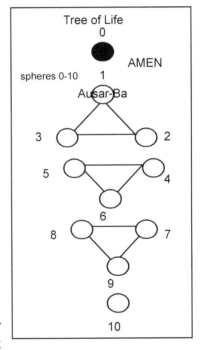

Sphere 0 is known by many names including, THE NAMELESS.
It is AMEN, NETER NETERU in Kemetic terminology. It is the
SUPREME BE-NESS, the ALL IN ALL, THE ROOT
CAUSELESS CAUSE, THE BEGININGLESS BEGINNING,
THE FOUNT OF ALL POSSIBILITIES, THE BOUNDLESS,
THE INFINITE, GOD, SPIRIT. It is AIN in Kabalistic
terminology. These are just a few names for the – ABSOLUTE
REALITY.

The AMEN in the Kemetic system and the Ain in the Kabalistic
system both correspond to the '0" sphere in the Tree of Life.
AMEN is known as 'the concealed' or 'hidden' in the Kemetic
System of Ausarian Spiritual Transformation and Resurrection.
The AMEN is the "SUPREME ALL,' the ever invisible Spirit.
The Hindus call this PARABRAHMAN.

We recognize immediately the total inadequacy of words in our
feeble attempt at *describing the indescribableness* of AMEN. Not
only do *words* begin to fail, we also cannot 'properly' represent AMEN, The ABSOLUTE with
any kind of *symbology*. Nevertheless, those who have come before us and have transmitted the
Ancient wisdom teachings down through the ages have shed light by their efforts to 'describe' in
order to aid our understanding. Likewise, what follows is a humble effort in that same Spirit of
transmission.

So, what symbol may serve as a cognizable bridge to understanding the 'uncognizable'?
A **Black** empty sheet of paper (ignoring its 4-sided boundaries of limitation) or the DARKNESS
we experience in closing our eyes to meditate may help bridge the imagination. In order to make

a cognizable bridge to understanding the uncognizable, the symbology used is the Divine cipher '0' - Zero

The Ancient Wisdom teaches that[*] AMEN is the BEGININGLESS BEGINNING, THE ETERNAL and INFINITE ALL IN ALL. It has no beginning and no end. There is no-thing that has come before it. There is no-thing that comes after it.

AMEN is THE ROOT CAUSELESS CAUSE. There is no-thing outside of the AMEN that *caused* it. There is no-thing outside of ITSELF that could cause its beginning or its end.

The AMEN is THE UNCONDITIONED CONDITION, the IMMUTABLE (CHANGELESS). There is no-thing outside of itself that could impose condition upon it or change the INFINITE ALL. IT is changeless having no attributes. Its absoluteness precludes any idea of finite or conditioned being.

AMEN is the FOUNT OF ALL POSSIBILITY. In its unqualified and unconditioned state of BE-NESS all may be drawn from it. It is paradoxically THE EVERYTHING AND NO-THING. AMEN is EVERYTHING-NESS in ITS potential, inexhaustible supply. It is also latent NO-THING-NESS, void, non-definable, non-discernible.

AMEN is NETER NETERU (All Qualities) in its LIMITLESS POTENTIAL for the expression of all quality, yet is ITSELF – unqualified. In order for the AMEN to latently possess all quality IT must also latently posses the 'quality of being unqualified.'

AMEN is THE ONE WITHOUT A SECOND and the ALL IN ALL.
There is no other thing created that is outside of the AMEN. The All is in all and all is within the All.

AMEN is ABSOLUTE CONSCIOUSNESS CONSCIOUS OF ITSELF. There is no-thing outside of the AMEN that the AMEN may be conscious of or who could be conscious of IT.

AMEN is THAT WITHOUT POINT OR CIRCUMFERENCE. IT is without dimension. IT is the BOUNDLESS ALL. There is no-thing outside of itself that could define, limit, restrict or contain IT.

But *how* and *what* does AMEN create?
According to: *The Secret Doctrine.*

There is one Boundless Immutable Principle.

---

[*] See *Kyballian; Infinitizing of Self hood; Secret Doctrine;* Budge et al.

KaAbBa Building The Lighted Temple
The Spiritual B(ARK)

And from this –

According to Dr Michael Robbins, *The Infinitization of Selfhood*, p. xx.
"The BOUNDLESS IMMUTABLE PRINCIPLE, the INFINITESSENCE' 'APPEARS' periodically, as a single *finite* Universe. IT has done so cyclically forever, is doing so Now, and will do so, cyclically, forever. Thus, there has been a *beginningless/endless* infinite sequence of successive finite Universes."

All objectivity or thing-ness 'seemingly' arises in Spirit or no-thing-ness to give the 'appearance' of an individualized or expressed entity. From the ONE LIFE, ETERNAL, INVISIBLE, yet OMNIPRESENT, WITHOUT BEGINNING OR END, a Universe is 'breathed out' in its periodic manifestation. It is endowed with Spirit/Life-Consciousness-Form/Matter.

The exhalation of The Great Breath produces vibration. As Spirit vibrates at a higher rate this substance is more subtle and refined. As Spirit vibrates at a lower rate this substance is more coarse, dense and material. After its cycle of manifestation the Great Breath is withdrawn and the Universe is abstracted back into Pure Spirit. In this 'inhalation' all resolves in Spirit and once again, DARKNESS reigns.

What happens through the process of Meditation?
This is your:
1. Re-identification with INFINITE ALL and ALLNESS – UNDIFERENTIATED, CONDITIONLESS, FORMLESS, BOUNDLESS
2. Re-absorption in consciousness into the Indivisible Unity
3. Ausarian access is getting 'set back to zero – that is the '0' of AMEN
4. DARKNESS found within you is the inexhaustible supply for all that is needed in your Spiritual journey
5. Re-identification as the Indivisible Unity you have access to the FOUNT OF ALL POSSIBILITY – the NU.

In a previous diagram of the continuum of Spirit/matter we have seen the return journey of Spirit in-form to Spirit in-form-less-ness depicted. This Spirit/matter continuum is likewise described in the following accordingly: Ra Un Nefer Amen. *Metu Neter, V.II,* p. 30-31.

> The energy/matter out of which all things are formed must be in its essential state, unformed, undefined, undifferentiated, etc. If the material basis of the world had any essential definitions (formations) these would act as limiting factors to its ability to be transformed infinitely. Its essential lack of definition is an absolute requirement for God's creative omnipotence. The Kamau metaphorized this state of energy/matter as an infinite expanse of water which they called "Nu" or less frequently" Nun.

H.P. Blavatsky, *The Secret Doctrine*, uses Parabrahman/mulaprakriti as equivalent terms, accordingly:

> Mulaprakriti is precosmic root substance. It is homogeneous, undifferentiated primal substance and has the possibility for differentiation. In its absoluteness, the One Principle under its two aspects (Parabrahman and Mulaprakriti) is sexless, unconditioned and eternal. Mulaprakriti is co-eternal with Parabrahman and moves into becoming a Universe.

So we can see here that ALL IS SPIRIT. Spirit/matter are co-eternal. As a *'stirring'* arises within the ABSOLUTE, the Spirit/matter or primordial substance used to create arises as a differentiation within ITSELF. Spirit/matter, Parabrahman/mulaprakriti and Energy/Matter are all equivalent terms. Throughout this discourse I will use the term Spirit/matter to describe this creative process continuum. The paradoxical NO-THING-NESS and EVERY-THING-NESS of *Spirit/matter* out of which creation arises is known by various names. The correspondence between the different systems is revealed as follows:

AMEN/Nu –Kemetic
Parabrahman/Mulaprakriti – Hindu
Ain/Soph – Kabalistic

We may extend this further in comparing the terms Prakriti and Nut. These terms reflect how the inactive principle (latent activity) in Mulaprakriti and Nu has now become Prakriti and Nut, the active creative, creating, and created substance. So we have:

Mulaprakriti (latent)	Prakriti (active)	- Hindu
Nu (latent)	Nut (active)	- Kemetic

In DARKNESS within THE ABSOLUTE, THE ALL, NETER NETERU, AMEN, THE SUPREME BE-NESS, THE FOUNT OF ALL POSSIBILTIES, THE INFINITE, just a few names for the ABSOLUTE REALITY – **CREATION** *Stirs*. Out of the DARKNESS OF NO-THING-NESS, Light emerges. Light itself is a manifestation and arises out of the One.

Accordingly: *Metu Neter,V.II,* p. 37.

> Nu is in a state of complete darkness which is called *Kekui*. Since light involves activity (propagation, hence differentiation) that takes place through time, there can be no light in the Subjective "0" which is a substance devoid of forms, structures, etc.

And Similarly –

Accordingly: Secret Doctrine, p. 64.

> Darkness radiates Light, and Light drops one solitary ray in the waters, into the mother deep. The ray shoots through the virgin-egg; the ray causes the eternal egg to thrill, and drop the non-eternal (periodical) germ, which condenses into the world egg.

KaAbBa   Building The Lighted Temple
The Spiritual B(ARK)

Ibid. p. 77

> Where was the germ, and where was now darkness? …The germ is that, and that is light; the white brilliant son of the dark hidden Father.

So we see that:

Sphere 0, AMEN, is the formless and unmanifested. Spirit/matter is the Divine Father/Mother locked in an eternal embrace. It is *latent* energy – because it is yet to-be *'stirred'* into creative activity. The Tree of Life is the raying forth of Spirit/matter into an *active* creative cycle. In our focus on sphere 0, AMEN we have been focusing within the Subjective realm. The invisible realm of no-thing-ness – unqualified, undifferentiated, and unconditioned. As creation stirs within the AMEN the creative process goes forth giving rise to the Universe from which myriad forms will emanate in the to-be created World(s). Here we move from the ONE REALITY to participate in the 'play and display'of the many. Accordingly: G.R.S Mead, *Thrice Greatest Hermes, The Virgin of The World. The Sacred Books of Tehuti,* p.71.

> He spake; straightway in cosmic order there began the differentiation of the **up-to-then black unity {of things}.** And Heaven shone forth above tricked out with all his mysteries; Earth, still a-tremble, as the Sun shone forth grew harder, and appeared with all the fair adornments that bedeck her round on every side. For beautiful to God are even things which men think mean, in that in truth they have been made to serve the laws of God.

> And God rejoiced when now He saw His worlds a-moving; and filling full His Hands, which held as much as all surrounding space, with all that Nature had produced, and squeezing tight the handfuls mightily, He said: "Take [these], O holy Earth, take those, all-honoured one, who art to be the mother of all things, and henceforth lack thou naught!

It is through your return to DARKNESS, BLACKNESS in consciousness that all things are made Anu - new. In our gradual loss of re-mem-brance of The ONE REALITY we loose sight within the Eternal.

Let's dispell the word Eternal:
 # 1. Oracle Metaphysical Dis-spelling Key:
Put letters of word or words together in a circle, like a serpent putting its tail in its mouth. Coming full Circle.

#2. Oracle Metaphysical   Dis-spelling Key: Read letters, putting together words, going forwards, backwards and in zig-zag patterns.
#3. Oracle Metaphysical Dis-spelling Key: You may crossover in order to use a letter more than once. Place re-used letter in parenthesis ( ).

#4. Oracle Metaphysical Dis-spelling Key: You may add a letter to complete a word. Place added letter in parenthesis ( ).

#5. Oracle Metaphysical Dis-spelling Key: Letter substitution-you may substitute a letter. Place substituted letter in parenthesis ( ).

#6. Oracle Metaphysical Dis-spelling Key: Make a list of derived words. Try to make the longest continuous unbroken word or string of words.

Derived Word List:

Neter al, Al(l) Neter

#7. Oracle Metaphysical Dis-spelling Key: Look up definition (dictionary, glossary, reference texts, etc.)

Definition: Neter al – Neter or Neter(u) plural are the Divine qualities of God.

Derived Word List Continued:

A Retn El – El means Angel, Divine Being. A ret(ur)n(ing) (Ang)El.

#8. Oracle Metaphysical Dis-spelling Key: Meaning. See the relationship and oracle or story of the Neteru – Put word list together to tell a story.

Meaning:

As the Retn El, the Returning Angel, we bring our awareness to the Neter Al(l) which is the Fount of all Divine qualities, the Everlasting Livingness of God, *Neter Neteru.* We enter within our Eternal Home.

But What is Created?

Understanding the creative process brings us to the next Metaphysical Key:

Chapter 8
Cosmogony and Cosmogenesis
What is Universal Ba?

> **Metaphysical Key to:**
> The Number 1
> **Universal Ba**
> The World   The World Soul   Comes Into Being
> **Cosmogony and Cosmogenesis**

In understanding of Cosmogony and Cosmogenisis we understand that:

1. Within the INFINITE, BOUNDLESS ALL, AMEN   there is a *Stirring.* Within this INFINITE, BOUNDLESS, BLACKNESS, DARKNESS OF SPIRIT, The ABSOLUTE ALL AND ALL *Stirs* within the limitless unconditioned substance of ITSELF.

2. This Spirit/Matter is called – Nu. By the Kemetians.• It is the waters of space. It is called Mulaprakriti by the Hindus.• AMEN – sphere 0, ABSOLUTE ALL AND ALL takes within the limitless unconditioned substance of ITSELF.

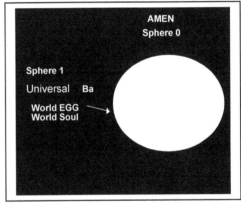

3. The fires of Ra thrills across the primordial Spirit/Matter, Father/Mother. The twin creative forces, called Shu & Tefnut by the Kemetians, are set to work.

4. These are the children of Ra. They are the centrifugal and centripetal twin forces at work in nature producing air, heat, light, and moisture.

5. Together they engage in an infolding and unfolding, play and display between themselves, like the yin yang symbol.

6. Through their interweaving dance, Spirit emanates outward to pervade ITSELF in all matter.

7. The circumgyration of the fires of Ra upon the waters raises a 'mound' within Nu. As the fire circles, flames leap and seek to pierce the mound or 'egg,' just as the male sperm seeks to penetrate the female ovum. At last, one solitary spark leaps high above all other flames. It takes aim, makes its descent and shooting forth as a solitary Ray of the ABSOLUTE this fire penetrates and impregnates the primordial, mother/matter. From this stirring within AMEN,

---

• See Budge, *Prt Em Hru. (The Egyptian Book of the Dead).*
• See H.P. Blavatsky, *Secret Doctrine.*

THE ALL sphere 0, there is a raying forth of Light and the One issues forth as Creator – sphere 1, Ba. The One egg now fecundated (fertilized) becomes the One Universal Ba.

8. The One Universal Ba is humbly pictured in the diagram, on the preceding page, as no image can adequately capture the Divine movement. The One Universal Ba is also called the World Egg and the World Soul.

9. In the Kemetic system, sphere 1 is known as Ba and Ausar. •

10. It is referred to in this text alternately as Ba, Ausar and Ausar Ba. This is pictured by the colored sphere in the Tree of Life at right.

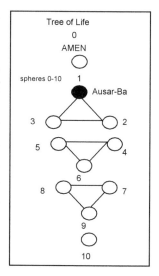

11. Here is when God the INFINITE is reflected forth as God the Creator. Thus Universe is created with all its multiplicity within of Super Cosmic Galaxies, Constellations, Suns, Planets, humans, animals, and so on. Just as God indwells you as an individual man or woman, God indwells the Planet, Suns, Constellations, Galaxies, and so on up to and including the Universe in total called the Universal Ba. God is reflected in all that is created. God transcendent becomes God indwelling. As man and woman you are made in the Image and Likeness of God. Therefore, man and woman have all the Divine attributes of God. These Divine qualities or attributes are called Neter or Neteru which is the plural.

12. Ba or Ausar Ba is The One True Self Realized Being-ness and Identification. Within the raying forth from AMEN – sphere 0, Ausar Ba sphere 1, comes into subjective being with the Divine archetypal design and creative substance rayed forth and complete within to become The Self Realized Being-ness that *IT* already *IS*.

• See Ra Un Nefer Amen, *Metu Neter*; Israel Regardie, *The Tree of Life;*
in the 'naming of the Spheres'.

KaAbBa   Building The Lighted Temple
The Spiritual B(ARK)

This brings us to the next

> **Metaphysical Key To:**
> Cosmogony and Cosmogenesis
> **Universal Ba *To***
> **Individualized Ba** Man and Woman

1. The One Universal Ba arises within the ABSOLUTE (AMEN) and begins its periodic cycle of manifestation. This is likewise pictured in the diagram pictured on the preceding page as sphere 1 – Universal Ausar Ba in the Tree of Life. Ba° is individualized Spirit and gives the breath of life.

2. The dance of the twin forces Shu and Tefnut enables the coming into manifestation of myriad Life-forms.

3. From this egg which is the Universal Ba (also called, Logos, Kosmos, Monad, Kether, Nebertcher) all spheres arise. Thus Super Galaxies, Galaxies, Constellations, Suns, Planets, Man and tiniest Atom come into created being. Therefore Ba is tiniest Atom, Ba is ultimately Universe, and Ba is everything in between.

What is Khepera?
4. The One Universal Ba is symbolized by the Scarab beetle Khepera. (See Budge) The Kemetians used this symbol to try to express the inexpressible. Numberless, and Eggless it is the stirring within the birthing sub-stance of Mulaprakriti or Amen/Nu which gives rise to Khepera the 1st Sun-Son/Daughter, or eye of Ra. In accord with the Law of Periodicity Khepera is Kosmos, Universal Ba, Universal Logos or Periodical Universe.

5. Within the One Universal Ba there is the particularization into the many. This is symbolized by the numerous eggs within the beetle Khepera which are the myriad to-be created forms, to-be birthed forth.

6. The Kemetians used picture images or ideagraphs from nature all around them to communicate ideas which is the language called MTU NTR. These symbols were called Hieroglyphic by the Greeks. The Kemetians used the symbol Khepera, which powerfully expresses this Divine creative process. Khepera is a beetle that lays eggs, then rolls them up in dung and pushes them along in a ball. Khepera is pictured in the diagram at right. If we

---

1. See Isha Schwaller De Lubicz, *The Opening of The Way. Her-Bak.*

dispell the word ball, we see that these eggs are 'ba'-lls within the greater 'Ba'-ll or Egg that contain the germ of life which in due course of time will become living creatures.

Metaphysical Key To:
Dispelling Illusion

Let's dispell the word Khepera:
#7. Oracle Metaphysical Dis-spelling Key: Look up definition (dictionary, glossary, reference texts, etc.)

Definition: According to E.A. Wallis Budge, *The Gods of The Egyptians, V.I,* p. 295-296. (Papyrus of Nes-Amsu) "The Book of Knowing the Evolutions of Ra, and of Overthrowing Apepi."

> Khepera –"The word here rendered by "Evolutions" is kheperu, being derived from the root kheper which means "to make, to fashion, "to produce, to form, to become, and in a derived sense "to roll," so that the title might be translated the "Book of knowing the "Becoming of Ra," i.e., the things which were made, or created, or came into being through Ra.

Here, we are seeing what comes into being as the fires of Ra moves upon the waters of space – Nu.

Ibid.

In the Kemetic creation story Nebertcher Saith,
> I am the creator of what hath come into being, and I myself came into being under the form of the god Khepera, and I came into being in primeval time. I came into being in the form of Khepera, and I was the creator of what came into being, that is to say, I formed myself out of the primeval matter, and I formed myself in the primeval matter. My name is Ausares, who is the primeval matter of primeval matter. I have done all my will in this earth, I have spread abroad therein, and I have made strong (or, lifted up) my hand. {He is described as the pautet pautti}. I was alone, for they (i.e., the gods) were not born, and I had emitted from "myself neither Shu nor Tefnut. I brought my name into my own mouth, that is to say [I uttered it as] a word of power *hekau,* and I forthwith came into being under the form of things which were created and under the form of Khepera.

Here we see the beginningless and endless 'extent' of the name **Ausares** in the words, 'I was the creator of what came into being, that is to say, I formed myself *out of* the primeval mater, and I formed myself *in the* primeval matter. **My name is Ausares, who is the primeval matter of primeval matter'.** Thus we see that no date can be given to the 'reign' of Ausares. It is through the Ausarianization of consciousness that you are resurrected in Spirit and made Anu (anew).

KaAbBa   Building The Lighted Temple
The Spiritual B(ARK)

The beginningless and endless can only be sensed in meditation as consciousness is re-polarized Anu and you gain Nu-standing in the higher Ba triangle of your Spiritual equipment.

And Continuing –

> I came into being from primeval matter, and I appeared under the form of multitudes of things from the beginning. Nothing existed at that time, and it was I who made whatsoever was made. I was alone, and there was no other being who worked with me in that place. I made all the forms under which I appeared by means (or, out of) the god-soul which I raised up out of Nu, out of a state of ineptness (or, out of the inert mass).

> I found there (i.e., in Nu) no place wherein I could stand. I worked a spell on my heart, and I laid a foundation before me, and I made whatsoever was made. I was alone. I laid a foundation in (or, by) my heart, and I made the other things which came into being, and the things of Khepera which were made were manifold, and their offspring came into existence from the things to which they gave birth. It was I who emitted Shu, and it was I who emitted Tefnut, and from being one god (or, the one god) I became three, that is to say, the two other gods who came into being on this earth came from myself, and Shu and Tefnut were raised up from out of Nu wherein they had been.

#1. Oracle Metaphysical Dis-spelling Key:
Put letters of word or words together in a circle, like a serpent putting its tail in its mouth. Coming full Circle.

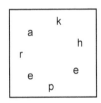 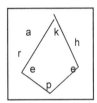

#2. Oracle Metaphysical Dis-spelling Key:
Read letters, putting together words, going forwards, backwards and in zig-zag, and crossover patterns.
#3. Oracle Metaphysical Dis-spelling Key: You may crossover in order to use a letter more than once. Place re-used letter in parenthesis ( ).
#4. Oracle Metaphysical Dis-spelling Key: You may add a letter to complete a word. Place added letter in parenthesis ( ).
#5. Oracle Metaphysical Dis-spelling Key: Letter substitution-you may substitute a letter. Place substituted letter in parenthesis ( ).
#6. Oracle Metaphysical Dis-spelling Key: Make a list of derived words. Try to make the longest continuous unbroken word or string of words.
<u>Derived Word List:</u>
<u>Ka</u>
<u>Ra</u>

Keep(e)r
Reaper

#8. Oracle Metaphysical Dis-spelling Key: Meaning. See the relationship and oracle or story of the Neteru – Put word list together to tell a story.

Meaning:

Ra keeper – (or holder) – The Sun is known as Ra to the Kemetians. Ra is not exhausted by the One creative act of the Universal Ba, as Khepera's body holds the myriad to-be birthed Suns/Ra*s* inside.

Ka reaper – (or holder) – Each individualized Sun-Son/Daughter must come to reflect its Divine or Spirit Ka which is the Image and Likeness of God. Thus do we ultimately reap the Image and Likeness of God without distortion through the lives we live.

1. Accordingly: The Ba {Monad which is two in one – Spirit-Matter or Pilgrim is "the only immortal and eternal principle in us, being an indivisible part of the integral whole – the Universal Spirit, from which it emanates, and into which it is absorbed at the end of the cycle." *(Secret Doctrine, V.I,* p.16 footnote).

2. If Ba ceases its individualized expression it returns to its source – Pure Spirit. As long as Ba is *in-form*, in manifestation, - the ONE of Pure Spirit has emanated into the THREE of Spirit, Soul and Matter. There is that continuum of Spirit, Soul and Matter within every individualized Ba. This is symbolized by the Kemetians as BKA.

3. The dance of these twin forces Shu and Tefnut next enables the One Life temporarily encapsulated in-form to be abstracted back into the One of SPIRIT. Thus, the Great Cycle of activity is followed by a cycle of rest called a Pralaya by the Hindus.

4. This Pralaya continues until Ba is breathed out for the next 'cycle of necessity' a finite Universe in an infinite chain of Universes.

5. It is through Ba that man and all living entities are At-Oned with/as the Universal Ba. It is within the great spiral of time when the fullness of consciousness has been realized that all is reabsorbed into the Universal Ba. The Universal Ba is then abstracted 'back' into the ABSOLUTE ALLNESS of Spirit (AMEN) from which it 'seemingly' arose. Ba then discards the temporary Temple or vehicle it has donned during its manifestation. Consciousness is conscious of the ALL SELF, ITSELF, NO-THING-NESS AND EVERY-THING-NESS *at rest, unstirred.*

KaAbBa Building The Lighted Temple
The Spiritual B(ARK)

How is Ba - Universe, Man/Woman and everything in between?
Lets Look at Ba. The creative process ensues and from the One Universal Ba the many to-be created forms arise. Both diagrams below seek to represent the same view but from a different angle. Ba is seen in each diagram as 'refractiles' throughout all levels of the created Universe. Within Ba is a still greater Ba – within a still greater Ba – until the Universal Ba is realized.

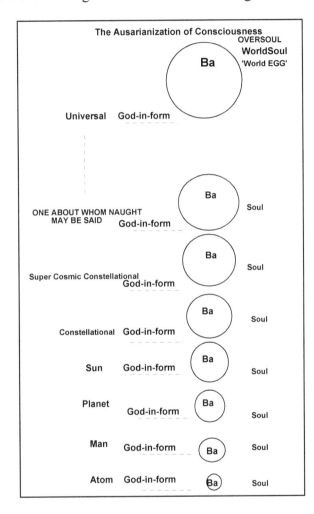

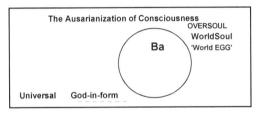

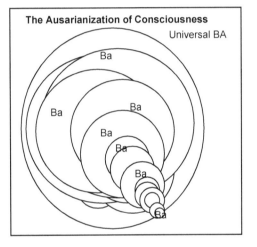

Let's appreciate the limitation in any diagram representing the evolutionary advancement in consciousness. In these representations, innumerable entities on every rung of the evolutionary ladder of conscious Spiritual development are left out. Nevertheless, the idea is to see the same *'essential'* Ba at every level of its immersion. This is expressed accordingly: E.A. Wallis Budge. *The Gods of the Egyptians, V.II,* p. 299.

The mythological and religious texts contain indications that the Egyptians believed in what may be described as a "World-Soul," which they called Ba; its symbol was a bearded man-headed hawk…

This Kemetic Mtu Ntr symbol is pictured in the diagram. The Universal Ba is referred to as the World-Soul by the Kemetians and the Oversoul by the Esoterisists. Each successive Ba takes its place along a great scale of entities, both vast and small. Each Ba is referred to as an individualization of Spirit. As such, each Ba, represents a level of conscious activity which is called Soul by the Kemetians.

What is Consciousness?

Consciousness is unfolding throughout the whole created Universe or Kosmos. In the diagram, on the preceding page, each circle represents an entification of Ba or Ba as an entity. God is indwelling Ba at each level. There is a Great Being who is ensouling or having consciousness within each circle. Whether a Planet, a Sun, a Constellationa, a Galaxy – all are Ba. Ba has existence on the micro level as Ba Atom and as Ba Man. Likewise, Ba has existence on the macro level of Super Cosmic Constellational Being on up to the Universal Ba in total.

By its extension into form, Ba is immersed at various levels of manifestation in forms/vehicles which range from the most coarse and dense – having a lower Spiritual vibration – to the most refined and subtle – having a higher Spiritual vibration. The Universal Ba arises and extends from the macrocosmic level of manifestation all the way down into the microcosmic level of manifestation.

As an individualization of Spirit, whether Man, Planet, Sun, Galaxy and so on:
a. Ba at each level of manifestation is seeking to reveal the fullest co-measure of God's Divinely
    intended design and plan at its own level of immersion in matter/form.
b. Ba at each level of manifestation has its own space/time continuum for the unfoldment of its fullest potential.
c. Ba is soul and soul is consciousness.
d. Ba at every level becomes an object of perception for the *One* and the *same One* who is doing the looking.
e. The Oversoul or Universal Ba itself becomes an object of perception.

All Souls are One and the Worldsoul or Oversoul is the All Soul into which all Souls are resolved. Soul is the Karest principle within each Ba. The Karest is later called Christ by the Christians. It is a cosmic principle that arises with the Universal or World Ba Itself. This same Karest/Christ or Soul makes its appearance felt at every level of immersion of Ba in matter. Just as the president holds an office; so does the Karest/Christ hold an office within each circle, governing each entity whether Man, Planet, Constellation and so on.

It is at the level of the Universal Ba Itself or Oversoul that the biblical words, 'HE so loved the World that HE gave HIS Only begotten Son – may have fullest meaning. On the individual level of man and woman the Heru or Christ has an office within you. That office within you may be *unoccupied* or operating under bad administration and government when you make poor choices and mismanage the affairs of daily living. Nevertheless, the 'Only begotten Son is resident within each one of us. Ka is Spirit. It is the double of the Soul. If we dispell the word Karest it reveals the words, 'Ka' and 'rest.' It means that Ka – the Divine Image and Likeness of God seeks rest within each one of us.

What about all the Bas at levels not filled in on the previous diagram?

This brings us to return again to our next

Metaphysical Key To:
The Law of Correspondence
"As above, so below; as below, so above."

The Ancient Kemetic Law of Correspondence is expressed accordingly: The Three Initiates, *The Kybalion*, p.113.

> As above, so below; as below, so above.

This law guides us to take what we can know on a micro level and use it as a bridge in order to have *knowingness* on a macro level. The Ancient wisdom teaches that the Universe is within man and woman and that by 'Knowing Thyself' man and woman may know Universe. Each Ba is an individualized Son/Daughter and Sun of God, or unit of the Divine Self. Ba is Spirit bestowing Life, and Consciousness in Form. Each Ba is an exact replica in miniature to the One Universal Ba the All Self, who is ITSELF the totality of all the miniature sons, of all the individualized Selves (See *A Treatise on Cosmic Fire*, p. 229; *Secret Doctrine*).

The Esotericist use the term, 'The One About Whom Naught May Be Said' as a bridge in consciousness – and – to give name to those Great Cosmic Entities we may contemplate upon – on up to *and* including – the Universe in total – called Universal Ba. This bridge is indicated by the vertical dotted line in the previous diagram. You can see here how Ausar Ba is likewise 'A ONE' About Whom Naught May Be Said.

As stated previously, within Ba is a still greater Ba – within a still greater Ba – until the Universal Ba is realized. Smaller 'worlds' within larger 'Worlds' represent differing space/time schedules of unfolding consciousness in the great spiral of time. The 7 Planes of Consciousness and the sub-planes within these greater planes help us to understand that planes are like stations or platforms in which a certain conscious awareness may be realized. As you use the Law of Correspondence to scale the ladder or planes of consciousness of the Tree of Life you will see that:

1. Ba is all the way up the scale
2. Ba is all the way down the scale

Ausarian Resurrection is to ascend the scale to embrace in consciousness that which expands you to the *whole* of the *SELF* that you are and have always been from the beginningless beginning.

So, Where in the 'World' are we?
In order to answer this question we must first look at the arising of the Number or Neter 1 – The Universal Ba. This brings us to our next

---
Metaphysical Key To:
Location in Space
Form, Spheres, Worlds

To glimpse the focus of our present consciousness we want to understand where we are in space. For now it is important to note that in the ongoing fecundating process myriad forms, spheres or worlds are created and birthed forth from within Universal Ba just like many eggs within the body of Khepera are eventually birthed forth. Or, to continue the analogy, just as many eggs may be birthed from the ovaries of a single woman. Out of the movement within DARKNESS *creation stirs* and there is the appearance of a 'World', Sphere or form that is ensouled or having consciousness.

What is a World or form?
A 'World' may be as all inclusive and *macrocosmic* as the *entire* manifested Universe itself. This is called the Universal Ba in the Kemetic tradition or World Soul.
A 'world' may be as *microcosmic* as a Planet, Man, Mineral or Atom.
Thus within Universe we have the appearance and disappearance of 'Worlds'.

So we see that:
Ba, is the macrocosmic World
Ba is the microcosmic world and
Ba is all that lies in between
Ba is sphere 1 and relates to the Spiritual development of man, woman and all creation.

The One entity indwelling as Ba is personified and called by many names. Since all is ultimately Ba, then Ba is synonymous with and finds correspondence with the following terms within various Spiritual traditions:

Terms Synonymous with Ba	Tradition
Ausar, Khepera, Nebertcher, Ra, Ptah	Kemetic
Monad, Logos, Lord, Pilgrim, Ancient of Days,	Esoteric
The One About Whom Naught May Be Said, Sanat Kumara	Esoteric
Lord, Pilgrim, Ancient of Days, God, Lord of the World(s)	Christian
Kether	Kabalistic
Allah	Islamic
Obatala	Yoruba

KaAbBa Building The Lighted Temple
The Spiritual B(ARK)

These terms relate to Spiritual Transformation and the Ausarianization of Consciousness of all creation, whether an Atom, Mineral, a Man, a Planet, a Super Galaxy, a Super Constellational Being and so on. Whenever we have 'world' or 'form' we have consciousness. Whatever the scope – the world of form or material manifestation is the immanent expression of God indwelling. In short, GOD indwells Ba.

Chapter 9
What Is Ka Ba?

This brings us to the next

> **Metaphysical Key To**:
> Number 1 and 2
> *Ka*Ba Unity/Two-Oneness Ka and Ba/Duality Or Diad
> Out of the '0', Zero –
> Whenever:
> There is the arising of the 1 as unity Ba (Monad)
> There is the arising of the 2 of Duality – BaKa or KaBa (Diad)

For the Kemetians Ka means Spirit and Ba means Soul. We are told that Ka precedes Ba. This is expressed in the following accordingly: Alvin Boyd Kuhn, *The Lost Light*, p. 588.

> "The Ba comes forth upon earth to do the will of its Ka.

This is derived from the Ritual Text of the *Prt Em Hru* which is expressed accordingly: E.A. Wallis Budge. *The Egyptian Book of the Dead*, p. 359.

> The souls come forth to do the will of their Ka's and the soul of Ausar Ani cometh forth to do the will of his Ka.

The above quotes may be re-stated as follows:
The Soul-Ba comes forth upon the Earth to do the will of its Spirit-Ka.

KaBa As Unity. What is the arising of the Number 1?
The above quotes may seem contradictory at first since in the last section it is Ba that arises from the stirring within the ABSOLUTE ALL, The AMEN. What we must remember is that *Ka*Ba is Unconscious-Consciousness and cannot be separated. This Unity is expressed in the diagram at right. As seen, *Ka*Ba enfold and circle upon each other, like the serpent that bites its own tail. Where one ends and the other begins, challenges our ability to discern. All 'seeming' divisions between Ka and Ba are arbitrary and merely useful for helping us to find our way back *Home* from a Spiritual Journey in Unfolding Consciousness that we never really went on, except in an illusion we came to believe as 'Real.'

Ka and Ba As Duality. What is the arising of the Number 2?
According to Albert Churchward, *Signs & Symbols of Primordial Man,* p. 211.

> This [the duality, the first differentiation] was the original, and the Egyptians worked out from this first two things – that is, the Ka, the Spirit, and the Ba, the Soul.

KaAbBa Building The Lighted Temple
The Spiritual B(ARK)

As Two in One or Two-Oneness, whenever we see Ba we recognize that Ka is implied also. This two-oneness or double-sexed nature is within us. It is expressed in our primal ancestors accordingly: Alvin Boyd Kuhn, *The Lost Light,* p. 468.

> Some tribal legends retain descriptions of primeval ancestors of humanity who were half male and half female, and were unaware of their unlikeness and innocent of sexual desire until a god created a longing to eat of the earth. Tasting earth's fruit, they lost the power to fly back to heaven. One Arunta legend tells of ancestors who were double – sexed when they first started on their journey, but before they had proceeded very far, their organs were modified and their mothers "became as other women are". The races emerging from Paradise were hermaphrodite.

Thus, we see that *Ka*Ba is One and unaware of any unlikeness. As we emerge from 'Paradise' as Ka *and* Ba, we *fall* into a sense of 'seeming separation', temporarily losing our ability to 'fly back to heaven'. We see in the three diagrams below:

1. *Ka* Ba as a circle **(Diagram A).**
2. Ka and Ba are next revealed in the Tree of Life and visually laid out in a straight line **(Diagram B).** Thus duality arises as a seeming 'above and below' within our Spiritual equipment.
a. At first, Ba – sphere 1 in the Tree of Life is pictured as arising with Ka
b. Next this Two-Oneness is now reflected as a duality in an upper Ba 1st Aspect of Divinity triangle and a lower Ka 3rd Aspect of Divinity triangle.
3. We now return to a previous Metaphysical Key **(Diagram C)** where Ka and Ba are seen as revealed within the Spirit/Matter Continuum. We have learned that Spirit vibrates along a continuum from high to low (low to high) within our Spiritual equipment.

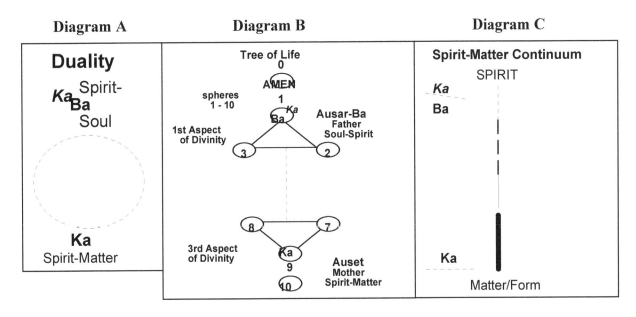

These diagrams seek to deepen insight within the Tree of Life. As the 'serpent bites its tail', the seeming below 3rd aspect 're-becomes' the seeming above 1st aspect. This is further described later. We will likewise learn more about the nature of Ka which is now reflected and seen as 'double'.

What is the relationship between Ka and Ba?
According to Isha Schwaller De Lubicz, *The Opening of The Way Her-Bak,* p. 201.
1. "Ba, [read here: 1st aspect triangle] in relation to Ka is the animating spirit.
2. Ka [read here 3rd aspect triangle] in relation to Ba, is the individualization of consciousness in the more or less gross or subtle states of being, and makes it possible to stabilize the animating spirit.
3. Ba gives the breath of life; its characteristic is nonfixity, and it always needs a support.
4. Ka is a principle of fixity, of fixation and attraction; it is the power which can attract, stabilize, and transform the vital or animating principle, Ba."

Additionally we read: Ibid. p. 202.

> Ka as cosmic power is in essence the idea of the hieroglyph of the Bull. As bearer of the generative power it provides the inherited individual quality, whether in the original creative source or in terrestrial procreators. Ka therefore is the bearer of all the powers of manifestation, the motive force of the universal functions.

So we see here as much as Ka is defined by the Kemetians as Spirit it is also defined as a principle of fixity and attraction. Ka expresses an:
1. In –Spiriting function and a
2. Materialization and manifestation function

It is through Ka that the human Ba of an individual soul, becomes an Entity. This principle fixity of Ka (Auset – sphere 9) and its association with the process of manifestation is further described in the following accordingly: Ra Un Nefer Amen. *Metu Neter, V.I,* p. 72.

> The next faculty created, the 9th sphere, uses all of the preceding shaping factors to make a vehicle that will serve to coordinate physical energy matter into the physical thing or event. This vehicle is the soul of the individual thing or event. In the Kemetic tradition it is called the "ka," and in the Hindu tradition, the "Jivan Atma." Because this faculty is directly in charge of the organization of physical energy/matter into the creature, it is referred to as "the Mother Goddess creator of all the living, and of the Earth" (Auset, Yemaya, Nana, Esse, etc.).

Ibid. p. 58.

> Also found here is the 9th sphere in relation to which is generated the vehicle that defines each thing or event as an individuated spiritual existence. This individuated spirit is called a

KaAbBa Building The Lighted Temple
The Spiritual B(ARK)

"Ka" in the Kemetian tradition. The division of the spirit that contains all of these spheres (7th, 8th, and 9th) with their respective Neteru is called the Sahu by the Kemetians, the lower Ruach by the Canaanites....

How is Ka Spirit and Matter? What is this Double Nature?
1. Ka is how Spirit expresses its right of descent into matter and its re-ascent into pure Spirit. It is the right to take of the sub-stance of Itself in order to see Itself reflected in matter/form.
2. Ka is the attraction of matter for Spirit and Spirit for matter.
3. Ka is the source of all appetites. Since All is Spirit –
4. Ka is ultimately the attraction of Spirit for Spirit.
5. Ka is the Law of Vibration in action.

The double nature of Ka is seen in the diagram at right.

According to Isha Schwaller De Lubicz. *The Opening of The Way. Her-Bak*: Ibid.
1. "Originally, Ka is the Formal Element which gives form to Substance and thus creates Matter.
2. It is the spiritual principle of fixity, which will become the basis of all manifestation, and
3. Through the ages of Becoming will undergo innumerable modifications
4. From the basest of forms to the perfection of the indestructible body."

What is BKA?
The Kemetians called the Divine qualities of God Neter or Neteru for plural. Letters and numbers are Divine beings or deities that speak and convey qualities of God. When the Neteru are put together they invoke both quality and name. According to Isha Schwaller De Lubicz, *The Opening of The Way Her-Bak*, p. 201.

"The word bka or beka, meaning the impregnation or fecundation of a female, shows how these two factors Ba and Ka must be brought together for there to be a conception. Conception is an incarnation of:
1. The essential Ka which is Spirit and
2. The specific Ka, given by the seed, and animated by the vital breath of the b-."

Instead of the words essential Ka and specific Ka, I will use the words Spirit or In-Spiriting Ka and Approximate or Approximating Ka as these serve as better Ausarian Spiritual Transformation and Resurrection ASTR descriptors to indicate the double nature of Ka. This is pictured in the diagram at right. Ka is called the double and is therefore reflected as both:

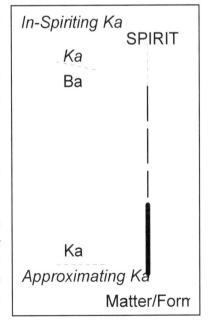

1. Spirit Ka – the essential and eternal Image and Likeness of God.
2. Approximating Ka – the specific 'snapshot' of how much you have been able to put together in consciousness of the right relationship between Spirit and matter.

In the diagram at right, this Neteru is placed in a circle to reveal it as an oracle that speaks throughout creation. The Spirit/Matter continuum cannot be separated. They are the Father/Mother in eternal embrace. It is only in appearance that Spirit/Matter or Father/Mother are seemingly separated to reflect that which is Spiritual and material in man and woman.

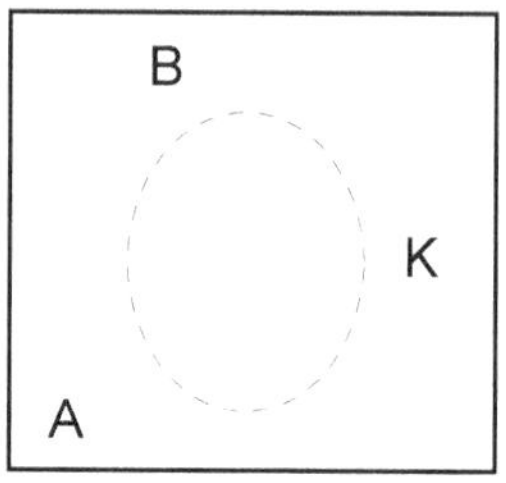

Ka Ab Ba As Trinity. What is the arising of the Number 3?
The interplay between the Divine Neteru of B-K-A is shown in the diagram at right. This is the interplay between Spirit and Matter, Father and Mother. Throughout this interplay you are the Sun- Son/Daughter or Soul who is:
1. Born of the Father and the Mother
2. Becoming fully conscious of the perfected relationship
    between Spirit and Matter

B K A is a Soul infusing process, whereby man and woman can be put back together again in consciousness. It is how the pieces within you are made to 'fit' together again as you re-connect within your own Spiritual equipment. It is how our Spirit is made whole. The Soul infusing process is described in greater detail later. For now

This brings us to our next

Metaphysical Key To:
Number 1, 2 and 3
Three-Oneness KaAbBa
Out of the '0' , Zero –
 Whenever:
 There is the arising of the 1 as unity Ba (Monad)
 There is the arising of the 2 of Duality – BaKa or KaBa (Diad) and
 There is the arising of the 3 of Multiplicity BaAbKa or KaAbBa (Triad)

 The 1, 2 and 3 are The Divine Trinity, The 3 Aspects of Divinity
                    Ausar, Auset and Heru

The process of BKA gives rise to Ba Ab Ka or Ka Ab Ba, depending upon where along the Spirit/Matter continuum we are focused. There is now the arising of a Spirit/Soul – Soul/Consciousness – Spirit/Matter Continuum. In the Kemetic Spiritual system the Three

85

KaAbBa   Building The Lighted Temple
The Spiritual B(ARK)

Aspects of Divinity are revealed in the terms Ka Ab Ba. These terms give insight into the purpose and function within our Spiritual make-up and offer the first basic structures for our study.

They likewise correspond to the Divine Trinity revealed in the Tree of Life of Auset – sphere 9,

Heru – sphere 6, and Ausar – sphere 1, pictured in the diagram at right. The 2nd Aspect of Divinity, known as Ab by the Kemetians is symbolized by the human heart. The heart is the seat of the Soul and growing Self conscious identity. The Ab Soul is the conscious experience of how Spirit and Matter are relating. It is how Father-Spirit has a conscious experience of Mother-Matter. As man's consciousness develops he must also develop a 'conscience'. This is Heru or the Karest/Christ principle within that guides you to be and act in accord with the Universal Law of Right Relationship. Through

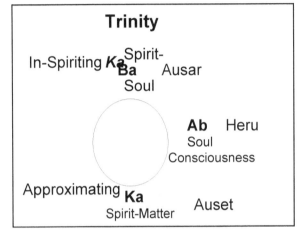

the relating aspect of Ab, the 'seeming' duality between Spirit-Matter with its myriad objective forms in play and display as Ba Ka are seen as ONE. Thus through Ab Soul consciousness the same One True Self is seen in every other Self.

The author concedes that any study of Ka Ab Ba or efforts to schematically represent the respective character of this profoundly enigmatic and mysterious concept must be humbly and cautiously approached. It must be recognized that descriptions and diagrams cannot adequately represent the dynamically moving play and display between Ka Ab Ba. Nevertheless, we must seek to penetrate the veil, thereby deepening understanding. So we do our best. This concept reveals the relationship between Matter, Soul and Spirit.

We will look first at the arising of the 3 – called the trinity, triad or triune. We learn from this Metaphysical Key that when there is the arising of the 1, we have the arising of the 2 of duality followed by the 3. In manifestation, the 1 sees itself reflected giving rise to the 2. Through the interaction between the 1 and 2 the Intelligent activity of creation is expressed, giving rise to the 3. We will first bring our focus to the arising of the 3 – making two different divisions within the Tree of Life.

Level 1 Division into 3
The emanation of Spirit is pictured in the diagram at right as the arising of the 1 and the 3, which form the upper geometric triangle in the Tree of Life. These are sphere 1 – Ausar, sphere 2 – Tehuti and sphere 3 – Seker. We see here that spheres 1, 2 and 3 are respectively the 1st aspect, 2nd aspect and 3rd aspect, the Divine trinity. These are the first 3 of the 7 Souls (later described)

The Ausarianization of Consciousness Series 1
Metaphysical Keys To the Tree of Life & Oracle Keys to Dis-spelling Illusion
The Spiritual Journey in Unfolding Consciousness

86

Kemetically called Ba, Khu, Sekhem (*See Metu Neter, V.I,* in re-claim-ation process in Kemetic naming of the spheres).

Level 2 Division into 3

The next level division into 3 is made as the 1 of the Ba triangle – emanates as 2 additional triangles, which now total 3 distinct triangles, pictured at right. The 3 aspects of Divinity, one for each triangle are now represented. Taken in total – they complete the Tree of Life and again the Divine Trinity is seen. The enumeration of Spirit into the 1 of Ba and the movement of the 1 into the 3 are seen in these two divisions that can be made within the Tree of Life. As we proceed in our story we will concern ourselves for now with the Level 2 Division – the 3 Triangles of Emanation – the 3 Aspects of Divinity in the Puat Neteru.

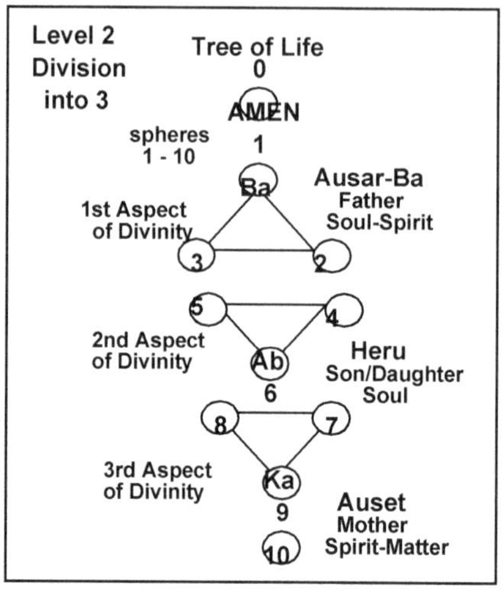

We turn our attention now to these three main divisions within the human Spiritual Constitution or Economy.

Throughout all major religions this concept of the three aspects of Divinity are variously expressed. In Christianity these are: Father, Son, and Holy Ghost. In Eastern Religion these are Shiva, Vishnu and Brahma. In Esoteric tradition these are Monad, Soul and Personality, or Spirit, Soul and Matter. These three triangles are also referred to as, The Knower, The Process of Knowing, and the Known. In the Kemetic system they are called Ba Ab Ka. Or Ka Ab Ba. In the chart on the next page, the Kemetic terminology precedes a list of terms commonly used by other traditions to give 'Name' to the Three Aspects of Divinity – the three divisions of Spirit/Soul-Soul/Consciousness-Spirit/Matter Continuum:

KaAbBa Building The Lighted Temple
The Spiritual B(ARK)

Three Aspects of Divinity
Spirit/Soul-Soul/Consciousness-Spirit/Matter Continuum

1st Aspect	2nd Aspect	3rd Aspect	
Ba	Ab	Ka	
Ausar	Heru	Auset	
Sphere 1	Sphere 6	Sphere 9	Ka-Ra-actor, Ka-erect-or (Character, Personality) producing the Sahu Body – Lighted Temple
•Neshamah	Rauch	Nephesh	
Kether	Tif(p)ereth	Yesod	
•Spirit	Soul	Matter	
Monad	Soul	Personality	
Monad	Spiritual Triad	Personality	
Life	Quality/Consciousness	Form	
Father	Son	Holy Ghost	
Father	Son/Daughter	Mother	
Shiva	Vishnu	Brahma	
Will/Power	Wisdom/Love	Intelligence/Activity	
Shamballa	Hierarchy	Humanity	
Knower	Process of Knowing	Known	

Understanding this Kemetic/Ancient Egyptian concept helps us to understand the Spirit/Soul – Soul/Consciousness – Spirit/Matter continuum and its correspondence with the Kemetic Law of Vibration. This is expressed accordingly: Tibetan, *A Treatise on Cosmic Fire,* p. 228.

> Man is the product of the approximation (at present imperfect) of the two poles of Spirit (the Father in Heaven) and of matter (the Mother). The result of this union is an individualised Son of God, or unit of the Divine Self, an exact replica in miniature on the lowest plane of the great Son of God, the All-Self, who is in Himself the totality of all the miniature sons, of all the individualised Selves, and of each and every unit.

This is the interplay between Spirit and Matter, Father and Mother and how the Son/Soul of Self consciousness is born of the Father and the Mother. Through the play and display of Ka and Ba that *Self* or Ab consciousness is born. This is the Trinity or Triune nature within your Spiritual make-up. This individualized Sun-Son/Daughter of God is Heru – sphere 6, in the Tree of Life.

We remember that all resolves into the One of Ba and finally the Infinite All of SPIRIT where all 3 aspects represented in the Kemetic Spiritual system as BKA or Ba Ab Ka, are at rest in the Eternal embrace of *indivisible* and *inseparable* Father-Mother or Spirit-Matter. Again, all 'seeming' divisions are arbitrary and are merely useful for helping us to find our way back *Home*

• Kabbalistic.
• The Books of the Tibetan, i.e. *A Treatise on Cosminc Fire*; *Esoteric Psychology;* et. al.

from a journey we never really went on except in an illusion we came to believe as 'Real'. We seek to unravel the unreality in our Ausarian Resurrection into the *REAL*.

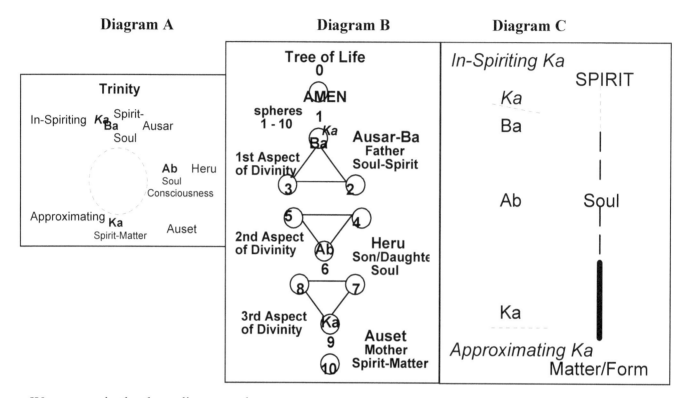

We can see in the three diagrams above:
1. KaAbBa as a circle **(Diagram A)**.
2. Ka Ab Ba are next revealed in the Tree of Life and visually laid out in a straight line **(Diagram B).** Thus Trinity or triune nature arises as a seeming 'above, middle and below' within our Spiritual equipment.
a. Three-Oneness is now reflected as the arising of Ba 1st aspect of Divinity triangle, Ab 2nd aspect of Divinity triangle and Ka 3rd aspect of Divinity triangle.
3. Ka Ab Ba are seen as revealed within the Spirit/Matter Continuum **(Diagram C)** as Spirit vibrates along a continuum from high to low (low to high) within our Spiritual equipment.

What are you as the Sun-Son/Daughter becoming fully conscious of?
As Ausar Ba son and daughter, you are becoming fully conscious of the perfect relationship between Father and Mother, between Spirit and Matter. To become fully conscious is to live the consciousness of Ausar Ba – that we are made in the Image and Likeness of God and All SELVES are but the ONE True Indivisible SELF.

These terms Ka Ab Ba help describe the Spiritual journey of man and woman who seemingly leave their Eternal Home and then 'return' This concept is critical in understanding the process

KaAbBa Building The Lighted Temple
The Spiritual B(ARK)

of Ausarian Resurrection. It assists you in 'knowing' and mapping out your straight-line course of Spiritual re-ascent. Your clarity of intention in your destination becomes your invocation – for Ausarian Resurrection. This clarity in direction assists you in Building The Lighted Temple, the Spiritual B-Ark or Ka Ab Ba, for navigating the Perfect Storm, in which we now live (See chapter on "The Spiritual Implications of The Perfect Storm – Understanding What Time It Is").

To gain understanding of Ka Ab BA is to gain understanding of the 'narrow middle way' or R/azor E/dged P/ath, as referred to by the Ancients. Those who follow it have a good R.E.P. or reputation. In the process of re-ascent, some will go around the wide base of the mountain for many lifetimes, gaining little altitude with each pass. Some will make a gradual but steady climb. Others will seek the narrow middle way, advancing to great heights in their climb, even in a single lifetime. The Pyramid symbolizes this concept.

Ka, Holy Ghost, Stool and Tool of God
The 'seeming' separation in consciousness of Ka and Ba has contributed to the subverting of the Mother principle by a patriarchal Western World. This is reflected in the discord between the male and female. Christianity uses the word 'Holy Ghost' as substitute for the Mother principle, the Kemetic Ka 3rd aspect of Divinity. Nevertheless, the letters or Neteru still reveal the Divine Mother in this word.

Let's dispell the word Holy Ghost:
#1. Oracle Metaphysical Dis-spelling Key:
Put letters of word or words together in a circle, like a serpent putting its tail in its mouth. Coming full Circle.

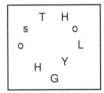 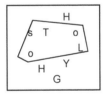 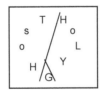

#2. Oracle Metaphysical Dis-spelling Key:
Read letters, putting together words, going forwards, backwards and in zig-zag, and crossover patterns.
#3. Oracle Metaphysical Dis-spelling Key: You may crossover in order to use a letter more than once. Place re-used letter in parenthesis ( ).
#4. Oracle Metaphysical Dis-spelling Key: You may add a letter to complete a word. Place added letter in parenthesis ( ).
#5. Oracle Metaphysical Dis-spelling Key: Letter substitution-you may substitute a letter. Place substituted letter in parenthesis ( ).
#6. Oracle Metaphysical Dis-spelling Key: Make a list of derived words. Try to make the longest continuous unbroken word or string of words.
<u>Derived Word List:</u>
<u>Stool Hy G</u> – Stool of High God

The Ausarianization of Consciousness Series 1
Metaphysical Keys To the Tree of Life & Oracle Keys to Dis-spelling Illusion
The Spiritual Journey in Unfolding Consciousness

90

<u>Tools Hy G</u> – Tools of High God
<u>Holy Host G</u> – Holy Host of God

#8. Oracle Metaphysical Dis-spelling Key: Meaning. See the relationship and oracle or story of the Neteru – Put word list together to tell a story.

<u>Meaning:</u>

It is out of the Divine Mother that Divine creation is fashioned. The 3rd aspect of Divinity – the Ka triangle provides the Tools of the Hy (High) G-(od) for building creation. All arises from the womb of the Divine Mother. It is the stool of the Most High God upon which Divine creation is placed. Within the Holy Host G-od indwells. The Ancient wisdom teaches us that the stool or throne is our Mother Auset – upon which Ausar the Father rests the Kingdom of God. Instead of moving within the 1st eye interiorly, the Spiritual Journey has been exteriorized and materialized so that humans sit on Ba® 'stools' imbibing alcohol trying to feel the 'Spirit' or Ka, trying to get high. They raise one arm up with a glass in it – instead of raising both arms up in the Ka posture, which symbolically mirrors how much of the Image and Likeness of God we are reflecting. This 'recreation' is but a distorted attempt at Ra-creation – which is trying to resurrect the Sun/Son within you, called Ra. The Ka symbol is shown in the diagram at right:

This process of 're-vivification', resurrection or raising up is expressed in the following accordingly: E. A. Wallis Budge. *The Prt Em Hru. (Egyptian Book Of The Dead*), Chap. XV, p. 247.

The word Ka means **"image"**, according to Greek (translation). The Ka seems to have been the **"ghost",** as we should say, of a man, and it has been defined as his abstract personality, to which, after death, the Egyptians [read here: The Kemetians] gave a material form. It was a **subordinate** part of the human being during life, but after death it became active and to it the offerings brought to the tomb by the relatives of the dead were dedicated. It was believed that it returned to the body and had a share in its **re-vivification.**

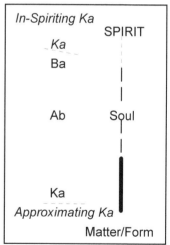

Let's dispell the word revivification:
#7. Oracle Metaphysical Dis-spelling Key: Look up definition (dictionary, glossary, reference texts, etc.)
<u>Definition:</u> Microsoft Word Thesaurus.
<u>Revivification</u> – Rebirth, renaissance, resuscitation, revival, reanimation, and resurgence.
In light of the above quote, we revisit an earlier diagram, which is shown at right and modified to further illustrate Ka in its 'double' aspect function.
At the top of the diagram we see:
1. <u>Spirit Ka or In-Spiriting Ka</u> – The 're-vivification' or resurrection function. The essential and eternal Image and Likeness of God.

KaAbBa   Building The Lighted Temple
The Spiritual B(ARK)

At the bottom of the diagram we see:

2. <u>Approximating Ka</u> – The 'subordinate' function in the human life. The specific 'snapshot' of how much you have been able to put together in consciousness of the right relationship between Spirit and matter.

To Summarize:

In our Metaphysical studies we begin with the Divine cipher called ZERO '0' sphere, in The Tree of life. This is The AMEN, The ABSOLUTE, ETERNAL, THE ALL, NETER NETERU, SPIRIT, - just a few of the many names.

From AMEN (Zero (0) sphere), - arises the ONE (1) which is Ba, Indivisible Soul-Spirit.

From the ONE (1) – Ba, the THREE (3) aspects of SPIRIT arise.

These represent The Three Aspects of Divinity. They are:

Ba – 1st Aspect (Soul-Spirit) – Will/Power of God

Ab – 2nd Aspect (Soul-Consciousness) – Wisdom/Love of God

Ka – 3rd Aspect (Spirit-Matter/Form) – Creative Intelligence/Activity of God

Taken together these 3 aspects are called the trinity, triad, triplicity or triune. Having arisen from the ONE, these 3 aspects are the 3 outpourings or emanations that make up your Spiritual faculty. Before penetrating deeper into the Trinity we must first turn our attention to the next Metaphysical Key to understand the divisioning into the 7 at work in man and woman.

Chapter 10
Divisioning Into The 7 – The Nature Of The Septenary At Work In Man & Woman

Having entered into the Trinity or Triune division in the Spiritual make-up of man and woman, we now turn to the Septenary. In order to gain insight into this altering in consciousness, we must understand the Divisioning into the 7 that is at work in the nature of man/woman and creation. This brings us to the next

---

Metaphysical Key To:
The Number 7
The 7 Planes of Consciousness, 7 Division of The Solar Systemic Planes
The Septenary/Heptanary Nature of Man and Woman and Creation

In this next pass down the Tree of Life The Planes are briefly described:
The Tree of Life is composed of 7 planes, numbered 1 – the highest, through 7 – the lowest (See *Treatise on Cosmic Fire*). These are outlined in the table below. Each of the 7 planes represents a 'World' in which a certain expanse in consciousness is taking place. Again, it is important to remember that even though we are looking at 7 discrete divisions in consciousness, the only separation is the one created by our own illusion of separative or broken consciousness.

The 7 States of Consciousness – 7 Division of The Solar Systemic Planes

Planes (systemic)	Worlds	Consciousness
Higher Planes		
1. Logoic (Divinity) Plane	World of Emanating Cause	Absolute Consciousness
2. Monadic Plane	World Divine	God Consciousness
3. Atmic (Spiritual) Plane	World Spiritual	Planetary Consciousness
Middle Plane		
4. Buddhic (Intuitional) Plane	World of Karest/Christ	Christ/Heru Consciousness/ Intuitional/Group Consciousness
Lower Planes		
5. Mental Plane	World of Mind & Soul	Mind Consciousness
6. Astral Plane	World of the Emotions	Kamic/Desire Consciousness
7. Physical Plane	World of Earth	Physical Consciousness

It is in studying the planes and sub-planes of consciousness that the subtle qualities of the Neteru and Soul Divisions are revealed. I give my deepest appreciation to Dr. Michael Robbins for his guidance here. The 7 Systemic Planes of Consciousness find relationship to the 7 divisions within the Tree of Life. In the Kemetic system, these planes are called the Arits. Each plane is a level of consciousness. Plane number 1 is the most Spiritualized. Plane number 7 is the most materialized. As man/woman makes his/her descent through the planes below, consciousness becomes more dense and materialized.

KaAbBa   Building The Lighted Temple
The Spiritual B(ARK)

The Ancients were very familiar with the 7 planes or Arits of consciousness. This is pictured in the diagram at right from the Papyrus of Ani. Seen here are the 7 Hathors or celestial cow goddesses. Het-Heru is also known as Hathor. Starting from the top down, each represents a plane in consciousness that must be ascended by the Bull of Heaven, Ausar, pictured at the bottom, who is you and me. Hathor glimpses the inner archetypal patterning of greater wholeness and beauty *upon each plane and* causes us – the Initiate – to aspire towards the Divinely intended design. When we are using the Het-Heru/Hathor part of our Spiritual equipment at a higher turn of the spiral or optimal level, we are magnetically attracting the higher ideal to be manifested in our lives.

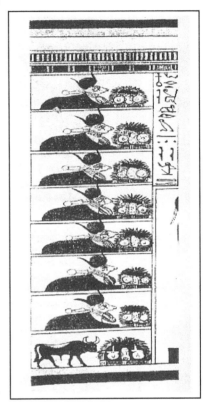

Let's dispell the word Arits:
 # 1. Oracle Metaphysical Dis-spelling Key:
Put letters of word or words together in a circle, like a serpent putting its tail in its mouth. Coming full Circle.

#2. Oracle Metaphysical Dis-spelling Key: Read letters, putting together words, going forwards, backwards and in zig-zag patterns.
#3. Oracle Metaphysical Dis-spelling Key: You may crossover in order to use a letter more than once. Place re-used letter in parenthesis ( ).
#4. Oracle Metaphysical Dis-spelling Key: You may add a letter to complete a word. Place added letter in parenthesis ( ).
#5. Oracle Metaphysical Dis-spelling Key: Letter substitution-you may substitute a letter. Place substituted letter in parenthesis ( ).
#6. Oracle Metaphysical Dis-spelling Key: Make a list of derived words. Try to make the longest continuous unbroken word or string of words.

<u>Derived Word List:</u>
<u>Stair</u> – That which we must climb, ascend
<u>Star</u> - A Luminous being as in the Sun Ra
<u>Aris(e)</u> – To ascend
<u>Stir</u> – To make movement out of slumber
<u>Star(e)</u> –The Bull and Cow Goddess are symbols connected with the Astrological sign of Taurus. Taurus relates to the 'eye of the Bull' or 'Bull's eye'. It is through the sign of Taurus that we may develop 'the eye that sees all' or 'the all seeing eye' of wisdom and illumination. So we see here that the word 'stare' relates to what the eye is focused upon. Biblically stated, if thine eye be single – beholding the One True Self as the Image and Likeness of God then thy whole body is full of Light.

<u>Istar</u> – Babylonian deity synonymous with Het-Heru (Hathor). Istar is the planet Venus. This planet rules in the sign of Taurus (and Libra) and under the Kemetic deity of Het-Heru – sphere 7.

<u>I.A.S.T.R.</u> – We undergo Initiation and our 'eye' is made whole through – 'I Ausarian Spiritual Transformation & Resurrection'.

#7. Oracle Metaphysical Dis-spelling Key: Look up definition (dictionary, glossary, reference texts, etc.)

<u>Derived Word List Continued:</u>

<u>Definition</u>

<u>Satir(e)</u> – A literary work in which human vice or folly is attacked through irony, derision, or wit.

<u>Definition</u>

<u>Sat(o)ri</u> – Buddhism. A state of spiritual enlightenment sought in Zen Buddhism.

<u>Definition</u>

<u>Strai(t), strai(ght)</u>

> <u>Straight</u> – Extending continuously in the same direction without curving. Erect.
> <u>Strait</u> – Strict, rigid, or righteous.

#8. Oracle Metaphysical Dis-spelling Key: Meaning. See the relationship and oracle or story of the Neteru – Put word list together to tell a story.

<u>Meaning</u>

Through our arduous climb up the 'stairs', we ascend the Tree of Life taking our place as a Luminous 'STAR' among the stars. Through 'satire' the whole story of our journey in unfolding consciousness is told of how we 'stir' from our slumber, opening more and more our eyes. In fixed 'star(e)' we finally behold the Image and Likeness of God that we have always been. At last we have undergone sat(o)ri (enlightenment) which is <u>I.A.S.T.R.</u> – 'I Ausarian Spiritual Transformation & Resurrection', becoming 'straight' as an arrow.

In reality these planes are interpenetrating and there is an *all at once-ness* and *simultaneity* happening. There is no 'this or that' or 'this and that' but rather 'All This is That'. However, what we can observe in the make-up of others is that it is possible to live in the physical or emotional plane of consciousness with little awareness of planes or Worlds of consciousness beyond. The practice of Ausarian Spiritual Transformation and Resurrection (ASTR) is to bring the consciousness into residence upon the higher Spiritual planes within your Spiritual equipment while using your mental, emotional and physical vehicles or Soul bodies made from the lower material planes to do your work in the outer World. By overlaying in the diagram at right, the 7 planes of consciousness are revealed within the Tree of Life. Here we see its divisioning into the 7 Systemic Planes of consciousness.

Metaphysical Key To:
The Overlay of The 7 Planes of consciousness

KaAbBa Building The Lighted Temple
The Spiritual B(ARK)

These planes of consciousness are also 7 Energy Fields. As man makes his descent to the more dense and materialized planes below he/she 'forgets' to identify *as/with* the fullness of the One True Self Identification as Ausar – sphere 1, and The Unlimited Access To All Potential that he/she *is*. The story of Ausarian resurrection that follows throughout this text is the story of understanding and transcending the fragmentation that occurs in consciousness as we make our descent from the higher planes of consciousness to the lower planes. This brokeness in consciousness manifests in our outer World as the pain of separation from our One True God-Self. We grow 'down' and 'up' the Tree of Life by our descent and re-ascent of the 7 planes of consciousness. Through this re-ascent in consciousness the 7 are made 1. This process of At-One-ing is the Ausarianization of Consciousness. It is where we may 'get an eye full' or know the fullest, 'I'.

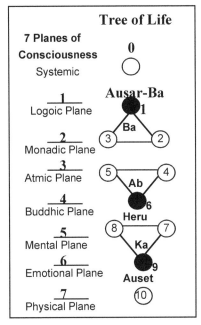

The Septenary is 7, and 7 is Number. Number is Ntr, or Neter to the Kemetians. Neter or Number provides the vehicle through which the Neteru or qualities of God may speak. The Septenate is one such numerological template in consciousness upon which unfolding events take place that express Divinity. The divisioning of the nature of creation and man into 7 discrete qualities of energy is the story of the Kemetic Goddess Ta-urt. The Divine Mother Ta –Urt is the first mother who was of no sex. She is provider of food and life and out of her, the 7 elemental powers are born. These 7 powers qualify all creation and guide material expression in life.

Let's dispell the word Ta-urT: This brings us to a new Oracle Metaphysical Dis-spelling Key:
#9.Oracle Metaphysical Dis-spelling Key: Take each letter one at a time or in combination with one or more letters and derive its meaning.
Derived letter or Neter list:
T – As the vertical and the horizontal line intersect to form the cross bar, we have creative potential arising within the Divine Mother
Au – Divine Breath
Ra – Fire of Ra, power of fecundation (impregnation) of the Mother substance
T - T – Ring of creation – Measure of fecundation of the Mother, the expanse of the Universe or manifested form. Enclosing 'ring pass not'.

#8. Oracle Metaphysical Dis-spelling Key: Meaning. See the relationship and oracle or story of the Neteru   Put word list together to tell a story.

Meaning:
The fecundating (impregnating) fiery breath of 'Ra' which is breathed 'Au' throughout the Mother within the manifesting ring 'T – T' giving rise to creation.

Churward states that the Great Mother – Ta-Urt who bore no children, was primary, and should be distinguished from the Great Mother who was later divinized as the Goddess Apt, who bore children and is also called Mut – the Vulture goddess, and Nu, Nut the Sky goddess. (See Churward. *Origin and Evolution of the Human Race*, p. 208). He states accordingly: Ibid. 235.

> …in the next phase of the mythology we find that the Great Mother "Apt" brought forth children and was given a constellation. She was divinized as both male and female, as "Apt", the goddess in human guise with the head of a hippopotamus; this was the next stage of development in evolution.

This emanation or divisioning into the 7 heptenary or septenary – is likewise later expressed as the body of consciousness of Ausar in the following accordingly: Gerald Massey. *Ancient Egypt The Light of the World, V.I*, p. 409.

> When the Supreme Being had been imaged or personified, the powers previously extant were represented as his offspring, his names, or members of his body. Hence the seven associate-gods, the Ali or Elohim, are now called the limbs, joints, the hands, the fingers, the lips, the teeth, the breath of god, or reversely stated, these parts of the one god become the associate gods, as a seven-fold emanation from Kheper-Ptah.
>
> Now Ptah was satisfied after his making of all things, and conferring all the Divine names. He formed the gods, he made the towns, he designed the nomes, he placed the gods in their shrines. He made their company flourish", " All the limbs moved when he uttered the word of wisdom which came forth from the tongue and worked a blessing upon all things". The word (lit *Speech*) became the *making of men* and the creation of gods for Ptah – Tatanen-Sepu.

Ibid. p. 407.

> The Put-company of the nine gods was preceded by that of the eight; the eight by that of the seven Ali, or associates; the seven Uraeus-divinities; the seven Khuti; and these by the Mothers Apt, Neith, Tefnut, and the seven cows or Hathors.

We see here in our story how the Great Mother and her seven elemental powers were now superseded by the combined god – Kheper-Ptah – in which both sexes were included in the one-Supreme Being who was now the Lord over all – Ausar. Ibid.

> The foundation of monotheism was laid when the various powers were combined in a single deity to be worshipped as the one true eternal spirit. These were primarily the Great Mother and her seven elemental powers. And when the goddess was superseded by the god Ptah, both sexes were included in the one Supreme Being who was now the Lord over all. It was the same with Osiris [read here: Ausar, Asar], as the pictures show. Asar was the mother and child (Hes-Ar) in one, and the perfect triune type was completed in God the father. There was no God the father without God the mother and God the child.

KaAbBa Building The Lighted Temple
The Spiritual B(ARK)

Ausar expressing as Kheper and Ptah is the opener and great architect in the Universe. In the process of creation there is the arising now of the 7 Primordial Conditioning Powers or energies that are called by many names which include: 7 Elohim, the 7 Glorious Spirits, The 7 Primordial Energies, 7 African Powers, 7 Khuti, 7 Ari, 7 Ali, 7 Spirits before the Throne, 7 Stars in Ursa Minor – The Little Bear, 7 Annuaki, 7 Angelic Powers, the 7 Ra(y)s, and the 7 Souls of Ra. This is expressed accordingly: Albert Churchward. *Origin and Evolution of the Human Race,* p.110.

> The seven elemental powers were afterwards, at the time of the Hero Cult and the Second exodus of the Nilotic Negro, divinized and represented by seven gods, two at first, Heru and Sut, then Shu, and afterwards the other four. There are two lists of these gods in the Ritual. These were given stars on high, and later represented the seven Pole Stars, and were called the Glorious Ones – The Khuti in Stellar Mythos. The first three were the heroes; they play a great part in the folk-lore tales found all over the world.

Creation arises out of the 'waters of space' called Nu by the Kemetians. Ausar expressing as Kheper-Ptah (Seker sphere 3):
1. Digs 7 holes in the waters of space and
2. Ultimately molds the to-be created Universe of forms and
3. Teaches matter *how to behave* according to 7 discrete streams of qualifying energies – 7 Deific powers

Through the Great Architect of the Universe, the Ancients knew that the 7 Elementary powers are a Divine template giving geometrical arrangement and quality to *all life* throughout manifest creation. This primal Seven is expressed accordingly by Levi, *Aquarian Gospel of Jesus The Christ,* p. 53.

> 20: From God's own Record Book we read: the Triune God breathed forth, and seven Spirits stood before his face. (The Hebrews call these seven Spirits *Elohim*.)
> 21: And these are they who, in their boundless power, created everything that is, or was.
> 22: **These Spirits of the Triune God moved on the face of boundless space and seven ethers were, and every ether had its form of life.**
> 23: These forms of life were but the thoughts of God, clothed in the substance of their ether planes.
> 24: (Men call these ether planes the planes of protoplast, of earth, of plant, of beast, of man, of angel and of cherubim.)
> 25: **These planes with all their teeming thoughts of God, are never seen by eyes of man in flesh; they are composed of substance far too fine for fleshly eyes to see, and still they constitute the soul of things;**
> 26: And with the eyes of soul all creatures see these ether planes, and all the forms of life.
> 27: Because all forms of life on every plane are thoughts of God, all creatures think, and every creature is possessed of will, and, in its measure, has the power to choose.
> 28: And in their native planes all creatures are supplied with nourishment from the ethers of their planes.
> 29: And so it was with every living thing until the will became a sluggish will, and then the ethers of the protoplast, the earth, the plant, the beast, the man, began to vibrate very slowly.

30: The ethers all became more dense, and all the creatures of these planes were clothed with coarser garbs, the garbs of flesh, which men can see; and thus this coarser manifest, which men call physical appeared.

This brings us to the next

Metaphysical Key To: **The Number 7** The 7 Souls of Ra, The 7 Soul Divisions or 7 Divisions of Spirit The Septenary Nature of Man and Creation	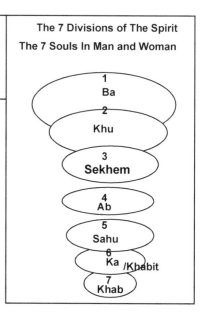

The 7 Souls of Ra, The 7 Soul Divisions, 7 Divisions of Spirit
Within the Kemetic Spiritual tradition there are Seven divisions of the Spirit or 7 Souls or 7 Soul bodies or vehicles. These are also called the 7 Souls of Ra (See Budge, Massey), (See the works of Ra Un Nefer Amen. *Metu Neter V.I & II,* who is the foremost pioneer in the correct naming and re-claim-ation of the Kemetic Neteru and Soul divisions in the Tree of Life or Paut Neteru). Each corresponds with and gives qualities to 1 of the 7 planes of consciousness. The 7 Divisions of Spirit – Soul are pictured in the diagram at right and briefly described below. Further detail is given later. These are as follows:

The Seven Divisions of Spirit-The Seven Souls of Ra
1. **Ba** – Soul.
2. **Khu** – Intelligence. The Divine ideation in the Mind of God. Luminous Beings of Light revealing the Divine archetypal design. Divine wisdom.
3. **Sekhem** – Power to achieve the fullest co-measure of God's Divinely intended design in manifested/ing form.
4. **Ab** – Heart expressing higher Divine Will and/or lower personal will and desire.
5. **Sahu** – Spiritual Body. (The Mental Body – a. Higher Abstract Mind b. Lower Mind). This is the body that has become the incorruptible body through its accumulation and attainment of a degree of knowledge, wisdom and intelligence.
6. **Ka/Khaibit**
a. **Ka** – The double, Spirit.   (The Emotional/Astral Body)
b. **Khaibit** - The shadow or overshadowing body. The Khaibit Soul division of Spirit may be thought of as an interpenetrating web between the 6th and 7th plane of consciousness, as shown in the diagram on the following page. The Khaibit is the scaffolding upon which the dense Physical body is built and the vitalizing source of the dense body. It is called the Astral or Etheric body by the Esotericists.
c. The Ka and the Khaibit are viewed as closely linked. This is expressed in the following quotes accordingly: Donald Mackenzie, *Egyptian Myths and Legends,* p. 90.

KaAbBa Building The Lighted Temple
The Spiritual B(ARK)

The Khaybet [Khaibit], or shadow, is evidently the survival of an early belief. It is really another manifestation of the Ka.

And likewise expressed in the following accordingly: E.A.Wallis Budge, *The Gods of The Egyptians.V 1*, p. 39.

> ...the "double" [the Ka] was an integral part of a man, and was connected with his shadow [the Khaibit], and came into being when he was born, and lived in the tomb with the body after death...

7 Khab – The dense living Physical body. (see also Khat – body of the deceased)

Metaphysical Key To:
The Overlay of The 7 Souls or 7 Divisions of Spirit in the Tree of Life

---

The Overlay of The 7 Soul Divisions or 7 Divisions of Spirit is revealed within the Tree of Life and have correspondence with the 7 Planes of Consciousness. Moving from left to right we can see in these four diagrams lettered A through D that:

| **A** | **B** | **C** | **D** |

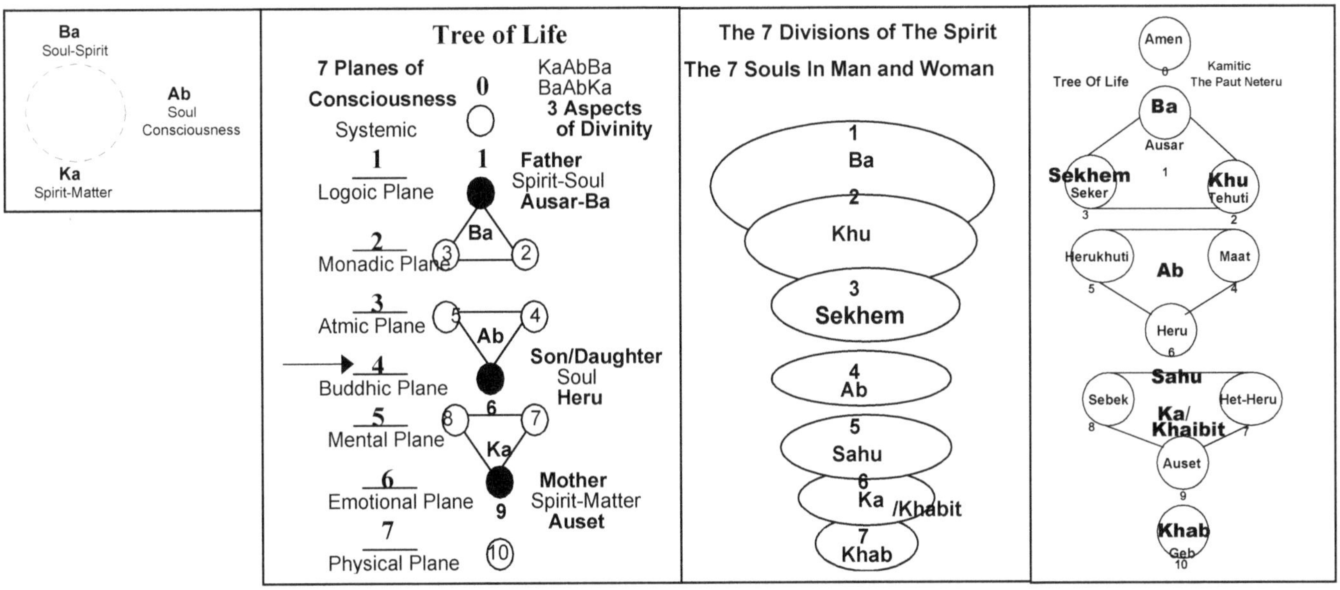

Diagrams A and B:
1. The Arising of the 1 and the 3 in the Divine Trinity, BaAbKa or KaAbBa.
2. The 7 Planes of Consciousness

Diagrams B, C, & D combined:
1. The Ba Triangle is the 1st Aspect of Divinity in the Tree of Life comprised of:
a. Ba Soul Body – Neter Ausar Ba, sphere 1
b. Khu Soul Body – Neter Tehuti, sphere 2

    c. Sekhem Soul Body – Neter Seker, sphere 3

    2. The Ab Triangle is the 2nd Aspect of Divinity in the Tree of Life comprised of:

    a. Neter Maat, sphere 4

    b. Neter Herukhuti, sphere 5

    c. Ab Soul Body – Neter Heru, sphere 6

    3. The Ka Triangle is the 3rd Aspect of Divinity in the Tree of Life comprised of:

    a. Sahu Soul Body – Neter Het-Heru, sphere 7 – Neter Sebek, sphere 8

    b. Ka/Khaibit Soul Body – Neter Auset, sphere 9

    c. Khab Soul Body – Neter Geb, sphere 10

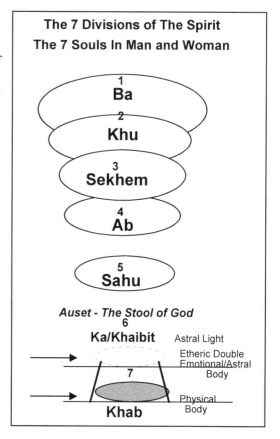

The **6th Ka/Khaibit** Soul Division and **7th Khab** Soul Division of Spirit are indicated by the arrows and further illustrated in the diagram at right. Here we see the 6th Soul Division Ka/Khaibit is Ast or Auset, the Astral Light. Auset is the Stool of God. She is the Tool of God. Auset has seen the Father/her husband in fullness and she has seen him in part (14 pieces). Auset is how God's creation is made visible. Love and devotion are her cohering powers. Spirit Ka individuates as approximating Ka/Khaibit and projects itself into physical form/creation which becomes the 7th Soul Division, or Khab.

Understanding Soul Ra(y) Energy
The 7 Souls of Ra or The 7 Ra(y)s of the Soul Continued:
Each one of us is sounding a sound or Soul note according to the particular Soul Ra(y) energy that sounded when we each incarnated. The Ab Soul Ra(y) is the predominating Soul note and indicates your Soul purpose.
For example:
Some people incarnate here on Earth with the express purpose of being leaders, teachers, artists, or scientists. It is in knowing the Ra(y) energy of the Soul that you are able to understand more clearly the work that you have come into the World to do. Knowing your Soul Ra(y) Purpose enables you to:

1. Harness the will of the Soul

2. Stand in empowered leadership, bringing your equipment into alignment

3. Build true to the Divinely intended design for your life

4. Be exquisitely and intimately familiar with the energy and power of your own Spiritual faculty

KaAbBa Building The Lighted Temple
The Spiritual B(ARK)

What is my Ab Soul Ra(y) Energy or Ab Soul Purpose directing in this incarnation?
Awakening and attuning fully to your Ab Soul purpose becomes an urgent inner stirring. It stirs us to a deepening self examination wherein we might ask and seek answers to the following:
1. What is my reason and meaning for being here?
2. Just what have I come to do in my Earth service?
3. What is it that I would do endlessly, effortlessly and tirelessly, even without pay?
4. What are the many qualities of this vibration – called Neteru by the Kemetians?
5. How is my Soul guiding me?

If there are 7 Souls, why is Heru – sphere 6, or the Ab Soul, a key division in my Spiritual Constitution that defines my Soul Ra(y) Purpose? Insight into this question is expressed accordingly:
In the Ancient text entitled, *The Virgin of The World,* **Heru – sphere 6**, is being initiated as he comes into maturity. We find him being instructed by his mother Auset – sphere 9 into greater knowledge. This instruction will aid him, as he must avenge his Father Ausar's death and ultimately be restored as rightful heir to the throne as King. In the discourse between Auset (mother) and Heru (son) we learn something about the early beginnings in the Spiritual journey of unfolding consciousness as she says accordingly:

> In the beginning there was just matter which had been emitted by God, devoid of that special essence which is called life…. The Great…thus began on these with use of holy arts as proper for the bringing forth of His own special work.

> He breathed into the gods, the Loves, and freely poured the splendor which He had within His heart into their minds, in ever greater and still greater measure that firstly they might have the wish to seek for that which is real, next they might yearn to find, and finally have power to win success in the spiritual search as well. But this, my Heru, wonder-worthy son, could never have been done had that seed in them been subject to death, for that as yet had no existence, but only with a soul that could vibrate responsive to the mysteries of Heaven.

What is this 'Soul' that could vibrate responsive to the mysteries of Heaven?
As we learned there are 7 divisions of the Spirit or 7 Souls. All 7 Souls must vibrate 'responsive to the mysteries of heaven' as stated in the above. But it is the Ab Soul or Heru – sphere 6, where the Son/Daughter is resurrecting within you.

Who is Heru?
You are Heru. This is further expressed accordingly: Albert Churchward. *Signs and Symbols of Primordial Man,* p. 124-125.

> I come before you and make my appearance as that God in the form of a man who liveth as a God'- or as Iusu, **[read here: the Kemetic *Iusu* is the Christianized *Jesus*]** the son of Atum Ra (chap. Lxxix.). "I repeat the acclamations at my success on being declared the heir of Seb [read here also: Geb] (chap. lxxxii.), 'Osiris [read here: Ausar] in Amenta, and Ra in heaven'. 'I descend to the earth of Geb and put a stop to evil' as a bringer of peace, plenty, and good-will on earth (Ritual, chaps xxii., xxiv., xxxii., xlii.). The *Ritual* proves that Seb, the god of Earth, was foster father of Horus [read here: Heru] when he was the child of the

The Ausarianization of Consciousness Series 1
Metaphysical Keys To the Tree of Life & Oracle Keys to Dis-spelling Illusion
The Spiritual Journey in Unfolding Consciousness

102

virgin mother only. In *Ritual*, chap. Lxxxii., Heru says that as the heir of Seb he was suckled at the breast of Isis [read here: Auset], the spouse of Seb, who gave him his theopanies. "After the life with Geb on earth Heru is reborn in the earth of eternity for the heaven of eternity (Ritual, chap. Lxxviii-xxv.). He is divinised with the substance of God (chap. Lxxviii.) by means of Heru, his manifester Ausar is said to relive, Heru is Ausar in his rebirth – Heru rises as god and is visible to the Divine spirits in his resurrection (chap. Lxxix.). He is the living soul of Ra in heaven.

Heru was the <u>only</u> one of the 7 great spirits born of the Mother who was chosen to become the only begotten son of God the Father when he rose up from the dead. This is he who says in the *Ritual*: 'I am the bright one in glory, whom Atum-Ra hath called into being and my origin is from his eye.... (Ritual, chap. Lxxviii., Renouf). **Those who were with him in glory were the 7 great Spirits, the Khuti or Glorious Ones, and amongst these Heru became the Divine heir of all things,** the Son of God who claims to have existed before Auset his Mother and was the manifester for the Holy Spirit Ra in all things. In *Ritual*, chap. Lxxii., Heru says, 'I have come forth with the tongue of Ptah and the throat of Hathor that I may record the words of my Father Tum with my mouth. I am Heru, prince of eternity'(chap. Xlii.). 'I am yesterday, to-day and to-morrow' (chap. Lxiv.). Tum, as the earlier form of Atum's name in the *Ritual,* is pre-eminently 'the Lord.' 'The Lord of Life', 'The Lord of all Creatures', 'The Lord of all'. He was also the patron of builders and architects, and his symbol is the Masonic square.

So we see here that as Heru, you become the 'Divine heir to all things'. By following your Ab Soul purpose and program, you make your descent to Earth which is Geb – sphere 10, 'to stop evil and bring peace' according to the particular Ra(y) qualities conditioning your Ab Soul, which you express. This is Spirit's movement into matter where your Ab Soul purpose and program may be revealed. Through your efforts of goodwill and good works on Earth you are solarized/divinised with the substance of God or respiritualized. By means of the Heru, whose manifester is Ausar, you are reconstructing the broken body of Ausar. You are Ausar in your rebirth and through you, Ausar is said to relive. Heru rises as Iusu, (Jesus) son of God who comes to know the *full conscious relationship* between Father (Soul-Spirit) and Mother (Spirit-Matter). It is through the Soul, or Heru - sphere 6, aspect of your Spiritual equipment that the birth of individual Self consciousness is taking place.

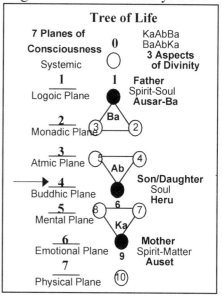

Through Heru, which is the 4th plane in the Tree of Life indicated by the arrow in the diagram at right, you come to relate the 3 Higher planes of consciousness (1-3, above) – the Higher Ego or Higher Manes with the 3 lower planes (5-7, below) – the lower ego or Lower Manes. Manes means mind. Heru is that aspect of your Spiritual faculty where you are linking the Higher Spiritual nature with the lower material nature – both within you. We will see that this relating by the Heru aspect in you is how you find your way back Home after you have made your descent down the Tree of Life. This is expressed accordingly: Gerald Massey, *Ancient Egypt The Light of The World*, p. 892.

> In his birth he says, "I am the babe" born as the connecting link betwixt earth and heaven, and as the one who does not die the second death (ch.42). He issues from the disc or from the egg. He is pursued by the Herrut-reptile, but, as he says, his egg remains unpierced by the destroyer.

As Spirit has a conscious experience of Mother-Matter, Heru is the 'Only begotten Son'. The Ab Soul is the conscious experience of the Divine marriage between the Father and Mother. Through the relating aspect of Ab, the *seeming* duality between Spirit-Matter with its myriad objective forms in play and display as Ba and Ka, are seen as ONE. This brings us to the next

> **Metaphysical Key To:**
> Understanding the 7 Ra(y) Qualities of Energy

What are the Ra(y)s?
A comprehensive study of the Seven Ra(y)s may be found in the writings of The Tibetan.
An abbreviated list of the qualities of The 7 Ra(y)s is given as follows accordingly: Michael Robbins. *Tapestry of the Gods, V.I & II.* (See Understanding Kemetic Energy/Appendix A for additional information on the 7 Ra(y)s)

The 7 Ra(y) Qualities of Energy
Ray 1 – Power and Will
Strengths: Strength of will, strong sense of purpose, power to lead, power to direct, power to govern, fearlessness, independence, power to liberate, courage.
Weaknesses: Arrogance, power-hungriness, domination, anger, violence, unrelenting ambition, control, suppression, impatience, willfulness, and destructiveness.

Ray 2 – Love/Wisdom
Strengths: Loving wisdom, power to understand and heal through love, empathy, sympathy, and compassion, inclusiveness, exquisite sensitivity, power to teach and illumine.
Weaknesses: Fearfulness, self-pity, oversensitivity and vulnerability, tendency towards an inferiority complex, over-inclusiveness, nonassertiveness.

Ray 3 – Active Intelligence
Strengths: Wide views on all abstract questions, rigorous analysis and reasoning, great mental fertility and creativity, ability to plan and strategize, ability to understand economy and handle money, executive and business aptitude.
Weaknesses: Intellectual pride, deviousness, perplexity and confusion, excessive thinking without practical action, manipulativeness, calculatedness, disorder and chaos, wasted motion, hyperactivity, restlessness, and tendency to "spread too thin."

Ray 4 – Harmony Through Conflict

Strengths: Facility for bringing harmony out of conflict, facility to compromise, mediate and bridge, love of beauty and capacity to create or express it, strong imagination and intuition, ability to amuse and entertain, fighting spirit, ability to make peace.

Weaknesses: Embroiled in constant conflict and turmoil, lack of confidence, worry, excessive moodiness, overly dramatic expression, confused combativeness, indecisiveness, moral cowardice, procrastination.

Ray 5 – Concrete Knowledge and Science

Strengths: Capacity to think and act scientifically, keen and focused intellect, detached objectivity, facility for mathematical calculation, powers of analysis, mechanical ability, practical inventiveness, technical expertise, research.

Weaknesses: Over-analysis, skepticism, irreverence, lack of intuitive sensitivity, excessive objectivity, rigid and set thought patterns, narrowness and prejudice, lack of emotional responsiveness.

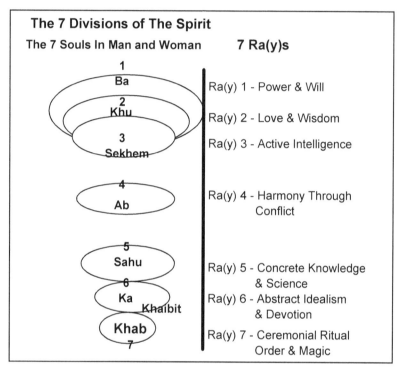

Ray 6 – Devotion and Abstract Idealism

Strengths: Intense devotion, unshakable faith and undimmed optimism, single-mindedness, utter loyalty, earnestness, profound humility, receptivity to spiritual guidance, unflagging persistence, power to inspire and persuade, purity, goodness.

Weaknesses: Rigid idealism, unreasoning devotion, blind faith, excess extremism, hyper-intensity, overdoing, ultra-narrow orientation, mania, selfish and jealous love, self-abasement, masochism, unnatural suppression of the instinctual nature.

Ray 7 – Order and Ceremonial Magic

Strengths: Power to create order, manifest and work upon the material plane, power to plan, organize and perfect form, keen sense of rhythm and timing, power as a magician (ability to bring form into manifestation), power to build.

Weaknesses: Rigid orderliness, excessive perfectionism, overconcern with rules, excessive conformity (or nonconformity), intolerance of anything new (or old), meaningless ritualism, superficial judgment based upon appearances.

KaAbBa Building The Lighted Temple
The Spiritual B(ARK)

A correspondence between the Seven Souls of Ra and the Seven Ra(y)s is shown in the diagram on the previous page:

The Ab Soul Ra(y) indicates your Higher purpose. It is this *sound* or *vibration* that guides you in knowing and fulfilling the work you have come to do in service to humanity and to the Planet. Attune to the inner wisdom within you for guidance in understanding your Ab Soul Ra(y) and purpose. This source or 'knowingness' is what the Kemetians call the oracle of Tehuti speaking through us (sphere 2) and what the Christians call the 'Still Small Voice'. Tap into this guidance now through your meditation, prayer, reflection, and quietude. See with which Soul Ra(y) qualities (strengths and weakness) you find resonance. (See Understanding Kemetic Energy/Appendix A, for determining your 14-Fold Kemetic Energy Formula and your Ab Soul Ra(y) Purpose). This brings us to the next

---
Metaphysical Key to: Understanding the 7 Principles of Kwanzaa
---

We are likewise honoring these 7 primordial qualities of energy when we celebrate the 7 Principles of Kwanzaa as reclaimed by another Chief among us Dr. Malauan Karenga. The 7 Principles of Kwanzaa, the Nguzo Saba, find correspondence with the 7 Ra(y)s. These are as follows:

Nguzo Saba   The Seven Principles of Kwanzaa

Umoja - **Unity** - To strive for and maintain unity in the family, community, nation and race.

Kujichagulia – **Self-Determination** – To define ourselves, name ourselves, and speak for ourselves, instead of being defined and spoken for by others.

Ujimaa – **Collective Work and Responsibility** - To build and maintain our community together and make our brother's and sister's problems our problems and to solve them together.

Ujamaa – **Collective Economics** – To build and maintain our own stores, shops, and other business and to profit together from them.

Nia – **Purpose** – To make as our collective vocation the building and developing of our community in order to restore our people to their traditional greatness.

Kuumbaa – **Creativity** – To always do as much as we can, in the way we can in order to leave our community more beautiful and beneficial than when we inherited it.

Imani – **Faith** - To believe with all our heart in our parents, our teachers, our leaders, our people and the righteousness and victory of our struggle. Last, but not least to believe in our God.

A correspondence between the Seven Rays and the Seven Principles of Kwanzaa is as follows:

The Seven Rays	The Seven Principles of Kwanzaa
Ra(y) 1 Power and Will	Umoja – Unity *(See also Kujichagulia)*
Ra(y) 2 Love & Wisdom	Kujichagulia –Self-Determination *(See also Umojo)*
Ra(y) 3 Active Intelligence	Ujamaa – Cooperative Economics
Ra(y) 4 Harmony Through Conflict	Kuumbaa – Creativity
Ra(y) 5 Concrete Knowledge & Science	Ujimaa – Collective Work & Responsibility
Ra(y) 6 Idealism & Devotion	Imani – Faith
Ra(y)7 Ceremonial Ritual, Order & Magic	Nia – Purpose

Note: Consider also that Principles Umoja and Kujichagulia may be interchanged in their correspondence with Ray(s) 1 and 2. This brings us to the next

---

Metaphysical Key To:
Understanding the 7 Energy Centers or Chakra

Our Spiritual equipment is composed of 7 Energy Centers or Chakras which are located along the spinal column which is called the Djed or Tet Pillar by the Kemetians. Each Chakra is a vortex of force. This fiery, vitalizing, life force called Ra, Kundalini or Chi is said to lie at the 7th Chakra at the Base of the spine. It is successively raised *through and qualified by* each Energy Center until we experience the full blending and glory of its crowning in our highest Head Centers. This is symbolized by the Uraeus Serpent of power rising upon the brow of the Initiated. We are like a flute with 7 notes. Three of our highest notes are located above the diaphragm, one is in the middle, and three are located below the diaphragm. We may focus on playing one note versus another. We may likewise play the full range of all our notes harmoniously blended. If we are focused upon playing the 3 notes or Chakras below the diaphragm then we live lives focused on survival and mere existence, disconnected from our greatest Spiritual potential, purpose and awakening. In the diagrams that follow we see:

1. A listing of the Kemetic Energy Centers or Chakras, Body Correspondences and East Indian Names are given. The Energy Centers are numbered 1-7 or 7-1 depending upon which direction from top to bottom or bottom to top you are counting from.

2. This is followed by a picture of the cow Goddess Het-Heru or Hathor who is symbolizing the journey of ascent through the 7 Arits with each Arit having its corresponding Chakra or Vortex of Energy.

3. This is followed by a description of each Chakra and a Meditation:

KaAbBa Building The Lighted Temple
The Spiritual B(ARK)

4. Kemetic Energy Centers	Body Correspondence	East Indian Chakras
Above the Diaphragm		
(1,7) Ikh	Crown, Head Chakra	Sahasrara
(2,6) Mer	1st Eye, Head Center	Ajna
(3,5) Sekhem	Throat Center	Vishudhi
Middle Chakra		
(4,4) Kheper	Heart Center	Anahata
Below the Diaphragm		
(5,3) Ab/Ob	Solar Plexus Center	Manipura
(6,2) Tekh	Sacral (sexual) Center	Swadhishtan
(7,1) Sefekht	Base (of spine) Root Center	Muladhara

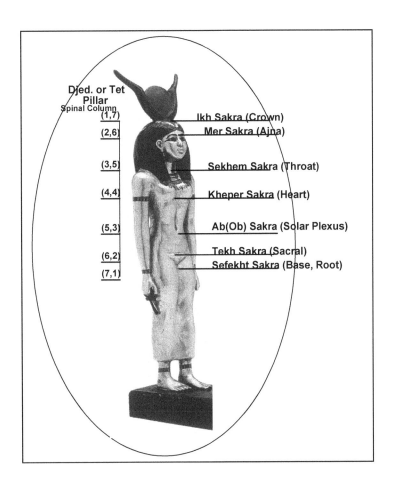

Through Het-Heru within our Spiritual faculty we ascend or descend from one plane of consciousness to the next. Like an elevator ride, she is how we push the button to arrive upon floors 1-7. Which floor we light upon and hang out the most, depends on what our heart most desires.

The Seven Energy Centers (Chakras) and Meditation
Sefekht Chakra
This is the Base or Root Energy Center located at the base of the spine. It corresponds with the Muladhara Chakra. Here is the power of manifesting your physical form and vitalizing that form with the life giving energy of Ra or Kundalini.
Meditation
I do the work of maintaining my physical form in a perfect state of health, vitality and well being. I draw the vitalizing energy of Ra for safety, protection, survival, sustenance, stamina, strength and functioning.

Tekh Chakra
This is the Sacral or Sexual Energy Center. It corresponds with the Swadhistan Chakra. It is the co-creative power of reproduction.
Meditation
I utilize some measure of my co-creative power through sexual expression and reproduction. I transmute some measure of my sexual energy through my higher centers so that I may vibrate as the WORD of power, work as a co-creative agency, playing my part in the great Divine plan to create Heaven on Earth.

Ab (Ob) Chakra
This is the Solar Plexus Energy Center. It corresponds with the Manipura Chakra. It is the center through which we are becoming a fully SELF conscious being.
Meditation
I express intelligent activity and use of the will in relating to self and others. As my conscience grows I recognize the same SELF in every other SELF.

Kheper Chakra
This is the Heart Energy Center. It corresponds with the Anahata Chakra. The heart is the seat of the Soul. Through forgiveness and compassionate understanding it is the Center in which your own pain and suffering may be transmuted into a healing balm that may heal and soothe others.
Meditation
I open my heart in an outpouring of love to humanity and all the kingdoms – mineral, vegetable and animal. I am One with my Brothers and Sisters. All Souls are but the One Soul.

Sekhem Chakra
This is the Throat Energy Center. It corresponds with the Vishudhi Chakra. The throat is like the womb. Through it we are co-creative agents in the great Divine plan.
Meditation
Through the throat center I give utterance to words of power (Hekau) that set in motion the vibratory field in which my highest and positive achievement may become realized. May every thought, sensitivity, and word issue forth from me on streams of golden living light and love

Divinely guided, so that power is wisely used and my deeds are pure of heart and in alignment with the Divine plan.

Mer Chakra

This Energy Center is the 1st eye. It corresponds with the Ajna Chakra. Through it we may glimpse the Divine ideation in the Mind of God. It is Divine Wisdom and Divine Love that sees all cohering in Unity.

Meditation

Through the 1st eye I behold the to-be manifested Divinely intended design in Seamless Unity of the One. In love and wisdom I work to uphold the underlying unity of the One/and the/Same Self that is reflected in all the diversity of Divine creation.

Ik/Ikh Chakra

This is the Crown Energy Center. It corresponds to the Sahasrara Chakra. This is where the Will of God is Known.

Meditation

In the Center of the Will of God I stand, immovable. Polarized here, I move out into the World of form in accord with Divine Will and Plan. This brings us to the next:

Metaphysical Key To:
The Overlay of The 7 Ra(y)s, The 7 Principles of
Kwanzaa, and The 7 Chakras within the Tree of

Up to now in our studies a process of *overlaying or appending* has been used in order to reveal:
1. The Metaphysical Keys within the Tree of Life
2. The correspondences and dynamics between the various Keys
3. We recall that this process of 'overlaying' is used to sequentially reveal the various correspondences that are *organic* within the Tree of Life.

With this foundation:
1. We see the overlay of the 7 Ra(y), The 7 Principles of Kwanzaa, and The 7 Chakras revealed in the Tree of Life
2. We now shift to a more comprehensive and larger map of the Tree of Life (*The Big Map*) to use as reference on the following page:

KaAbBa Building The Lighted Temple
The Spiritual B(ARK)

The Big Map

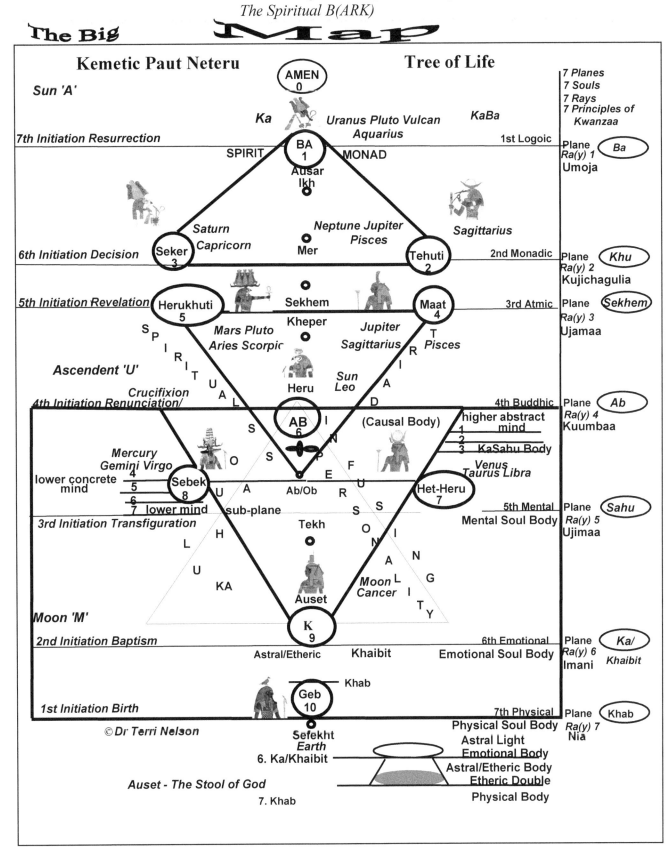

Kemetic Paut Neteru   Tree of Life

7 Planes
7 Souls
7 Rays
7 Principles of Kwanzaa

Sun 'A'

AMEN 0

Ka   Uranus Pluto Vulcan   KaBa
Aquarius

7th Initiation Resurrection   1st Logoic   Plane Ra(y) 1   *Ba*

SPIRIT   BA 1   MONAD   Umoja

Ausar Ikh

Saturn   Neptune Jupiter Pisces   Sagittarius
Capricorn

Mer

6th Initiation Decision   Seker 3   Tehuti 2   2nd Monadic   Plane Ra(y) 2   *Khu*
Kujichagulia

5th Initiation Revelation   Herukhuti 5   Sekhem   Maat 4   3rd Atmic   Plane Ra(y) 3   *Sekhem*
Kheper   Ujamaa

Mars Pluto   Jupiter Sagittarius Pisces
Aries Scorpio

Ascendent 'U'   Sun Leo

Heru

Crucifixion
4th Initiation Renunciation/   4th Buddhic   Plane Ra(y) 4   *Ab*

AB 6   (Causal Body)   higher abstract mind
1
2
3   KaSahu Body   Kuumbaa

Ab/Ob

Mercury   Venus Taurus Libra
Gemini Virgo
4
lower concrete 5
mind 6
7 lower mind   sub-plane

Sebek 8   Het-Heru 7   5th Mental   Plane Ra(y) 5   *Sahu*
Mental Soul Body   Ujimaa

3rd Initiation Transfiguration   Tekh

SPIRITUAL

FUSION PERSONALITY

Moon Cancer

Auset

Moon 'M'

K 9   6th Emotional   Plane Ra(y) 6   *Ka/*
2nd Initiation Baptism   Emotional Soul Body   Imani   *Khaibit*
Astral/Etheric   Khaibit

Khab

Geb 10

1st Initiation Birth   7th Physical   Plane Ra(y) 7   *Khab*
Physical Soul Body   Nia

© Dr Terri Nelson   Sefekht
Earth
6. Ka/Khaibit   Astral Light
Emotional Body
Astral/Etheric Body
Etheric Double

Auset - The Stool of God

7. Khab   Physical Body

Chapter 11
Building The Lighted Temple The Spiritual B-Ark
Ka Ab Ba

No matter what your Spiritual/Religious practice *we* are all challenged to do the work of *Building The Lighted Temple.* When you attune to your Soul purpose and let it guide you it radiates your whole Temple. Your Divinity is tangibly expressed on Earth through your Light and Service in the World.

We are all familiar with the arrangement and structure of a House. We can move within the simple patterning of a House in order to understand what it means to Build The Lighted Temple. This is expressed in the diagram below:

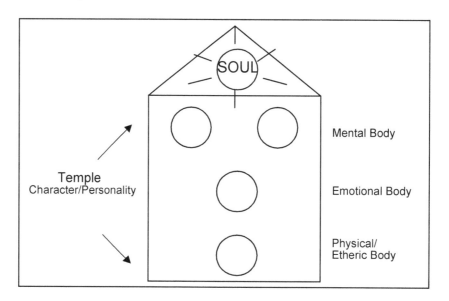

Because a house has different floors or levels, you would have a different awareness on each floor. For example you would have a different awareness in standing in the attic than if you stood in the basement. Like a house, your Spiritual constitution or equipment has different floors within which you have certain awarenesses.

1. We can use the simple patterning within a house to navigate and work within the deeper patterning of our Spiritual make-up and equipment by:
a. Cultivating a more Divine quality on each 'floor' or plane of consciousness upon which we hold awareness – *as well as*
b. Elevating our consciousness to the highest floor or plane.

This is indicated in the following exercise of Building the Lighted Temple or Spiritual (B) Ark:

KaAbBa Building The Lighted Temple
The Spiritual B(ARK)

The table below gives qualities or Neteru to cultivate in your awakening Spiritual equipment as part of your daily ASTR practice:

Physical	Emotional	Mental	Character/Personality	Soul
Relaxation	Calm	Clarity	Efficiency	Will Divinely aligned
Health	Peace	Mindfulness	Effectiveness	Love
Vitality	Receptivity	Intelligence	Courtesy Diplomacy	Intelligence/ Revelation/Right Knowledge
Flexibility	Clearness	Non-pre-occupation	Strength	Compassion/Right Relationship/Just-ice
Strength	Purity	Receptivity	Assertiveness Courage	Illumination/ Intuition
Grace	Reflective-ness (waters)	Fluidity	Stability Steadfastness	Wisdom
Beauty	Steadiness	Perspective	Disciplined	Joyfulness
Durability	Responsive-ness	Sight	Rhythmic Action Adaptable	Inclusiveness
Steadiness	Aspiration	Keenness	Coordinated/ Skillful	Peacefulness
Longevity	Sensitivity/ Empathy	Intuition	Integrity	Purpose/Right Action/Service

Metaphysical Key:
Affirming Lighted Temple Building – ASTR Daily Practice
As a stance in greater service to humanity -
That the Fire of my Highest Aspiration may burn brightly, Lighting the Temple and Fulfilling the Life Purpose that I have incarnated to do, I will work to improve the fitness of my Temple by cultivating *more* _____

An example of this may read as follows:
As a stance in greater service to humanity –
That the Fire of my Highest Aspiration may burn brightly, Lighting the Temple and Fulfilling the Life Purpose that I have incarnated to do, I will work to improve the fitness of my Temple by cultivating *more Health, Peace, Intuition, Discipline, and Wisdom*

Next –

2. We can use the simple patterning within a house to navigate and work within the deeper patterning of our Spiritual make-up and equipment by:

a. Moving within the more complex patterning of our Spiritual make-up which is symbolized by the Tree of Life.

b. Observing that the Tree of Life may be re-arranged to reveal that it is likewise a house as seen in the following diagrams.

c. Recognizing that we need these deeper Metaphysical Studies to accelerate our emergence from and through the *Spiritual Implications of The Perfect Storm.*

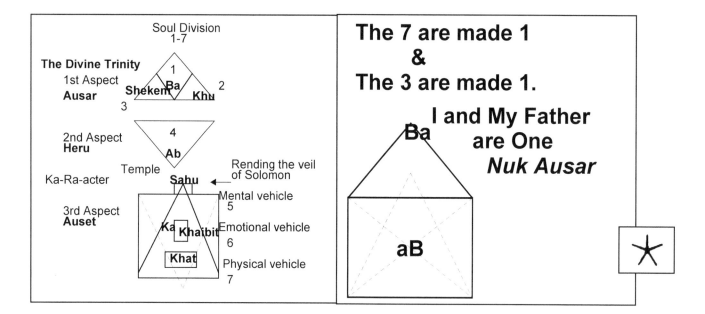

In the diagram at left we see 3 basic triangles that are trying to come together. This coming together is pictured in the diagram at right. These are KaAbBa, or BaAbKa depending on which direction (top-down or bottom-up) you are looking from. It is in the bringing together of Ba and Ka that Ab becomes the spark within you. It is at first a faint glimmer of light. Like any spark, flicker or flame it must be kept guarded until it grows into a brilliantly, raging glow of fiery luminous Light. It is how you Build a Lighted Temple. As the Ka triangle is infused with the Ab and Ba Soul, the 6 pointed Star is seen. As this infusing process in consciousness continues, the 6 pointed Star becomes the 5 pointed Star as seen the diagram above at right. This is called the *Amsu Heru* by the Kemetians. In a later chapter you will see how the Sahu vehicle or Soul body of your Spiritual equipment is involved in this work.

Let's dispell the word Amsu:

 # 1. Oracle Metaphysical Dis-spelling Key: Put letters of word or words together in a circle, like a serpent putting its tail in its mouth. Coming full Circle.

KaAbBa   Building The Lighted Temple
The Spiritual B(ARK)

```
┌─────────────┐
│      A      │
│  u       m  │
│      s      │
└─────────────┘
```

#2. Oracle Metaphysical Dis-spelling Key: Read letters, putting together words, going forwards, backwards and in zig-zag patterns.

#3. Oracle Metaphysical Dis-spelling Key: You may crossover in order to use a letter more than once. Place re-used letter in parenthesis ( ).

#4. Oracle Metaphysical Dis-spelling Key: You may add a letter to complete a word. Place added letter in parenthesis ( ).

#5. Oracle Metaphysical Dis-spelling Key: Letter substitution-you may substitute a letter. Place substituted letter in parenthesis ( ).

#6. Oracle Metaphysical Dis-spelling Key: Make a list of derived words. Try to make the longest continuous unbroken word or string of words.

#7. Oracle Metaphysical Dis-spelling Key: Look up definition (dictionary, glossary, reference texts, etc.)

Derived Word List:

AUM – Is the Most sacred word (See also, Aung, and OM) which is sounded by various religious traditions to most approximate the Great Divine Breath 'Au' and the vibration that hurls and keeps the Universe and all created beings within, in manifestation. Ausar is sounding the perfecting sound of AUM, drawing all within its 'ring-pass-not' to be At-Oned within the Universal Ba – the return of Spirit to Spirit.

Aum S

A Sum –

SUMA –

> **Definition:** Thesaurus:
> Sum – Amount, quantity, aggregate, tally, whole, entirety, worth

#8. Oracle Metaphysical Dis-spelling Key: Meaning. See the relationship and oracle or story of the Neteru – Put word list together to tell a story.

Meaning: To become a 5 pointed STAR – Amsu Heru, is to measure up, or become the fullest measure of what you have always been from the beginningless beginning. The Seker – sphere 3 aspect of our Spiritual equipment teaches us to 'measure up' and (a) achieve the fullest measure of the Divinely intended design and (b) sound the fullest measure of THE WORD we are and have always been from the beginningless beginning.

This brings us to the next

┌──────────────────────────────────────┐
│ **Metaphysical Key To:**   │
│ Character dispelled is   │
│ *Ka-Ra-acter and Ka-erect-er*   │
└──────────────────────────────────────┘

The Ancients called our great Solar Neter Ra. We are all Ra or Suns who are building character in the World. Character dispelled reveals the words, *Ka-Ra-Acter and Ka-Erect-er.* This is further described in this chapter. The distinction between the word Character and Personality is also further described. As we build character we see that we are all Ka-*Ra*-acters in the World. As Ka-Ra-acters we are all undergoing ASTR – Ausarian Spiritual Transformation and Resurrection to become a STAR. We are playing our part in choosing whether to build in accord or out of accord with the great Divine plan. We are under the guidance of The Great Architect of the Universe – GAOTU. All the while we are Ka-erect-ing our temples. These will either prove to be Lighted Temples in which God indwells, or that which is grotesque, hideous and full of **darkness.** As Heru – sphere 6, we are all co-creative in the building process. Therefore, the Lighted Temple extends to include our body, our environment and our Planet.

The synonymous nature between the words Ka and Character/Personality is expressed in the following accordingly: E. A. Budge, *The Prt Em Hru (Egyptian Book Of The Dead),* p.lxi.

> And in addition to the natural and spiritual bodies, man also had an abstract individuality or **personality** endowed with all his **characteristic** attributes. This abstract personality had an absolutely independent existence. It could move freely from place to place, separating itself from, or uniting itself to, the body at will, and also enjoying life with the gods in heaven. This was the Ka, a word which at times conveys the meanings of its Coptic equivalent and of image, genius, double, **character**, disposition, and mental attributes. The funeral offerings of meat, cakes, ale, wine, unguents, etc., were intended for the Ka; the scent of the burnt incense was grateful to it. The Ka dwelt in the man's statue just as the Ka of a god inhabited the statue of the god.

KaAbBa Building The Lighted Temple
The Spiritual B(ARK)

How Are You Building The Lighted Temple?

In order to address this question we must look within the 3rd aspect triangle which is now pictured within a square and indicated by the arrow. This square is traditionally referred to as your personality or character. Both geometric figures – the square and the triangle – are major keys in your Ausarian Spiritual Transformation and Resurrection – ASTR (STAR). You will recall from a previous quote:

> In Ritual, chap. Lxxii., Heru says: 'I have come forth with the tongue of Ptah and the throat of Hathor that I may record the words of my Father Tum with my mouth. 'I am Heru, prince of eternity' (chap. Xlii.). 'I am yesterday, to-day and to-morrow' (chap. Lxiv.) Tum, as the earlier form of Atum's name in the Ritual, is pre-eminently 'the Lord.' 'The Lord of Life,' 'The Lord of all Creature,' 'The Lord of all.' He was also the patron of builders and architects, and his symbol is the **Masonic square.**

The square itself represents the lower quarries in which you are fashioning an instrument for the use of the Higher Self or Ab and Ba Soul bodies so that you can be of greater service in the World. As an Ancient mystery and Masonic symbol, the square symbolizes the House, Temple or B-Ark that you are in the process of constructing so that the Spirit may consciously indwell. Each one of us has the onerous task of building a fit structure or Temple which will be able to bear the great impress and vibration of Spirit *without shattering.* This becomes a great challenge under the impress of the increasing Spiritual Tides now rising on our Planet Earth. Ready or not these Spiritual Tides are keying your instrument up to reflect greater Light and Ausarianization in Consciousness. They lead us all to address the Spiritual Implications of the Perfect Storm.

How do you raise your vibration and ascend the elevator through to higher planes of full Self Conscious living?

Man and woman are said to be 'building character'. The initial steps in building character are to cultivate:

Right Understanding	Right Thought
Right Speech	Right Action
Right Livelihood	Right Effort
Right Mindfulness	Right Meditation

But where in your Spiritual equipment or vehicles is this cultivation taking place?

This brings us to the next

> **Metaphysical Key To:**
> The 3 Soul bodies or Vehicles of Manifestation

The Character or Personality/Temple is composed of three vehicles or bodies. These are the vehicles or Soul bodies of manifestation. The work of ASTR is to transmute the sub-stance of your vehicles from a more dense, coarse material nature which has a lower vibration into a more refined solar substance of a higher vibration. These three vehicles or Soul bodies are briefly described here. A fuller description is given in *The Ausarianization of Consciousness Tablet Series – The Metaphysical Keys to The Tree Of Life with Oracle Keys to Dis-spelling Illusion,* (See *Esoteric Psychology, V.I & II; Metu Neter, V.I).* The more traditional names and the Kemetic names in the Tree of Life are as follows:

<u>The Soul bodies or Vehicles of Manifestation</u>
Mental vehicle or body which corresponds with the:
a. Sahu Soul body or 5th Soul/Spirit division
b. 5th Plane of Consciousness
c. 5th Ra(y) or Soul of Ra
d. Sphere 7 – Het-Heru. This is Higher Mind and is the faculty of abstract thinking, imagination and higher reasoning.
e. Sphere 8 - Sebek. This is Lower Mind and is the faculty of concrete mind and how you
    think, plan and reason.

Emotional/Astral vehicle or body which corresponds with the:
a. Ka/Khaibit Soul body or 6th Soul/Spirit division
b. 6th Plane of Consciousness
c. 6th Ra(y) or Soul of Ra
d. Sphere 9 – Auset. This is our feelings, desires, sentiency, and emotions. The emotional
    body is the watery, receptive and subconscious nature. The vitalizing body is called
    Khaibit by the Kemetians and the Etheric/Astral body by the Esotericists.

Physical vehicle or body which corresponds with the:
a. Khab Soul body or 7th Soul/Spirit division
b. 7th Plane of Consciousness
c. 7th Ra(y) or Soul of Ra
d. Geb – sphere 10. This is Khab in the Kemetic system. This is your physical form and
    faculty for activity and vitality

KaAbBa Building The Lighted Temple
The Spiritual B(ARK)

For now we see that: these three vehicles comprise the lower floors or the 5th, 6th and 7th planes of consciousness, their respective Chakra and the 5th, 6th and 7th Soul divisions respectively in your house or Temple building.

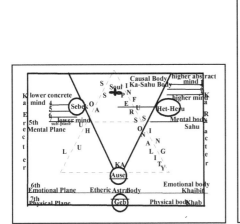

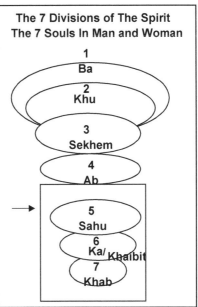

We are Spirit. In order to make an 'appearance' in the physical realm we need an instrument or equipment. Our physical, emotional and mental bodies are constructed for use from 7th, 6th, and 5th plane sub-stance. We can literally be focused from the waist down in these lower planes of consciousness, unrefreshed by the Spiritual livingness of the 4th, 3rd, 2nd and 1st planes of consciousness above. Like an extremity cut off from its blood supply, the cutting off of our lower equipment from our higher equipment can cause the setting in of atrophy, decay, and death. As Knower, you are called to Build the Lighted Temple. The Divine Image and Likeness is always present in you.

We must move with the awareness that we are Spirit even if that Spirit does not as yet don the (finest) form or vestiture. We do the work to purify the material form substance or vestitures enough to see, capture and reflect this image. You often hear talk of folks wanting the 'finest robes' or outfits. We feel that if we dress in the best finery it will reveal something of the quality of who we are. In reality, your best 'threads' are spun with a super atomic sub-stance *so fine* that scientists are still trying to figure out how to 'see' and identify it. The *next* finest robe in our evolutionary development is to:
1. Indwell our Sahu Soul Body, which is the body of Light that your Spirit is constructing while
2. Contacting more the Ab and Ba Soul within our instrument of manifestation

The Sahu Soul Body is also called the Glorified or Spiritual body. It is through the Sahu Soul body that you are re-born into the Spiritual body and able to escape death of the material body – the Khab. More will be said about the Sahu body as we go along in our study.

Through the process of Soul infusing later described:
1. The Ka Triangle/Square becomes a vehicle for the Ab Triangle
2. The Ab Triangle becomes a vehicle for the Ba Triangle
3. This is a re-amalgamation or putting back together the 3 Aspects of Divinity within us

Reascension Into Sacredness
In this very moment in which you now stand you are witnessing the shade starting to rise. You may behold the early glimmers of light. Spirit is rising, like the Sun just peaking on the horizon. The Spiritual waters of the Earth are rising and Earth is re-ascending into sacredness.

Yet The Elders know and await

Today the Elders stand perched upon the high planes heralding the dawn. They chant with triumphant resounding, *'The Spiritual tides are rising, The Spiritual tides are rising, The waters of Spirit are rising'.* They beckon us to awaken to the new cycle we are now entering. Can you feel the power of our Elders?

They tell us that eons ago they watched the Sun go down on the horizon. They knew of the darkness in the cycles that would come. That we would enter into the underworld called Amenta by the Kemetians. Now they herald that the Sun is coming over the horizon. That we are being resurrected out of the confines of material consciousness into a Spiritual re-awakening and that - *The rising Sun's in sight!* Know that you are the Rising Sun-Son/Daughter. You are a STAR. They teach us to chant the following:

Reascension Into Sacredness
     from the Elders
Communicated via Dr. Terri Nelson

Reascension into sacredness
All are gathering in
Reascension into sacredness
From the four winds

Our Elders are elated
By the dawning of this hour
They stand in witness to this day
Feel their great power   (*repeat 1ˢᵗ* *verse*)

We emerge from the darkness
Eons long was night
We come now to serve and save
The rising Sun's in sight. (*repeat 1ˢᵗ* *verse*)

The Ausarianization of Consciousness Series 1
Metaphysical Keys To the Tree of Life & Oracle Keys to Dis-spelling Illusion
The Spiritual Journey in Unfolding Consciousness

122

You are the rising Sun that is in sight. But what gets in the way of our recognition?
This brings us back again to a previous

Metaphysical Key To:
Know Thyself
Overcoming Impediment # 1
Not Knowing Our Way Home and
Not Taking Responsibility For
Knowing, Seeking, Finding and
Being *All Spooked Up*

As African American and Diaspora, we have a keen awareness of the horrors that have occurred in the darkness, particularly over the last 500 years of our enslavement. We are afraid of the darkness and we have become all *Spooked Up.* We must move within the DARKNESS to develop our own Ka-Ra-Acter in order to Build The Lighted Temple. We must take an inner look at the man or woman in the mirror to create a *Nu-being.*

What Is Personality and Character?
Is There a difference between Personality and Character?

Let's dispell the word Personality:
#7. Oracle Metaphysical Dis-spelling Key: Look up definition (dictionary, glossary, reference texts, etc.)

<u>Personality</u> – The quality or condition of being a person. 2. The totality of qualities and traits, as of character or behavior that are peculiar to a specific person. 3. The pattern of collective character, behavioral, temperamental, emotional, and mental traits of a person.

Let's dispell the word Character:
<u>Definition:</u>

<u>Character</u> – The combination of qualities or features that distinguishes one person, group, or thing from another. 2. A distinguishing feature or attribute, as of an individual, a group, or a category. See synonyms at quality, type. 3. *Genetics.* A structure, function, or attribute, as of an individual, a group or a category. 4. Moral or ethical strength. 5. A description of a person's attributes traits, or abilities. …11. A mark or symbol used in a writing system. 12. *Computer Science.* One of a set of symbols, such as letters or numbers, that are arranged to express information. 13. A style of printing or writing. 14. A symbol used in secret writing; a cipher or code. *Archaic.* 1. To write, print, engrave or inscribe. 2. Consistent with someone's character or behavior: [Middle English character, distinctive mark, imprint on the soul, from Greek *kharakter.*

We see that the word character is missing the Neter 'K' although it still maintains the sound when pronounced. Also note the Greeks (who so generously 'borrowed' from 'K'emet) retained the K in their spelling of character as *kharakter.*

#10. Oracle Metaphysical Dis-spelling Key: Letter replacement. Here we have replaced the 'k' which had been substituted by the letter 'c.'
 # 1. Oracle Metaphysical Dis-spelling Key:
Put letters of word or words together in a circle, like a serpent putting its tail in its mouth. Coming full Circle.

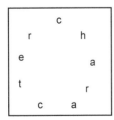 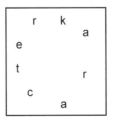

#2. Oracle Metaphysical Dis-spelling Key: Read letters, putting together words, going forwards, backwards and in zig-zag patterns.
#3. Oracle Metaphysical Dis-spelling Key: You may crossover in order to use a letter more than once. Place re-used letter in parenthesis ( ).

#4. Oracle Metaphysical Dis-spelling Key: You may add a letter to complete a word. Place added letter in parenthesis ( ).

#5. Oracle Metaphysical Dis-spelling Key: Letter substitution-you may substitute a letter. Place substituted letter in parenthesis ( ).

#6. Oracle Metaphysical Dis-spelling Key: Make a list of derived words. Try to make the longest continuous unbroken word or string of words.

Derived Word List:

A re-arrangement of the letters renders two key words or derivations which are:

Ka-Ra-acter

Ka-erect-er

#8. Oracle Metaphysical Dis-spelling Key: Meaning. See the relationship and oracle or story of the Neteru – Put word list together to tell a story.

Meaning:

So we see here that the most prominent discernment of this oracle is:

Ka – is the <u>erector</u> of <u>Ra.</u> Ra is the Sun God to the Kemetians. Ra is the Sun- Son/Daughter in matter or form.

Ka is <u>Ra-acter</u>. As the developing Self conscious entity, Ka-Ra-acter is what is erect-ing the Sun/Son within you. As the Ra-acter or Ra-actor, you are trying to *act* like Sun-Son/Daughter who at first can only approximate the Sun. It is through your efforts as Heru – sphere 6, that you are striving to be fully Self Conscious. As Heru, the Son/Sun is fully *erected* to then fully reflect the Father- Ausar sphere 1, who is now *re-surrected.*

Derived Word List Continued:

<u>Ka-teacher</u> – When someone is of great moral character they are a teacher or demonstrator of God on Earth by their example. This was the case when the Ancient God Kings walked among us on Earth. They embodied truer reflections of the Image and Likeness of God.

<u>Ka-reache(r)</u> – Through successive approximations to the ONE, your Approximating Ka finally reflects Spirit Ka, which is the fullness of the Image and Likeness of God.

<u>Carat or Karat</u> – We become a unit measure of a precious stone (diamond). We are a diamond in the rough until we do the work to unveil the Jewel within us.

<u>Rate</u>

<u>Rat</u>

<u>Ka-ta-ract or Cataract</u> –

> **Definition**: Thesaurus, dictionary
> 1000 Torrents, currents, rapids, floods, deluge
> 1000 Pathology. Opacity of the lens or capsule of the eye, causing impairment of
>   vision or blindness. [Middle English cataracte, from Greek katarraktes.

<u>Ark</u> - a vehicle, temple of God.

<u>Charter or Kharter</u>-

> **Definition**:

A document outlining the principles, functions, and organization of a cooperate body; a constitution. 3. To hire (a bus or an airplane for example) for the exclusive, temporary use of a group of travelers. [From Latin chartula, diminutive of charta, paper made from papyrus. See card.

Card –

> **Definition:** 1. A flat, usually rectangular piece of stiff paper, cardboard, or plastic, especially: a. One of a set or pack bearing significant numbers, symbols, or figures, used in games and in divination. D. One bearing a person's name and other information used for purposes of identification or classification. To check the identification of.

Meaning:

So we see here that the words Ark, Charter, Card and Character reveal how you are identified as a *traveler* in this World. Today there is much distortion and preoccupation with the acquisition of credit 'cards' and 'cars'. Both of these words dispelled reveal the word Ka. You are impressed with certain information or codes that: a. 'rate' you as to who you are or b. 'rat' you (as in 'rat you out'), as to who you are. You are enabled or prohibited from attaining a 'silver or gold' credit card based on your 'good credit, merit and trustworthiness'. Likewise, we may have come to believe that we can tell something about a person by the car they drive – as if this could be some kind of external, measure of character. You are building your Lighted Temple – your Ark and the covenant. Biblically this is, "God's promise to the human race". It is the promise that you will be in the end, what you have always been, from the beginningless beginning, The Image and Likeness of God, The One True Self – Ausar.

Derived Word List Continued:

Heart – Great Ka-ra-acter is revealed through the purifying of the heart. To purify the heart is to purify your physical, emotional and mental vehicles or Soul bodies.

Earth – Notice here that heart and earth are spelled using exactly the same Neteru. Just as there are cells that make up your body, humanity itself are the cells that make up the body of the Earth. If your heart is polluted with regret, anger, selfishness, etc., (all violations of the law of Maat-sphere 4) you are contributing to the pollution of:

Khab/Geb – In the Kemetian tradition Khab, Geb – sphere 10, is your individual body. On a larger scale Geb is the Earth which is our Planetary body or Khab. As your individual heart is made pure you are contributing to the purification of the Earth.

Hear – to hear is to register your changing vibration.

Heat – is involved in the purification process. As the fire of Ra, also called Kundalini, is raised up the spinal column you are raising your Spiritual vibration.

Tare –

> **Definition**:
> 1. Any of various weedy plants of the genus vicia, especially the common vetch. 3. Tares. An unwelcome or objectionable element. To determine or indicate the tare of, especially to weigh in order to find out the tare. [Middle English, from old French, ultimately from Arabic *tarhah,* that which is thrown away, from *taraha,* to reflect.]

The Ausarianization of Consciousness Series 1
Metaphysical Keys To the Tree of Life & Oracle Keys to Dis-spelling Illusion
The Spiritual Journey in Unfolding Consciousness

126

Meaning: We are separating the wheat from the tares in our own constitution or equipment. As we develop Ka-erect-ter and Ka-Ra-acter, we come forth to hear the words spoken by God Ausar to Christ-Heru, '*This is my son in whom I am proud*'. Note: The Old English practice of 'tar – ing and feather-ing' an 'offender' would suggest itself to be an inverted practice of trying to get people to re-member their duty before the scales of Maat.

Throughout this text the words Ka-Ra-acter and Ka-erect-ter will be used interchangeably, recognizing in each instance that there is an *actor* and *erector* involved.

Let's look at the distinction between Ka-ra-acter and Per-son-ality.
Ka-erect-er development is at work within your Spiritual equipment. As such, your Ka-Ra-acter is expressing itself through who you are and who you are becoming. Through your Ka-Ra-acter, others are able to see how Ra is in action upon the stage of life as the *emerging* Sun (Son/Daughter) of God in you.

On the one hand, the terms personality and Ka-Ra-acter are synonymous. For example:
You may observe a 5 year old and say, 'She is quite a Ka-Ra-acter'. This implies that some distinct kind of 1) quality and 2) organizational structure is pervading as you experience this child in action. You may also say, 'She has quite a little personality'. This likewise implies recognizable quality and organizational structure. Both statements are expressing the idea that this little girl is able to coordinate and move her physical body, her emotional body, and her mental body in such a distinct way that some quality is being conveyed to the observer about who she is becoming – such as being intelligent, delightful, creative and entertaining.

On the other hand there exists some subtle difference between the terms. Ka-erect-er is built or 'erected. *It is the blended essence or bouquet of fragrant qualities* that arise once the personality structure is blended, coordinated and balanced. After even a partial dispelling of the word Ka-Ra-acter, the vital importance of its development can not be overemphasized in the Spiritual Journey of unfolding consciousness and Ausarian Resurrection. You can not get where you think you are going without great moral Ka-erect-er. This is why the Manes or also spelled as Manas in his/her prayers to the Gods beseeches them '*not to make his/her Name to Stink*'. (Refer to page 172 of this text for *Ritual* verse from, *The Prt Em Hru (The Egyptian Book Of The Dead)*. The Lotus petals unfold as Ka-Ra-acter is developed. The story of Ausar and Auset reveals insight into the meaning of:
1. Scent or odour of Ka-Ra-acter
2. Re-gaining immortality by passing through the purificatory fires in order to transmute the more coarse, material substance of your vehicles into a more refined, Solar substance.

Auset travels to Byblos in search of her deceased husband Ausar. This is expressed accordingly:
E. A. Budge, *The Prt Em Hru (Egyptian Book Of The Dead)*, p.l.

> Soon after she learned that the chest [read here: sarcophagus] had been carried by the sea to Byblos, where it had been gently laid by the waves among the branches of a **Tamarisk** tree, which in a very short time had grown to a magnificent size and had enclosed the chest within

KaAbBa   Building The Lighted Temple
The Spiritual B(ARK)

its trunk. The king of the country, admiring the tree, cut it down and made a pillar for the roof of his house of that part which contained the body of Ausar.

In a different account the story is continued accordingly: E. A. Budge, *Osiris. The Egyptian Religion and Resurrection,* p. 5.

Meanwhile the waves had carried the box to the coast of Syria and cast it up at Byblos, and soon as it rested on the ground a large **Erica** tree sprang up, and growing all round the box enclosed it on every side. The king of Byblos marveled at the size of this **tree,** and had it cut down, and caused a **pillar** for his palace to be made of that portion of the trunk which contained the box.

When this news reached Auset she set out at once for Byblos, and when she arrived there she sat down by the side of the fountain of the palace and spoke to no one except the queen's maidens, who soon came to her. These she treated with great courtesy, and talked graciously to them, and caressed them, and tired their head, and at the same time transferred to them wonderful **odour** of her own body. When the maidens returned to the palace the queen perceived the **odour** which emanated from their hair and bodies, and learning from them that it was due to their contact with Auset, she sent to her and invited her to come to the palace.

After a conversation with her she appointed her to be the nurse of one of her children. Auset gave the child her finger instead of her breast to suck, and at night she burned away in fire his mortal parts, whilst she herself, in the form of a swallow flew around and around the pillar which contained the body of Ausar, uttering mournful chirpings. After she had treated the child thus for some time, the queen one night saw her son burning in the fire, whereupon she uttered a piercing cry, and so prevented him from obtaining the gift of immortality which was about to be bestowed upon him.

In each account a different name for the tree or pillar is given. Let' look at both names:
Let's dispell the word tamarisk:

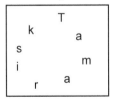

#10. Oracle Metaphysical Dis-spelling Key: Letter replacement. Here we have replaced the 'k' which had been substituted by the letter 'c.')
Derived Word List:
Kristmas, C(h)ristmas – as in Christmas Tree.

Let's dispell the word Erica:

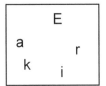

The Ausarianization of Consciousness Series 1
Metaphysical Keys To the Tree of Life & Oracle Keys to Dis-spelling Illusion
The Spiritual Journey in Unfolding Consciousness

128

Derived Word List:

Eri(c)(t)ka, Er(e)(c)(t)ka

E(u)r(e)ka – to express triumph upon finding or discovering something.

#8. Oracle Metaphysical Dis-spelling Key: Meaning. See the relationship and oracle or story of the Neteru – Put word list together to tell a story.

Meaning:

The word Tamarisk reveals the word Christmas. If we dispell the word Erica we see that it reveals Erect-Ka or Ka-erect. It is the Tree symbolizing how you 'erect-Ka'. It also reveals the word Eureka which is to express triumph upon finding or discovering something. The greatest find we can make is to discover the SELF. In both instances, the Evergreen Tree symbolized eternal life. It is the Ka-rest-mas Tree that is later called the Christmas Tree.

So we may see from our story that:

1. Immortality comes from successively raising the fires of Ra up the spinal column
2. This is our elevator ride up the djed/Tet Pillar through the 7 planes of consciousness
3. By moving through the fires we purify our mortal parts

Those who have moved further along the path may be detected by their fragrant odour or aroma, having burnt off the dross of dense matter. Ka-erect-er/Ka-Ra-acter and personality speak to the quality, structure, function, fragrance, luminescence and purity of the instrument through which the Soul may operate and do its work in the World.

KaAbBa   Building The Lighted Temple
The Spiritual B(ARK)

What Are Some Of The 3ʳᵈ Aspect Functions Of The Ka-erecter Or Ka-Ra-acter?

1. The Ka-erect-er or personality becomes the Temple or instrument that the Ab-Soul and later Ba-Soul uses to do its work in the World. The physical, emotional and mental Soul bodies are each qualified by a particular Ra(y) energy (See Seven Ra(y)s Key). These energies need to be raised to their optimal level, balanced and blended so that the vehicles are working together in a complimentary and harmonious manner. These fused, blended and balanced energies can become a single functioning coordinated unit. The Ka-Ra-acter or Ka-Ra-actor coordinates the energies of the physical, emotional and mental vehicles. The mere presence of these three vehicles does not in itself constitute what is known as a Ka-Ra-acter or Personality/Temple. (See *Esoteric Psychology*). The designation applies only after the energies of the three relevant vehicles have been blended and become subservient to the Ka-Ra-acter or Personality. When this occurs, the Ka-erect-er emerges as a distinctive state of consciousness.

2. All along the journey, you come to identify as a 'self' that is less than our ONE TRUE SELF IDENTITY. Yet, each stage of initiation causes you to relinquish your identity and attachment with that lesser 'self'. You transcend beyond the bound or boundary of that lesser 'self' into an identification with a still greater 'self' until you re-turn to your full identification with the ONE TRUE SELF – Ausar Ba. So you can see that it is important to have a *sense of self* – lower ego, in order to transcend into the greater sense of Self – Higher Ego. This is Ka-erect-er building.

How does this work?

3. The Ka-Ra-acter is how you *get your act together* and *keep it together*. What does it mean when we say someone has their act together? It means that you are able to coordinate your life. You are able to move your physical, emotional and mental vehicles in such a way that you able to do something meaningful in your immediate life sphere like going to work, managing a home and attending to a family. How each person does this allows them to make a statement about who they are and to express their unique I-dentity. On any given day when you awaken and are still lying in bed your thoughts may be going one way, your feelings another, and your body may be saying, 'frankly I do not want to get up and go at all'. Yet, it is your Ka-Ra-acter or Personality that coordinates these vehicles, brings them into alignment and *gets them out the door* to do something in your immediate life space. Thus, the Ka-Ra-acter becomes a dominant force.

4. Many lifetimes are spent gaining mastery over the physical, emotional and mental vehicles. Humanity may become polarized in any one of these vehicles such that developing overall integration and co-ordination is delayed. Remember that it is through these 3 vehicles that you have manifestation in the physical World. You may be over-emphasizing (or under-emphasizing) one vehicle or lower Soul body at the expense of overall development and coordination of all the vehicles in your ASTR practice. For example, men and women may become too emotionally polarized or focused. As such, they are easily overcome by their emotional tides to the point where doing something meaningful in their immediate life space feels like an impossible feat. As a Metaphysician, Holistic Psychotherapist, Healer and Teacher, I am aware that many people have major challenges getting out of the door or even

The Ausarianization of Consciousness Series 1
Metaphysical Keys To the Tree of Life & Oracle Keys to Dis-spelling Illusion
The Spiritual Journey in Unfolding Consciousness

130

out of bed. This is due to their being emotionally polarized with fear, depression, anxiety, trauma, etc. Likewise, someone may be so mentally polarized they appear to have 'all the answers' yet they lack emotional sensitivity and empathy with others. Such a person may 'get out the door' but they interface with the World with major part(s) of their equipment underfunctioning and uncoordinated with other parts of themselves.

5. The diagram at right demonstrates that the work of Ka-Ra-acter building is to balance, blend, and coordinate the energies of the physical, emotional and mental Soul bodies with the Ab Soul and Ba Soul which are Higher consciousness and conscience. In this process you may experience:

Ka	Ka	
Ra	erect	Mental vehicle
acter	ter	Emotional vehicle
		Physical vehicle

Working to:
1. Build
2. Balance
3. Blend the energies of
4. Coordinate
5. Align
the lower Mental, Emotional & Physical
Souls bodies or vehicles

a. Misalignment
b. Polarization in one of the lower vehicles with diminished awareness of the higher
c. Leakage of energy that comes from
d. Lack of disciplining of the vehicles for maximal performance as an instrument for the higher Ab and Ba Soul

1. **What gets in the way of you coordinating your physical body, emotions and mind so that you can 'get out of bed', 'get out the door' and do something meaningful in your immediate life space?** You are encouraged to make a list at this point as this will indicate the work of Ka-erect-er Building for you. See also Table on page 113.

Ka-erect-er Development and Building List:

_____

_____

2. As man/woman re-ascends, the Ka-Ra-acter/Temple becomes the vehicle for the Ab-Soul. As the Personality becomes completely Ab-Soul infused it becomes a lighted vehicle for the Ba Soul. You must develop Ka-erect-ter in order to have a fit instrument in service of the higher Ab and Ba Soul program. The Ka-erect-er is the lower self or ego. Lower egoic consciousness must be transcended into the Higher Egoic consciousness of the Ab and Ba Triangles. Re-ascension into sacredness is consciousness in its *inner-ing return* as THREE in ONE.

3. Just because a Ka-erect-er or Personality is able to get out the door in the morning does not mean this will bring healing and upliftment to humanity and the World. A Ka-Ra-acter can be 'doing its own thing' which is working for the limited and personal self interest of the lower ego. Moreover, a well-coordinated Ka-erect-er that is disconnected from the Ab Soul light may be extremely ambitious, selfish, sadistically inclined, and even dedicated to evil, as has been amply demonstrated in the World by numerous so called Ka-Ra-acters.

How is personal will used?

KaAbBa Building The Lighted Temple
The Spiritual B(ARK)

4. The approximating Ka is what you are known for and how you are remembered, whether through greatest fame or greatest infamy. As you journey along, the Ab Soul and the Ba Soul knocks, expanding your conscious awareness, and it beckons you to a wider sphere of radiance and service beyond your personal sphere. The Ka-erect-ter can surrender to or resist the higher calling and impress of the Ab and Ba Souls. This is your use of *personal will and choice.*

What happens when the Ka-erect-ter is brought under the Higher Ab and Ba Soul program?

We do not want to just build the first three floors of our house as previously shown in the diagram at right. We want this temple to be lighted, which means we must gradually unpack our entire Spiritual Equipment, which are the Soul levels, floors or planes of consciousness within the Ab and Ba Soul Triangles above. You are Heru – sphere 6, the rising and erect-ting Sun. As you unpack the Self, you develop and awaken the *purified heart* and the 1st *eye that sees and knows.* This is pictured in the 2 diagrams that follow on this page and the next:

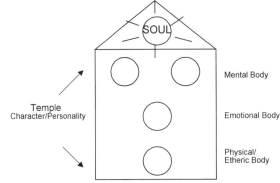

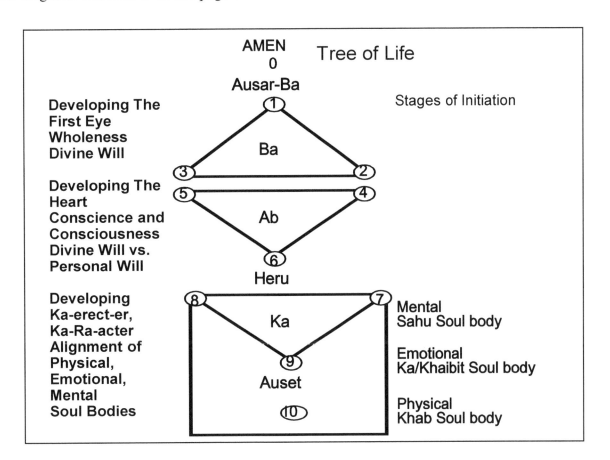

The Ausarianization of Consciousness Series 1
Metaphysical Keys To the Tree of Life & Oracle Keys to Dis-spelling Illusion
The Spiritual Journey in Unfolding Consciousness

132

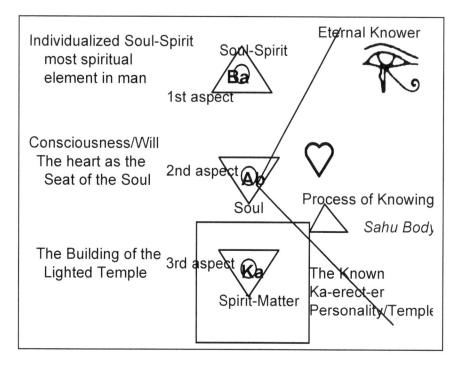

In Ka Ab Ba – the THREE aspects of Divinity within your Spiritual faculty come to act as ONE. These expansions in consciousness bring you back into your re-member-ance of your ONE TRUE SELF.

You must undergo ASTR in order to become a STAR. Holding your intent, directing your course and knowing where you are going (destination) *is* your daily ASTR practice. What is occurring within your Spiritual Equipment through practice is the:

1. Alignment of the Ab Soul with its instrument or Temple – the Ka-erect-er/Temple
2. Relinquishing of the limited agenda of the Ka-erect-er or Personality/Temple
3. Surrender to the Higher calling of the Ab Soul which urges you the initiate into a wider field of influence and World service
4. Rendering your Ka-erect-er/Temple a fit instrument for the Ab Soul and Ba-Soul
5. Blending and uniting in your consciousness of the THREE into the ONE.
6. Abstracting of your conscious awareness back into the ONE
7. Returning to Unity or God Consciousness
8. Living in awareness that the THREE of KA AB BA is the ONE of Spirit
9. Sustaining of this pervading awareness in your daily life

The Ausarian Spiritual Tradition and writings teach much about the Spiritual journey and Ausarian Resurrection. That is, the resurrection of immortal man who has now 'seemingly' become a mortal and knows 'death,' as he comes to experience 'a separated self'.

The Ancient wisdom tells us that man and woman will stand within the Hall of Amenta before Ausar, Lord of all the Worlds – the God who dwells within you. Here, your heart will be weighed on a scale against the feather of Maat – sphere 4. Maat is the Neter or Divine qualities within us of truth, justice, harmony and right relationship whose symbol is the ostrich feather. Upon her scales of justice your heart is weighed against the lightness of the feather. When the scales of balance tip, you incur Karma and become bound upon the wheel of birth and death.

You will make recitations from the papyrus of the sacred text which are accordingly: E. A. Wallis Budge. *The Prt Em Hru (Egyptian Book Of The Dead), Nebseni Papyrus* Chapter 125, p. 351.

KaAbBa Building The Lighted Temple
The Spiritual B(ARK)

Homage to you, O ye gods, I know you and I know your names. Cast me not down to your knives of slaughter, and bring not my wickedness into the presence of the god whom ye follow, and let not the time of my failings come before you. I pray you, declare me right and true in the presence of the Universal God, because I have done that which is right and true in Ta-mera; I have not cursed the god…

Homage to you, O ye gods who live in the hall of Right and Truth, and who have no evil in your bodies, who feed on your own substance in the presence of Heru who liveth in his disk… on the day of the great judgment which shall be holden by you. I have come unto you; I have committed no faults; I have not sinned; I have done no evil; I have accused no man falsely; therefore let nothing be done against me. I live in right and truth, and I feed my heart upon right and truth. That which men have bidden I have done, and the gods are satisfied there at. I have pacified the god, for I have done his will I have given bread unto the hungry and water unto those who thirst, clothing unto the naked, and a boat unto the shipwrecked mariner. I have made holy offerings unto the gods; and I have given meals of the tomb to the sainted dead. O, then, deliver ye me, and protect me; accuse me not before the great god. I am pure of mouth, and I am pure of hands. May those who see me say, 'Come in peace, come in peace…

You will respond to the "42 Negative Confessions" – statements of innocence, regarding your conduct during your Earthly journey.

This brings us to the next

Metaphysical Key To:
The 42 Admonitions
The Laws of Maat

The 42 Laws of Maat are also known as the:
The 42 Declarations of Innocence
The 42 The Admonitions of Maat
The 42 Negative Confessions

They are found in *The Prt Em Hru (The Book of Coming Forth by Day)* which has been misnamed, *"The Egyptian Book of The Dead"*. Our African Ancestors used these Universal laws of right relationship to maintain harmony and balance in society. They serve to guide right thoughts, acts, and deeds in life. Later the biblical Moses would reveal just ten of these Laws in the form of the 10 Commandments that he had learned in the Ancient Mystery schools of Kemet. These Laws are to be recited daily as a way to bring ones' daily life into alignment. As you recite these, make whatever corrections are deemed necessary so that your daily life may reflect the principles of Maat which are: truth, justice, harmony, balance and right relationship. *To work in accord with Divine Law is to Build the Lighted Temple*. These are listed on the following page accordingly:

The Ausarianization of Consciousness Series 1
Metaphysical Keys To the Tree of Life & Oracle Keys to Dis-spelling Illusion
The Spiritual Journey in Unfolding Consciousness

134

THE 42 DECLARATIONS OF INNOCENSE *The Admonitions of Maat*

1. I HAVE NOT DONE INIQUITY.	22. I HAVE NOT POLLUTED MYSELF.
2. I HAVE NOT ACTED WITH VIOLENCE (TO ANYONE OR ANYTHING).	23. I HAVE NOT CAUSED TERROR.
3. I HAVE NOT ROBBED WITH VIOLENCE.	24. I HAVE NOT SPOKEN EVIL.
4. I HAVE DONE NO MURDER, I HAVE DONE NO HARM.	25. I HAVE NOT BURNED WITH RAGE.
5. I HAVE NOT DEFRAUDED TEMPLE OFFERINGS.	26. I HAVE NOT STOPPED MY EARS AGAINST THE WORDS OF RIGHT AND TRUTH (MAAT).
6. I HAVE NOT DIMINISHED OBLIGATIONS.	27. I HAVE NOT WORKED GRIEF.
7. I HAVE NOT PLUNDERED THE NETCHER.	28. I HAVE NOT ACTED WITH INSOLENCE.
8. I HAVE NOT SPOKEN LIES.	29. I HAVE NOT STIRRED UP STRIFE.
9. I HAVE NOT SNATCHED AWAY FOOD.	30. I HAVE NOT JUDGED HASTILY.
10. I HAVE NOT CAUSED PAIN.	31. I HAVE NOT BEEN AN EAVESDROPPER OR PRIED INTO MATTERS TO MAKE MISCHIEF.
11. I HAVE NOT ABUSED MY SEXUALITY.	32. I HAVE NOT MULTIPLIED MY WORDS EXCEEDINGLY.
12. I HAVE NOT CAUSED THE SHEDDING OF TEARS.	33. I HAVE NOT DONE HARM NOR ILL.
13. I HAVE NOT DEALT DECEITFULLY.	34. I HAVE NOT DISHONORED THE ANCESTORS.
14. I HAVE NOT TRANSGRESSED OR ANGERED GOD.	35. I HAVE NOT FOULED OR WASTED THE WATER.
15. I HAVE NOT ACTED GUILEFULLY.	36. I HAVE NOT SPOKEN SCORNFULLY.
16. I HAVE NOT LAID WASTE THE PLOUGHED LAND.	37. I HAVE NOT CURSED THE NETCHER.
17. I HAVE NOT BORN FALSE WITNESS.	38. I HAVE NOT POLLUTED THE EARTH.
18. I HAVE NOT SET MY LIPS IN MOTION (AGAINST ANYONE).	39. I HAVE NOT DEFRAUDED THE OFFERINGS OF THE NETERU.
19. I HAVE NOT BEEN ANGRY AND WRATHFUL EXCEPT FOR A JUST CAUSE.	40. I HAVE NOT PLUNDERED THE OFFERINGS OF THE BLESSED DEAD.
20. I HAVE NOT COMMITTED ADULTERY (not taken the wife of any man, the husband of any wife).	41. I HAVE NOT MISTREATED CHILDREN.
21. I HAVE NOT LUSTED NOR COMMITED FORNICATION.	42. I HAVE NOT MISTREATED ANIMALS.

KaAbBa   Building The Lighted Temple
The Spiritual B(ARK)

Again, Heru is the use of the will to choose whether to live a life in accord with Divine will or not. You may choose to use the will to build askew or in alignment with the Divinely intended design for your life. The will governs the heart. The heart is the seat of the Soul.

When the will is aligned with Divine purpose the heart is made light, and purified. The heart is the symbol that reflects how much personal will has been transmuted into Divine will. Heru is the guidance of your Soul, the accumulated wisdom of many lifetimes. Therefore Heru is the wisdom – the Spiritual essence, that has been garnered in your long pilgrimage to Ausarian consciousness.

Next-

We will look first at Ba or Ausar Ba as God indwelling Man and Woman. Making descent down the Tree of Life we will seek to understand the dynamic movement within:
1. The 3 primary triangles Ba Ab Ka and
2. Each of The 7 Souls or 7 Divisions within the Spiritual economy

Metaphysical Key To: Ausar Ba	1. Ba Man/Woman God-in-form Ausar Ba

Sphere 1
Ba   Symbol – Bird with Human Head
Kemetic Neter – Ausar Ba
Man & Woman
Kabalistic Name - Kether-Crown
1st Aspect of Divinity Triangle
Ba Triangle - Kemetic
Monadic Triangle – Esoteric
Spheres 1, 2, & 3
Initiation: 7th degree Resurrection

What is Ba?

1. Presently as Earth inhabitants, we are attaining *to-be* conscious as the God indwelling the Planet is conscious. Through your expanding consciousness as Ausar Ba man or woman, your attainment to the consciousness of Ausar Planetary Ba enables you to 'come forth' and say, I and my Father are One – *'Nuk Ausar'* which is Kemetic for, *'I am Ausar'.*

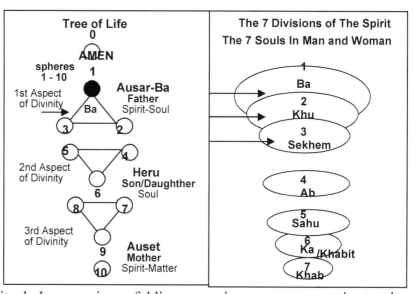

As you continue the Spiritual Journey in unfolding consciousness you attain to the consciousness of that Great Being ensouling our Sun – Ausar Solar Ba. Again, in this way you 'come forth', and say, 'I and my Father are One' and so, on up to and including your At-One-ment as Ausar Universal Ba, Itself.

Indicated by the arrows in the diagrams, we see within the Ba 1st aspect triangle that:

a. Ba, Khu, and Sekhem are the 1st, 2nd and 3rd Soul divisions of Spirit respectively, which are part of our Spiritual constitution.

b. They likewise correspond to the Kemetic Neteru Ausar Ba – sphere 1, Tehuti – sphere 2, and Seker –sphere 3 in the Tree of Life.

KaAbBa Building The Lighted Temple
The Spiritual B(ARK)

2. As Ausar Ba man and woman, you are a spark of Divine Spirit. Ba is individualized Spirit and the most Spiritualized element in Man. Like the spark that arises from the flames, Ba arises from the infinite, boundless, ALL and begins its 'seeming' journey into manifestation. The nature of Ba is Spiritual and it is indivisible. Ba is not Pure Spirit while it is manifested in-form. It is however the Spiritualizing element in man and woman and throughout the entire manifested Universe. In attaining to the Consciousness of/as Ausar Ba you are expressing the Divine will of God.

3. As Ausar Ba you are The Drawer from the Fount of All Possibility with Unlimited Access to All Potential. You are The Drawer of All Power (Omnipotence), All Wisdom (Omniscience) and All Pervading Presence (Omnipresence). When man is living his Ausarian consciousness then he is fully expressing the God that dwells within. He may express all of the Divine qualities of the One True Reality, The Supreme Being. He knows full Godhood and Self realization. He knows unity of Spirit and he knows the underlying unity between all created Beings. Unity of Spirit is full consciousness of the whole of the Tree of Life. As you identify within Ausarian consciousness, your entire Spirit is unified and transcends the brokeness that occurs when you identify as the 'lesser self'.

4. As Ausar Ba man and woman you are the exiled God who walks the Earth trying to remember your Divinity, Godliness, eternal Home and the SELF as Life eternal. By your extension into form, you are immersed at various levels of manifestation in vehicles or bodies which range from the most coarse and dense to the most refined and subtle. This coarseness or refinement influences the degree to which we consciously register Divinity. By knowing 'Thyself' at every level of immersion in matter you become Ausar Ba.

5. The more coarse and dense your vehicles for manifestation, the lower your Spiritual vibration, the further you are from living your full, conscious Ausar Ba awareness. The more refined and Spiritualized your vehicles for manifestation, the higher your Spiritual vibration and the closer you are to living fuller Ausarian consciousness. It is through your temporary 'garment' or temple that you may *register the livingness of the OneTrue Self and know God as dwelling within you.*

6. Currently, man and woman as a microcosm are evolving in the three Worlds of form which are the physical, emotional and mental Soul bodies or vehicles. Ba is Spirit bestowing Life and Consciousness in-form during its cycle of incarnation. Each Ba is both Sun and Son/Daughter, an individualized Son of God, or unit of the Divine Self. You as Ba man or Ba woman are a tiny replica of the One Universal Ba, though limited by your level of Self conscious awareness of the ONE GOD in-form, that you are. As man or woman on your own plane of manifestation, you are striving for full Self conscious realization of the One True Self as Ausar Ba – sphere 1.

7. As Ausar Ba, you are a measure of the fullest achievement of God's Divinely intended design and plan even if as yet unrealized by you in your limited 'self conscious' awareness at your

present level of immersion in matter/form. As Ausar Ba, you have your own space/time continuum for the unfoldment of your fullest potential, which is the Self Conscious Realization of the One True Self – The Image and Likeness of God that *you are* and have been from the beginningless beginning.

8. It is through the full unfoldment of Self Conscious Awareness and the practice of meditation that you are At-One-ed with yourself as Ausar Ba, which is to be At-One-ed with all created entities and finally At-One-ed with/as Universal Ba Itself. Thus, full Self conscious realization is gained at every level of manifestation. This is expressed in the following very *condensely compacted* quote which starts out *complex* and ends *simply a*ccording to Michael Robbins, *The Infinitization of Selfhood*, p. xx.

> The Purpose of all Life in Cosmos is the *realization of* and *identification with* the BOUNDLESS IMMUTABLE PRINCIPLE, the 'INFINITESSENCE', the INFINITE SELF/NON-SELF, *and* the *perfected,* reflected *SELF-Objectification* of the One 'EXTRUDED' 'infinitessentialized Possibility' which the Universe Is. All beings or identities, therefore, are REALLY, no particular beings or identities but, instead, only the ONE AND ONLY INFINITE BEING/NON-BEING, the ONE AND ONLY INFINITE IDENTITY/NON-IDENTITY, the ONE AND ONLY INFINITE SELF/NONSELF. Therefore every apparent *being* is, *REALLY,* every 'other' apparent *being.* Thus, every-one is, REALLY, everyone else, and every-thing is, REALLY, everything else.

9. As the Divine emanates forth and makes it descent into matter, the consciousness of your unlimited potential becomes dimmed if you identify your self as these limiting conditions. It is only when your consciousness is polarized within the Ausar Ba faculty of your Spirit that you re-gain interior-sightedness – the IS-NESS of All Neteru, Divine qualities, - whose potential may be actualized within a to-be Circumscribed Field of Expression. This full return in consciousness is Ausarian Resurrection. This is the awareness of boundlessness within a boundaried field of expression.

10. With the *stirring* within the AMEN, the Infinite All takes the unqualified, unconditioned sub-stance within itself and God as BE-NESS becomes God as Creator. *Ausar is a Ray of the Absolute Spirit that penetrates into the dark depths of matter then raises and redeems every aspect of Itself back into Itself in its return as Pure Spirit.* When your consciousness is resident within this sphere, you experience an Unlimited and Unconditioned state of Being-ness in a To-Be-Conditioned State of Becoming.

11. As you reside within your Ausarian consciousness, which is your One I-dentity, you move beyond the duality that arises in awareness. This 'seeming' duality leads to states of pleasure and pain in your experience. When you are polarized within your Ausarian consciousness you are continually imbued with inner Peace – *Hotep.* Perched above the rising and falling states of normal awareness your consciousness is that of peace and Light Supernal, even in the midst of changing outer circumstance.

KaAbBa   Building The Lighted Temple
The Spiritual B(ARK)

12. As Ausar Ba you are The Eternal Witness and Knower who moves out into manifestation *while* standing upon your own High plane of consciousness. You are The One True Self Realized Being-ness. When you live this reality you are living God Consciousness. You have 'returned' to reside upon your heavenly thrown while establishing the Kingdom of Heaven on the Earthly plane. It is from the heavenly heights of Ausarian consciousness that you stand resurrected and able to solve all of life's problems.

13. When you are not bringing the awareness to the Ausar Ba part of your Spiritual equipment you experience Disconnection from All Power, All Wisdom, All Pervading Presence. This is the diminished state of conscious livingness of/as God – actualizing in the physical World (Geb).

14. As Ausar it is your 'Ba' Aspect of Divinity that is the only immortal and eternal principle in you, being an indivisible part of the integral whole-the Universal Spirit, from which it emanates, and into which it is absorbed at the end of the cycle.

15. As long as Ba is in-form, in manifestation, the ONE of Pure Spirit has emanated into the THREE of Spirit, Soul and Matter. If Ba ceases its individualized expression it returns to its source – Pure Spirit.

A beautiful rendition of the Ba, Khu and Sekhem Soul bodies is expressed accordingly: E.A.Wallis Budge. *Osiris. The Egyptian Religion of Resurrection,* chapter on, "The African Doctrine of Last Things," p. 116 –147.

What is Ba?

> The Ba, its seems, was connected closely with the Ka with which it dwelt, and appears to have been regarded as the soul of the Ka. It was not incorporeal, though its nature and substance were somewhat ethereal. It was gratified by the offerings made to the Ka of the dead body in the tomb, and perhaps it partook of their spirit entities. It revisited its Ka and the body in the tomb, and it could take up its abode there at pleasure; it was free to travel all over heaven, and to mix with and to hold converse with souls there, and it could take any form it pleased. The Ba of a man was represented by a bird with a bearded human head.

What is Khu?

> …there is no doubt that it [the Khu] was supposed to be eternal. The Pyramid Texts prove that the Khu of the gods lived in heaven and thither wended the Khu of a man as soon as ever the prayers said over the dead body enabled it to do so. King Unas stood at the head of the Khu," i.e., he was the chief of all the Khu; and when the souls of the gods transferred themselves from their own spirit-bodies to Unas, their Khu were before Unas. The god received the king as a brother and placed him among the "imperishable Khu." The last passage is important, for the hieroglyphic determinatives suggest that the Khu were beings of light, comparable to the stars, and the evidence of other passages supports this view, and

indicates that the Khu of a man was the intangible, ethereal, transparent portion of his immaterial economy to which modern nations have given the name of spirit.

We have learned previously that Khus are the Divine ideation in the Mind of God. As Divine Intelligence they are the Luminous Beings of Light revealing the Divine archetypal design. The Khus reveal the whole moving geometry and architectural design in the Mind of God. This is further described later in relationship with Tehuti – sphere 2.

Let's Dispell the word Kumara or Khumara:
#7. Oracle Metaphysical Dis-spelling Key: Look up definition (dictionary, glossary, reference texts, etc.)
Definition: Barborka, *The Divine Plan.* HP Blavatsky, *Theosophical Glossary*. When these reference sources are unveiled the following is derived:
Kumara – (a Sanskrit word) An aspect of the Solar Neter/ancestor Ra who incarnated in/as the Afican/Lemurian 3rd Root Race.

This brings us to a new Metaphysical Dis-spelling Key:
#11. Oracle Metaphysical Dis-spelling Key: What does the word sound like? Say the word out loud and then silently in a meditative state.
Sounds Like:
Khu- mer (r)a or Khu mirror

Mer - face, image, likeness, pyramid
> **Definition:**
> Mirror – Something that faithfully reflects or gives a true picture of something else. From Old French *mireor,* from *mirer*, From Latin *mirari.*
> **Definition:** E.A. Wallis Budge. *Hieroglyphic Glossary, VI*, p. 307.
> Mer – like, as.
> Mer – lake, any collection of water, lake, pool, cistern, reservoir, basin, canal, a particle of prohibition.
> Mertt – copy, likeness.
> Mer – a sea-going ship, inundation, flood, stream, libation tank, swampy land
> Merit – celestial lake, heaven, sky.

#8. Oracle Metaphysical Dis-spelling Key: Meaning. See the relationship and oracle or story of the Neteru – Put word list together to tell a story.
Meaning:
This word dispelled is Khu mirror. It is the face or image of Ra. A Khu mirror is one who is revealing the face of a Divine ideation in the Mind of God. The 'wended' Khu is the one who has made his/her way to Heaven. The returning Khus reflect what has been seen of God's design. The returning Khus *together* reveal the whole moving geometry and architectural design in the Mind of God. When the disciple has attained to the consciousness of the Khu Soul he/she is

called a Kumara or Khumara in the Eastern tradition and a Khu in the Kemetic tradition. Thus do we become a Mer Khu Ra – mirroring the image likeness of God/Ra.

What is Sekhem?

> The word means "power," and it may be an immaterial personification of the energy of a man. To King Pepi it is said: "Thy Sekhem cometh among the Khu, Thy Sekhem is pure among the Khu;"…Ausar and every god had his Sekhem, and Ra is called the "Great Sekhem, the Sekhem among the Sekhemu.

The word Sekhem is further dispelled later in this work and in *ACTS 2.*
We now move to the Ka triangle.

The Ausarianization of Consciousness Series 1
Metaphysical Keys To the Tree of Life & Oracle Keys to Dis-spelling Illusion
The Spiritual Journey in Unfolding Consciousness

142

Metaphysical Key To:
Understanding Ka

Sphere 9

Ka   Symbol – Upraised Arms

Kemetic Neter – Auset

Kabalistic Name - Yesod-Foundation

3rd Aspect of Divinity Triangle

Ka/Ka-erect-er/Triangle - Kemetic

Personality – Esoteric

Spheres 7, 8, 9, & 10

Initiation: 2nd degree Baptism

1. Ka is Spirit. It is the Eter-nal Image and Likeness of God.

2. Ka is how we are made to remember that we are made in the Image and Likeness of God, perfect and without distortion.

3. Indicated by the arrows in the diagrams at right, we see within the Ka 3rd aspect triangle that:

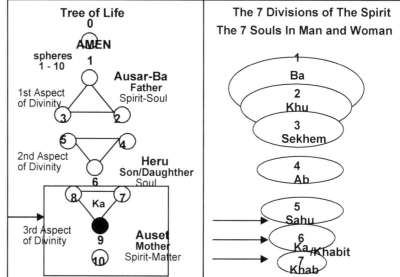

a. Sahu, Ka/Khaibit and Khab are the 5th, 6th and 7th Soul divisions of Spirit respectively, which are parts of our Spiritual constitution.

b. They likewise correspond to the Kemetic Neteru Het-Heru – sphere 7, Sebek – sphere 8, Auset - sphere 9 and Geb – sphere 10. The 10th sphere completes the square or the quarternary.

The above is further substantiated by the following accordingly: Alvin Boyd Kuhn, *The Lost Light,* p. 262.

KaAbBa   Building The Lighted Temple
The Spiritual B(ARK)

In an address to Pepi it is written that the god "setteth his remembrance upon men and his love before the gods". Indeed the Ritual records the fact that the deceased in Amenta was shown his Ka (higher soul body) and assured that it accompanied him through the lower earth in order that he might not utterly forget his Divine moorings, or as he says, "that he might not suffer loss of identity by forgetting his name". Man is on earth like one stricken with amnesia. Showing him his Ka bestirs the Manes to recall his Divine name and nature.

4. Ka is called the double of the dead.

5. As *'In-Spirit-ing'* Ka: Ka is Spirit. It is the fullness of the eternal Image and Likeness of God.

6. As *'Approximating' Ka*: Ka in its entifying function is the fullness of the Image and Likeness of God that can be reflected or contained in the garment or vestment that you are using as an individualized Ausar Ba man or woman, who has achieved a certain point of Self consciousness.

7. Ka is the Spirit-matter continuum substance from which you must build the Lighted Temple. The temple is the Ka-Ra-acter and the Lighted Temple is the Ka-Ra-acter that is being Ab and Ba Soul infused. This is described later.

8. Ka as Spirit makes its deepest descent into matter. IT asserts its right to live and indwell the most wretched of forms that are unillumined and in which consciousness is dimmed.

9. Yet all the while, Ka reminds the life indwelling these forms, whether wretched or refined, that they are all made in the Image and Likeness of God.

10. *Spirit as matter* at its lowest vibration and *matter as Spirit* at its highest vibration *is* the playfield of Ka. What is imaged by Ka is at times more Spiritual – the in-Spiriting Ka – and at times more material – the approximating Ka. Yet Ka is Spirit and never ceases as the Image and Likeness of God. Ka is like the film in a camera.

Let's dispell the word camera:
#10. Oracle Metaphysical Dis-spelling Key: Letter replacement. Here we have replaced the 'k' which had been substituted by the letter 'c.'

Derived Word List:
Kam – Black, the substance out of which we make and remake ourselves in the Image and Likeness of God.

Make Ra – The making of the Sun-Son/Daughter
Mer, Mera - face, image, reflection
#11. Oracle Metaphysical Dis-spelling Key: What does the word sound like? Say the word out loud and then silently in a meditative state.

> **Sounds Like:**
> Mirror - See previous dispelling of mirror.

Makera, Maker(u) – When we are found justified, made whole as Ausar.
Karma – What you have made of the God Ra – the Sun-Son/Daughter through your thoughts, words, acts and deeds.

#8. Oracle Metaphysical Dis-spelling Key: Meaning. See the relationship and oracle or story of the Neteru – Put word list together to tell a story.
Meaning: Ka finds correspondence with the Kemetic Neter Auset – the Divine Mother.
As Auset, the Divine Mother within you is impregnated and impressed with the All Potential of the Father Ausar. Within her Black womb the Image and Likeness of God appears. Only she can *hold* and *reflect* the Image and Likeness in fullness. As the collective unconscious Auset is:
a. The fullness of the Image and Likeness of the One True Self and
b. All successively approximating Ka snapshots to the One True God Realization
c. Absolute and utmost devotion to the regathering of the broken body of Ausar until the full image of Ausar is reflected unbroken and undistorted.

11. Ka 'seemingly' entifies (creates entities) along the Spirit-matter continuum without itself being entified or limited. What is 'seemingly' entified is called Ba. Ba, a pure and formless Spirit, must always have the support of Ka in order to manifest. This is expressed accordingly: Isha Schwaller De Lubicz. *The Opening of The Way Her-Bak*, p. 202.

    > Egyptians also called it the "Father of the fathers of the Neters", for Ka is the principle which realizes (makes real) continuous creation; without it the Father would have no effective power, and by it the Son reveals the face of his Father. By it all things receive their "names".

12. Ka and Ba are in *play and display* through all the myriad, created forms within the One Universal Ba.

13. As man and woman you are made in the Image and Likeness of God. It is the 'Spirit Ka', which holds this image, as Spirit becomes immersed at all levels of manifestation, more subtle or more dense. Ka is how each entifcation, or – Ba – knows and expresses its Divine essence and has rehearsal in fully radiating the Glory of God in whatever garment it temporarily dons.

KaAbBa Building The Lighted Temple
The Spiritual B(ARK)

14. Ka is the Spirit-Matter continuum substance from which man must fashion an instrument that reflects his Divine Image and Likeness of God. That instrument must bear up under the Ka-in-Spiriting impress.

15. The approximating Ka offers the *snapshot* on the inner realm of how much you have been able to put together in consciousness about the right relationship between Spirit and matter. To 'see' the right relationship between Spirit and matter is to express the livingness of Heru/Christ – sphere 6, in form. The Soul seeks to garner, bit by bit, treasure by treasure, snapshot by snapshot and essence by essence the Ka-rest or Christ reflection and livingness. When the Approximating Ka within you at last reflects Spirit Ka – the eternal Image and Likeness of God without distortion – you take your stand and affirm: 'I and my Father are One'.

Let's dispell the word snapshot:

 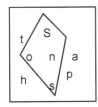

Derived Word List:
Sons Ptah – Sons of Ptah

Let's dispell the word Photo and Photograph:

This brings us to a new Metaphysical Dis-pelling Key:
#12. Oracle Metaphysical Dis-spelling Key: Take out duplication of letters so that each letter appears only once.

#5. Oracle Metaphysical Dis-spelling Key: Letter substitution-you may substitute a letter. Place substituted letter in parenthesis ( ).

 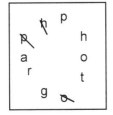

Derived Word List:
Ptah o R(a) G - Full circle God.

#8. Oracle Metaphysical Dis-spelling Key: Meaning. See the relationship and oracle or story of the Neteru – Put word list together to tell a story.

Meaning: As described earlier, Ptah is synonymous with the Names Ausar, Khepera, Nebertcher, Ra and Seker which is sphere 3 in the Tree of Life. Ptah is the Kemetic Neter that digs 7 holes in the waters of space or Nu and teaches matter how to behave, according to 7 discrete streams of qualifying energies - 7 Deific powers. Ausar expressing as Kheper-Ptah-Seker is the opener and great architect in the Universe. We are becoming Sons of Ptah, or Suns who move out along a path and then return as One and the Same Everliving God.

16. Ka is the erector of Ra the Sun- Son/Daughter in Matter-form.

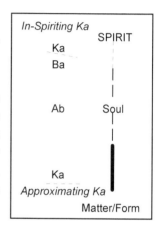

17. The Kemetic equivalent for eternal life is the permanent personality or Ka-erect-er which was imaged by or in the Ka.

18. Ka is what helps you not to loose your way. We note that Ba is reflected a 'little lower' in our diagram at right. This is because Ba is what arises into manifestation out of SPIRIT, AMEN – sphere 0. As long as Spirit is in a body of manifestation as Ba, no matter how subtle or refined, it is still in-form. This includes tiniest atom as Ba Atom, man as Ba Ausar, Sun as Ba Sun, up to and including the entire manifested Universe itself as Ba Universe.

A beautiful rendition of the Khab, Ka/Khaibit and Sahu Soul Bodies is expressed accordingly: E.A.Wallis Budge. *Osiris.The Egyptian Religion of Resurrection,* chapter on, "The African Doctrine of Last Things," p. 116 –147.

What is Khab/Khat?

> The physical body of man was called the Khat, a word which sometimes has as its determinative a mummy, or a mummy lying on a bier. When the body was born, there came into existence with it an abstract individuality or spiritual being, which was wholly independent and distinct from the physical body, but its abode was the body, whose actions it was supposed to direct, and guide, and keep watch over, and it lived in the body until the body died.

What is Ka /Khaibit?
Ka

> …in late times Ka simply meant "person" or "self". When the body died the Ka did not die with it, but continued its existence; whether it was supposed to live for ever cannot be said. The body was preserved in a tomb, so that the Ka might come and visit it whenever it pleased, but it could not be considered the dwelling-place of the Ka after its death. Therefore the Kemetians prepared a figure or statue of the dead person to whom the Ka belonged, taking great pains to give it all the characteristics of the deceased, so that the Ka might

recognize it as an image of its body and be pleased to enter into the figure and take up its abode there.

Khaibit

Closely associated with the body was its shadow and the Kemetians appear to have thought it one of its most important attributes. We do not know what ideas they held about its functions when the man to whom it belonged was alive, but it is quite certain that they did not believe the resurrection of the spiritual body to be complete unless that phantom form was in possession of its shadow. The texts lead us to suppose that the Sahu was an immaterial form of the physical body, and it seems that the Kemetians thought it to be material enough to cast a shadow! In the text of Unas the shadow is mentioned in connection with the "form". In The Theban Book of the Dead the deceased prays that his Ba and Khu and Shadow may not be shut in the Other World, and elsewhere we read, "O keep not captive my Soul (Ba), O keep not ward over my Shadow, but let a way be opened for my Soul and for my Shadow, and let [me] see the great God in the shrine, on the day of the Judgment of Souls, and let [me] recite the words of Ausar, whose habitations are hidden, to those who guard the members of Ausar, and who keep ward over the Khu (Spirits), and who work evil against me, lest they work evil against me." …The shadow is a recognized portion of man among modern African peoples. In West Africa the natives told Dr. Nasau that it was possible for a human being to have his *nsisim*, i.e., shadow, stolen or otherwise lost, and for him to exist in a diseased or dying state…The shadow enters and leaves the body by mouth, and is then likened to the breath of a man.

Let's dispell the word Khaibit:

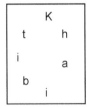

Ka
Ba
Hit
Hab
Tab –
Bait – That which lures. That which is used to get one hooked, or upon a hook.
Habit –

Definition: 1. A. A recurrent, often unconscious pattern of behavior that is acquired through frequent repetition. B. An established disposition of the mind or character. Customary manner or practice: a person of ascetic habits. 3. An addiction, especially to a narcotic drug. 4. Physical constitution. 5. Characteristic appearance, form, or manner of growth, especially of plant or crystal. 6.a. A distinctive dress or costume, especially of a religious order. b. A riding habit. To clothe; dress. [Middle English, clothing, from Old French, clothing, behavior, custom, from Latin Habitus, from past participle of habere, to have.

Bit –

Definition: 1. A small portion, degree, or amount: Something that controls, guides, or curbs. A unit of information storage capacity, as of memory.

#8. Oracle Metaphysical Dis-spelling Key: Meaning. See the relationship and oracle or story of the Neteru – Put word list together to tell a story.

Meaning: We have learned previously that Auset is absolute and utmost devotion in re-gathering the broken body of Ausar until the full image of Ausar is reflected unbroken and undistorted. The Ka/Khaibit, which is the 6th division of the Soul, finds correspondence with: (1) the 6th Ray, which is the Ray of Idealism and Devotion and (2) the 6th plane of consciousness. On a higher turn of the spiral, the 6th Ray brings in the qualities (Neteru) of: intense aspiration, dedication, reverence, utter loyalty and adherence to reflecting the purity and goodness of the Divinity within. On a lower turn of the spiral, the 6th Ray brings in qualities of: blind faith, unreasoning devotion, ill-considered loyalty and overattachment. (See next section on the 7 Ra(y)s). This is the part of our Spirit where we can become as fish trapped in a net. It happens when we go for the bait of lesser self identification. The work within the Ka/Khaibit 3rd aspect triangle is to reflect the full Image and Likeness *bit by bit* or *part self by part self* all the while being *habituated* on the *whole Self*.

What is Sahu?

The fact that the Kemetians and many peoples of the Sudan were in the habit of drying the body in the sun or embalming it, and swathing it in cloth of some kind, proves that its preservation was in some way necessary for the eternal welfare of its spiritual constituents. …There is no proof that they ever expected the physical body to rise again; on the contrary, the texts state clearly that the "soul is in heaven, the body in the earth," and "thy essence is in heaven, thy body in the earth"…Thy soul liveth, thy body without defect, like [that of] Ra, for ever and ever." These statements taken together prove that the Kemetians believed that some kind of body rose from the dead, and continued its existence in the Other World. The pictures of the beatified as seen in papyri show us that this risen body had the form and appearance of the physical body which had been mummified and laid in the grave…**The word "sahu" seems to mean something like "free", "noble", "chief", and in this case it appears to be used as the name for a body which has by means of the religious ceremonies that have been performed over it, obtained freedom from the material body and power whereby it has become incorruptible and everlasting.** Hence arose the great importance of funeral ceremonies and offerings, which caused a spiritual body to spring from the physical body, and the Ka to continue its existence after the death of the body to which it belonged.

The Sahu Soul body is further described later in the Transmigration of the Soul.
We now move to the Ab Triangle.

KaAbBa   Building The Lighted Temple
The Spiritual B(ARK)

Metaphysical Key To:
Understanding Ab

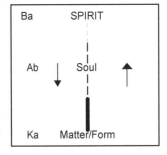

Sphere 6
Ab   Symbol – Human Heart
Kemetic Neter – Heru
Kabalistic Name – Tepereth –Beauty
2nd Aspect Triangle
Ab Triangle - Kemetic
Spiritual Triad - Esoteric
Spheres 4, 5, & 6
Initiation: 4th degree Renunciation/Crucifixion

1. Ab is the second aspect, or middle principle. It is the heart in the Kemetic Spiritual system. The heart is the seat of the Soul. As the seat of the Soul, it is the seed of the growing conscience and evolving consciousness of the relationship between Ka and Ba.

2. Indicated by the arrows in the diagram at right, we see within the Ab 2nd aspect triangle that:

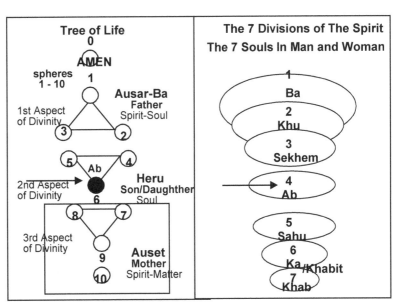

a. Ab is the 4th Soul division of Spirit, which is part of our Spiritual constitution.
b. The Ab triangle likewise corresponds to the Kemetic Neteru, Maat – sphere 4, Herukhuti – sphere 5, and Heru – sphere 6 in the Tree of Life.

3. The Ab Soul is the conscious experience of how Spirit and Matter are relating. This is indicated by the arrows in the diagram at right. The Soul-midway between Spirit and Matter relates the two. The Ab 2nd aspect triangle is how Father-Spirit has a conscious experience of Mother-Matter. Through the relating aspect of Ab, the 'seeming' duality between Spirit-Matter with its myriad objective forms in play and display as Ba Ka are seen as ONE. By your growing conscious awareness of the Divine

marriage between the Father and Mother, the Soul unfolds like the many petals symbolized by the Lotus flower, which was held as sacred to the Kemetians.

4. The Ab is the Will used to live a life in alignment and in accord with Divine Will. It is under the directive and governance of your Ab Soul that you build a Lighted Temple, environment and World that is in accord with the Divine Archetypal Design. In the long evolutionary journey, man and woman are accumulating experiences of being conscious of the *Self* as it is immersed in varying degrees of material form.

5. It is through the full unfoldment of the Soul that Daughter/Son-(Sun)ship is revealed. (Sun)ship is the Heru – sphere 6, called the Karest principle within. This is later called the Christ principle by the Christians. As the Heru or Karest, you are the Son or Daughter of God. Only through the Soul's growing awareness of the relationship between Ba-Ka, Spirit-matter and Father-Mother is Initiation taken. Initiation is expansion into greater states of consciousness. It is a re-uniting of the Higher Self – Ego and lower self – ego, that which is Divine and human within you. As you are becoming fully conscious of the perfect relationship between Father (Soul-Spirit) and Mother (Spirit-Matter) residing in *you* – your radiance as Son/Daughter of God is gradually realized. You are the living *Sun* called Ra by the Kemetians that comes over the horizon at dawn, having known a long Winter of death.

6. Only after a long evolutionary process involving many lifetimes is the resplendent glory of this realization finally stabilized in your daily conscious awareness. By taking the successive initiations into the One True Self I-Dentity you are able to boldly claim, My Father(Mother) and I are One. *Nuk Ausar*, I *am Ausar*.

7. The Ab Soul is the Higher Self or Higher Ego that seeks more and more to imbue your daily life with wisdom, intelligent living and selfless love. It guides you to perform a service in the World that is larger than just your limited personal sphere of existence. It is the purified heart, the Sun (Son) from which you radiate love outward into the World.

8. The Ab Soul is the light of consciousness. It is the garnered treasure of many lifetimes of experience. It is the jewel.

9. The full conscious measure of what is garnered by the Son/Daughter in the Ab triangle is what moves your development into the full measure of the Ba Soul-Spirit, 1st aspect triangle. Thus the 'essence' of Self conscious life in form is *Known*.

10. Ab Soul or Egoic consciousness is produced through the medium of two fires. Accordingly: The Tibetan. *Treatise on Cosmic Fire,* p. 506.

> In all manifestation, … we have duality producing triplicity. Spirit meets and contacts matter; the result of that contact is the birth of the Son, or the Ego, the consciousness aspect.

KaAbBa Building The Lighted Temple
The Spiritual B(ARK)

The egoic manifestation is therefore the middle aspect, the place of at-one-ment, and (after due evolutionary cycles) the place of balance, or of equilibrium.

These two fires which meet to produce the third are as follows:
1st aspect Ba: Electric Fire
3rd aspect Ka: Fire by friction.
2nd aspect Ab: Solar Fire.

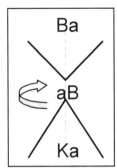

The third fire – Ab, is indicated by the arrow in the diagram at right.

11. The meeting of these two fires of Spirit-Father and Mother-Matter produces the Son (Sun) and is called Solar Fire or the Fire of Ra. This is the growing Light and illumination of the Sun- Son/Daughter. This is how Ab the Son, through the Mother, comes to reflect the Father as Ba. This is pictured in the diagram:

12. Ab is how we get to the heart of the matter(s). Through the Ab agency of the heart all matter becomes Solarized. As we become Soul conscious we come to Know the Self and see every other Self as *The One* and *The Same Self.*

13. The Ab is likewise the developing eye of Heru. In our story the eye of Heru is torn out in the fierce battle with Set but is later restored.

A beautiful rendition of the Ab Soul Body is expressed accordingly: E.A.Wallis Budge. *Osiris. The Egyptian Religion of Resurrection*, chapter on, "The African Doctrine of Last Things," p. 116 –147.

What is Ab?

> In Egyptian ab which literally means "heart" is used to express wish, longing, desire, lust, will, outrage, mind, wisdom, sense, intelligence, manner, disposition, attention, intention, etc., …regarded as the seat of life, and as the home of the passions, both good and bad, and as the seat of the pleasures derived from eating, drinking, and the carnal appetite. The importance of the heart to the deceased will be readily understood from the fact that no less than five Chapters of the Book of the Dead (xxxvi-xxx.) [read here: Book of Coming Forth by Day] are devoted to its preservation.

Heru is the will. It is the use of the will to choose. We choose whether to creatively and intelligently live a life *in* or *out* of accord with Divine will. It is the power to choose to build askew or in alignment with *the Divinely-intended design for your life.* The will of Heru governs the heart. Heru is the growing consciousness that you are the 3 in 1 – KaAbBa.

When I-dentified in the lowest aspect of your Spiritual faculty Heru is:
1. Your lower ego or self consciousness identity
2. You I-dentify as the personality or Ka-erect-er vehicle which comprises the physical

emotional and mental Soul bodies

    a. This personality instrument is seen as separate from the Higher Spiritual agency
    b. Divorcing you from the inner guidance of Higher Manes (Mind)
    c. You I-dentify as/with Lower Manes, which is a long series of lesser selves

When I-dentified in the highest aspect of your Spiritual faculty Heru is:
1. Your Higher Ego or Self conscious I-dentity.
2. You I-dentify as/with Ausar – Ba – the 3 made 1.

Chapter 12
Our State of Unitive Consciousness Changed Over Eons Of Time
3 Primary States of Egoic Consciousness

Our state of Unitive consciousness changed over eons of time and so did our relationship with ourselves, nature and the World around us. We are further told that along the journey of unfolding consciousness man and woman underwent a process of *individualization* wherein the 'spark of mind' was implanted.

What is Ego?
The implantation of the spark of mind is the birth of self-reflective consciousness in man and woman. As man and woman became self-reflective beings, the great game of subject-object was begun. Gradually they began to experience the self as separate from all other selves. This represents the great 'entification', 'objectification' or 'particularization' in consciousness. The birth of self-reflective consciousness is the power to *Know That You Know*. It is the Ego expressing as the Higher Self and the ego expressing as the lower self.

Our Story Continues…
In the story of Ausar, Auset and Heru we turn now to a discourse that is occurring between Auset and her son Heru. In it she is teaching him how to come into maturity so that he may avenge his Father's death and come into his rightful inheritance of the throne of his/her Kingdom. She speaks about this *spark of mind* or power *'to know'* and use the mind accordingly: *Virgin of the World. (G.R.S Mead, Thrice Greatest Hermes;* Dr. Muata Ashby, *Ausarian Resurrection).*

> O Heru, these were the souls, created out of God's very being. In time they came to be conscious of themselves and looked up at the Father of All. Being sparks of their creator as sun rays are emanations of the sun, souls have the power to create due to their ability to **know and use the mind**.
>
> O Heru, **this power became the source of pride and conceit.** The souls thought themselves to be equals to The God, and as their punishment, were enclosed in watery encasements. This is the nature of human existence and it is the reason why human beings are a blend of what is physical and what is Divine.

As our story continues we learn about:
1. These 'Souls' who have 'the power to create due to their ability to know and use the mind' which is called Manes by the Kemetians
2. How this power became the source of pride and conceit and
3. How we come to be a blend of that which is physical and Divine

The game of consciousness is to gain conscious awareness of the *seeming selves* against the backdrop of the *Seamless Unity of The One True Self.* This is accomplished as your awareness remains perched in your higher Spiritual equipment of the Ba and Ab Soul triangles, as/while you perform your work in the World using your Ka-erect-er Lighted Temple as an instrument.

However, when the One True Self as Ausar is forgotten then 'particularization' is seen and mistaken as the *self.* In our lesser self identifications we choose to build askew or out of alignment with *the Divinely-intended design.* This leads to the accumulation of regret, remorse, greed, fear and anger which weighs the heart like lead so that it is heavier than the feather of Maat – sphere 4. Upon her scales of justice the heart is weighed against the lightness of the feather. When the scales of balance tip, we incur Karma and become bound upon the wheel of birth and death. According to Ra Un Nefer Amen, *Metu Neter V1,* p. 228.

> Heru corresponds to our will, which is the freedom to follow or reject Divine law, and our emotions. This freedom is the crux of our Divinity. Without it, man would be compelled to follow the structural shaping forces of order which manifest in the 10th sphere as the "instincts" that compel all other creatures to obey the law, in which case he could not be held accountable to law, human or Divine, let alone be considered the "likeness of God".

The Kemetic Spiritual Tradition and writings teach much about the Spiritual journey and Ausarian Resurrection that is:
• The resurrection of immortal man
• Who has 'seemingly' become a mortal
• As he came to experience *a separated self*
• Who now knows *death*

This brings us to the next

Metaphysical Key To:
The 3 Primary Qualities of
Consciousness/Mind

The 3 primary Egoic States in Consciousness may be observed as follows:
1. Consciousness may remain unitive
2. Consciousness can become dualized and reconciliative/combative
3. Consciousness may become separative or particularized into many parts

How we perceive the 'outer World' depends upon which of these 3 primary Egoic states we find ourselves identified with. The qualities each expresses is shown in the following diagram:

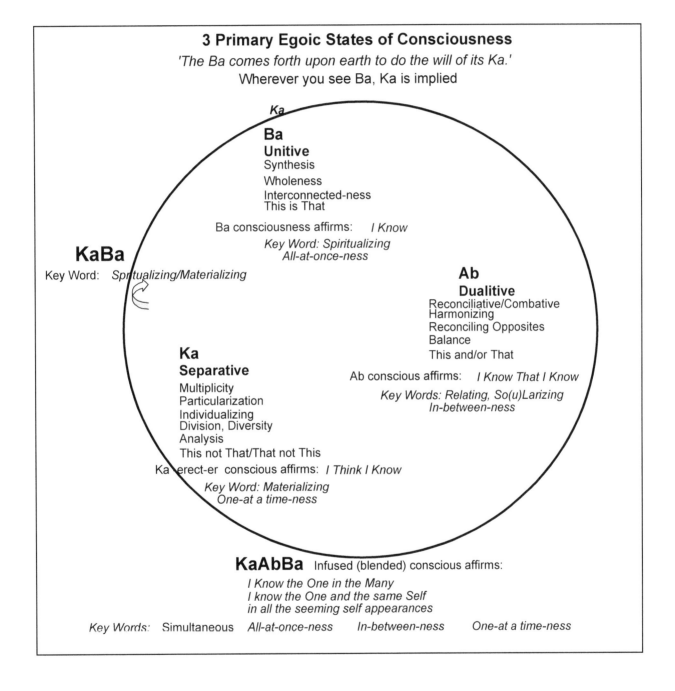

KaAbBa Building The Lighted Temple
The Spiritual B(ARK)

3 Primary Egoic States of Consciousness
'The Ba comes forth upon earth to do the will of its Ka.'
Wherever you see Ba, Ka is implied

Ka

Ba
Unitive
Synthesis

Wholeness

Interconnected-ness
This is That

Ba consciousness affirms: *I Know*
Key Word: Spiritualizing
All-at-once-ness

KaBa
Key Word: *Spritualizing/Materializing*

Ab
Dualitive
Reconciliative/Combative
Harmonizing
Reconciling Opposites
Balance
This and/or That

Ab conscious affirms: *I Know That I Know*
Key Words: Relating, So(u)Larizing
In-between-ness

Ka
Separative
Multiplicity
Particularization
Individualizing
Division, Diversity
Analysis
This not That/That not This
Ka erect-er conscious affirms: *I Think I Know*
Key Word: Materializing
One-at a time-ness

KaAbBa Infused (blended) conscious affirms:
I Know the One in the Many
I know the One and the same Self
in all the seeming self appearances

Key Words: Simultaneous *All-at-once-ness* *In-between-ness* *One-at a time-ness*

The Ausarianization of Consciousness Series 1
Metaphysical Keys To the Tree of Life & Oracle Keys to Dis-spelling Illusion
The Spiritual Journey in Unfolding Consciousness

156

As you may recall from the fields of Psychology and Psychoanalysis, Sigmund Freud is said to have coined the terms *Superego, Ego and Id* to describe on a more narrow scale the process of unfolding consciousness. This brings us to the next

> **Metaphysical Key To:**
> Ka Ab Ba and European Psychoanalysis

He was considered founder of psychological and psychoanalytic techniques used by counseling professionals (See Robert Bocock. *Freud and Modern Society*). As we see the terms Id, Ego and SuperEgo are derived from the Ancient Wisdom sources of our Black Ancestors and are called KaAbBa. I find Freud's choice of the word 'Id', which is the Ka 3rd aspect triangle, of interest.

Let's dispell the word Id:
#9. Oracle Metaphysical Dis-spelling Key: Take each letter one at a time or in combination with one or more letters and derive its meaning.
Derived letter or Neter list:
I D

#8. Oracle Metaphysical Dis-spelling Key: Meaning. See the relationship and oracle or story of the Neteru – Put word list together to tell a story.
Meaning:
If we dispell this word we see that:
1. It is the word 'eyed' or what is seen.

2. It is also the word (or acronym) 'ID', or what we 'I'Dentify as the self (temporarily) on the way to full Identification in our SuperEgo function as Ausar Ba. This is a World in which we are asked for our ID as proof of *who* we are or who we say we are. We need an ID to get through the door in certain outer plane establishments (organizations, clubs, bars, schools, etc). In other words we 'Ka-rd' people in order to seemingly know who they are.

3. ID is also ID – entity, or the 'eyed entity'. Because we have eyed this entity we come to believe what our eye sees. After all, 'It is in the eye of the beholder'.

4. The so called Freudian terms, SuperEgo, Ego and ID (or Id) are just substitutions of the Kemetic terms Ba, Ab and Ka respectively.

5. The term SuperEgo connotes the Highest Soul Consciousness Ba and is our 1st Aspect of Divinity. The term Ego connotes Ab Soul Consciousness, the 2nd Aspect of Divinity. It is the governing agency within that is relating the two of SuperEgo and ID, or the Divine and human. The term ID connotes the Ka Soul Consciousness and is our 3rd Aspect of Divinity.

KaAbBa Building The Lighted Temple
The Spiritual B(ARK)

This is expressed in the following which is testimony that other folks have known the 'stuff' of our Ancient Wisdom and called it something else, as seen in the table below:

African/Kemetic Term		Europeanized/Psychoanylitic Term
Ka	3rd Aspect of Divinity	ID (Id)
Ab	2nd Aspect of Divinity	Ego
Ba	1st Aspect of Divinity	SuperEgo

6. Essentially your ID should *read* that you are the SuperEgo. If it does not, then this reflects that you are off into the lower ego, calling yourself something less than who you really are. It is about growing up from:
a. The collapsing of the lower ego – lower case 'e', a state of blurred vision or blindness into
b. The expanding of Higher Ego - capital 'E', a state of Full Eyesightedness which is
c. The restoration of the eye of Heru –

This brings us to return to a previous

> **Metaphysical Key To:**
> The Law of Correspondence
> "As above, so below; as below, so above."

Just as –
Your passageway through doors on the outer physical plane depends on your ID Ka-rd, which will gain or block your admission into schools, businesses, clubs, organizations, government agencies, bank accounts, etc.
So too –
Your passageway through doors on the inner Spiritual plane depends on your ID Ka-rd, which will gain or block your admission if it does not reflect the *full measure* of who we are.

> **Metaphysical Key To:**
> The Overlay of The 3 Primary Qualities of Consciousness/Mind.

By overlaying the diagram at right, the 3 primary Egoic states of consciousness are revealed within the Tree of Life which are described as: Unitive, Dual (Relating), and Separative.

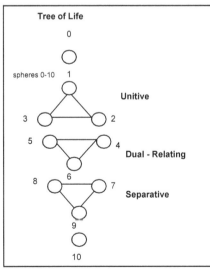

This brings us to our next

Metaphysical Key To:
Racial Names and Physical Characteristics

Each Root Race is known by various Names or racial characteristics. This is indicated in the diagram below:

Racial Names/Characteristics

Racial Names/ Characteristics	African/Negro Black	Semitic Brown/Red/Yellow	Aryan/Caucasian/European White
Kemetic Naming[2]	Nehesu/Nuhes/ Nashi/Neshi/Nahsi	Aamu/Hemu	Themehu/Tamahu
Esoteric Naming[3]	3rd Root Race Lemurian	4th Root Race Atlantean	5th Root Race Aryan

Does each Root Race contribute particular qualities in consciousness?
Seeking to address this question brings us to the next

Metaphysical Key To:
Read from the angle of consciousness and not just from the angle of the physical form/manifestation

In *The Ausarianization of Consciousness Tablet Series – The Metaphysical Keys to The Tree Of Life with Oracle Keys to Dis-spelling Illusion,* passages will be quoted which have been written by authors who have had access to the Ancient wisdom. These authors *have made a link* between Race and Consciousness. I did not make this link. It was made long before these present writings. What I do is make an earnest attempt to unscramble, ungarble and unveil what has been said, in order to wade through the tremendous racism, secrecy and veiling that has occurred in these reference sources. The different Racial Groups have responded differently to this event of 'individualization'. Although first occurring in the African 3rd Root, Race this event of individualization, would have its greater impact on the later Semitic 4th and Aryan/European 5th Root Races, who made their appearance on the Planet in a *later* and *descending* cycle of time. What is key in understanding these passages is to read them from the *angle of consciousness* and

not just from the angle of physical form/manifestation. In other words, an individual who belongs to or identifies with a Racial group and *tends to* express one of the three primary Egoic states of

---

[2] See Wallis. E. A. Budge. *The Gods of The Egyptians, V.I & II.*
[3] See Tibetan, *24 Books of The Tibetan*; Blavatsky, *Secret Doctrine;* Barborka, *Divine Plan;* Heindell, *Cosmo-Conceptions;* et al.

consciousness i.e. Unitive, Dual, or Separative, may likewise express all primary Egoic states of consciousness. Full consciousness in all its states belongs to no individual Race. This leads us to revisit an earlier

---

Metaphysical Key To:
The Impersonality of The Cycles of Time

This Key reminds us to seek to understand the *impersonality of the cycles* of time that *rise and fall*. It is important to see that whenever we look upon an event in Human history, we must simultaneously look at it upon the backdrop of time in which the event is occurring. Each Root Race has made its appearance upon a backdrop of time. Within each cycle certain qualities (Neters) of energy are available that qualify events. The Root Races and the process of Individualization are further described in, *ACTS 2.*

Our Story Continues…
What was this Unbroken Consciousness of the African/Lemurian?
This consciousness is called by many names which includes Unitive, All Consciousness, God or Ausarian Consciousness, Omniscient Consciousness. According to: Max Heindel, *Rosicrucian Cosmo-Conception,* p. 216.

> Before the beginning of the Saturn Period the virgin spirits who are now man, were in the World of Virgin Spirits, and were "All-conscious" as God in whom (not from whom), they were differentiated. They were not "self" conscious however. The attainment of that faculty is partly the object of evolution which plunges the virgin spirits into a sea of matter of gradually increasing density which eventually shuts it from the All-consciousness.

And Continuing: Ibid. p. 278:

> The Lemurian [read here: African 3rd Root Race consciousness] knew no death because when, in the course of long ages, his body dropped away, he entered another, quite unconscious of the change. His consciousness was not focused in the physical world, therefore the laying aside of one body and the taking of another was no more to him than a leaf or twig drying and falling away from the tree and being replaced by a new growth.

As indicated in the above quote, the African 3rd Root Race consciousness was focused within the higher spheres of its Spiritual equipment which comprise the more Divine aspect of man and woman. These are spheres 1 – 3, the higher Ba triangle in the Tree of Life.

You will recall from an earlier quote that:

> The Ba comes forth upon earth to do the will of its Ka.

This is restated as: The Soul-Ba comes forth upon the Earth to do the will of its Spirit-Ka.
Again this is seen in the three diagrams below:

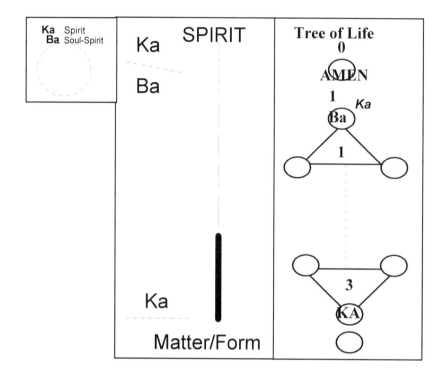

1.   The diagram at left reveals KaBa as One, the Primal couple or Two-Oneness
2.   The Middle diagram reveals the Spirit-Matter continuum or the descent of Spirit into matter
3.   The diagram at right is overlay of diagrams 1 and 2 as revealed in the Tree of Life

KaAbBa Building The Lighted Temple
The Spiritual B(ARK)

This brings us to the next

> **Metaphysical Key To:**
> Spirit came down from the higher Worlds and by
> concurrent action are the bodies built upward.

Ibid. p. 266-269.

> The Spirit came down from the higher Worlds during involution; and by concurrent action,
> the Bodies were built upward in the same period. It is the meeting of these two streams in the
> focusing Mind that marks the point in time when the individual, the human being, the Ego, is
> born – when the Spirit takes possession of its vehicles.

In the two diagrams below we simultaneously see:
1. KaAbBa as a circle
2. KaAbBa revealed in the Tree of Life and visually laid out in a straight line

This meeting of these two streams is indicated by Heru – sphere 6, which is the 4th plane of
consciousness in the Tree of Life This concurrent action of the Spirit coming down from the
Higher Worlds during involution and the bodies being built upward is indicated by the arrows.

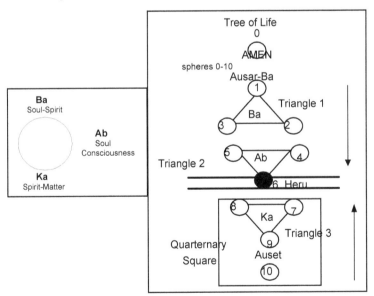

As the consciousness *remained* focused within the higher triangle, it used the lower Ka triangle
which is comprised of the physical, emotional and mental bodies in order to do its work in the
World. These are the Soul 'bodies that are built upwards'. In the diagram, on the previous page,
we see the Ka triangle within the geometric figure of the square or quaternary. These are spheres
7-10, the third triangle in the Tree of Life. This triangle and square are illustrated in the diagram
at right. It is within the 'square' or the quarries of life that character (Ka-Ra-acter or Ka-erect-er)

or the temple is built. It is within this aspect of your Spiritual equipment that you must fashion a temple, which will bear the light from the higher two triangles, the Ab and the Ba. The three triangles combined express the Divine Trinity within you whose name is Ka Ab Ba. When consciousness is poised within the higher or Ab and Ba Soul then the temple you fashion is the Lighted Temple.

It is only later, through a series of events, over the passage of time that this focus begins to shift. This shift in focus would:
1. Leave man and woman forgetful of their residence within the higher Soul realms and
2. Move the conscious awareness into the lower spheres which comprise the more material and human aspect of man and woman's Spiritual equipment
3. Instead of knowing that we are *Spirit Ka,* we would forget the fullness of our ID and wander in the World as an *approximating Ka* trying to re-member and reconstruct our proper ID-entification

So where in your Spiritual equipment is this ability still registered and accessible?
As we proceed down the Tree of Life, acknowledgment is given to Ra Un Nefer Amen in his tremendous re-claim-ation work in the 'Naming of the Spheres' in the Tree of Life - Paut Neteru by the Kemetians. The Tree of Life is your Spiritual equipment both human and Divine and a road map in consciousness. It has been veiled under Kabbalistic Names which has contributed to a disconnection with our Divine Trinity and African Neteru. We will begin our descent down the Tree of Life describing consciousness within the Three primary Triangles of Ba Ab Ka.

What was the consciousness of the Original Humans – The African Root Race when focused in the Ba Triangle of the Tree of Life?
Our Black Race Ancestors saw interiorly and in wholeness. This is a consciousness of Unity and Synthesis. Their consciousness was poised within the higher Ba and Ab Triangles of their Spiritual equipment, symbolized by the Tree of Life. They went out as *knowers* and populated the World. They possessed the 1st or inner eye, which gave them innersightedness and revealed to them the whole moving geometry within the Mind of God. Thus they were poised within Divine Mind, which is symbolized as the Kemetic Neter Tehuti - sphere 2. This sphere has correspondence with the 2nd Soul body called the Khu. As Divine Mind, Tehuti is like the Puzzle Box Cover of a 'seemingly' multitudinous piece puzzle.

Innersightedness allows you glimpses of the Puzzle Box Cover of the great architectural design and plan of creation and manifestation. Our Ancestors had inner-sight of the underlying unity in nature. Within the whole moving geometry of the Puzzle Box Cover of the Great Design of Creation, the seamless unity, interconnection and interdependence throughout creation is viewed. Wholeness and unbrokeness in consciousness is the Reality. This inner wisdom or Tehuti faculty within is the Synthesizing Power Of Love And Wisdom. This power holds and coheres the seeming myriad pieces or part-I-cularizations of the to-be created forms in *the seamless unity of the One*. This power keeps the *circle in consciousness unbroken*. We return to a previous.

KaAbBa   Building The Lighted Temple
The Spiritual B(ARK)

> **Metaphysical Key To**:
> Restoration of The 1st Eye
> ***Overcoming impediment # 2***
> Blindness

Within this sphere resides Divine Ideation or the archetypal lives called the Khus by the Kemetians. This is Divine intelligence. The African 3rd Root Race had inner-sight of the underlying unity in nature. The latter Races would lose this innersightedness which is registered through the power of the 1st eye. Today we are working to restore our 1st eye. This is indicated accordingly: H.P. Blavatsky. *Secret Doctrine, V.II,* p. 306.

> The possession of a physical third eye [read here: first eye], we are told, was enjoyed by the men of the Third Root-Race [read here: African/Negro] down to nearly the middle period of Third Sub-race of the Fourth Root-Race, when the consolidation and perfection of the human frame made it disappear from the outward anatomy of man. Psychically and spiritually however, its mental and visual perceptions lasted till nearly the end of the Fourth Race [read here: AfricanSemitic] when its functions, owing to the materiality and depraved condition of mankind, died out altogether before the submersion of the bulk of the Atlantean continent.

What is the 1st Eye?
As previously stated, this eye is erroneously called the 3rd eye. The 1st eye in man and woman has its correspondence with the eye of Ra. As Creation arises within the waters of space, called Nun by the Kemetians, it is the eye that *sees and knows.*

We have been using the more imperfect geometric square or Puzzle Box Cover to give example of the 1st eye. In order to understand the 1st eye we now move to the more perfect geometrical figure of a sphere. Imagine holding a soccer ball and noting its outer design of polygon shapes. Now imagine standing in the center within the soccer ball with each polygon shape in its patterning acting as a mirror. The 1st eye is like a sphere of reflecting mirrors. It is what gives us full circumference or full circle seeing – that we may *see* from all sides and in all directions. Standing within this magnificent mirrored spherical 1st eye, you are increasingly able to see that each mirror reflects its relationship to every other mirror. As you scan all around this sphere you are simultaneously able to:

1. Survey each mirror – seeing each individuated reflection, perspective and point of view it holds and
2. Glimpse the synthetic wholeness held in the full spherical sight of the entire moving geometry

When your awareness is poised within the Unbroken Omniscient consciousness of the Tehuti faculty – sphere 2, you are moving within 3rd Root Race consciousness and are able to behold in fullness – the whole moving geometry of the Divine Design. When poised within Unbroken Omniscient consciousness, our Ancestors were able to behold in fullness the Divine Design and were guided by this invisible inner patterning. The higher impress of Divine mind and ideation was at work within them. The way to arrange the affairs of life is revealed in order to manifest the Divinely intended archetypal design. They were able to intuit the design and to instantaneously *know* how the pieces fit. Thus, Divinity was made manifest in all that was constructed. They walked as Gods and Goddesses and Heaven and Earth were made one.

The latter Races would lose this innersightedness which is registered through the power of the 1st eye. Events would occur where man began to experience a 'brokeness in consciousness'.Man's consciousness gradually became more exteriorialy focused. His reality moved from:

1. Being one of inclusiveness, Spiritually and interiorly focused in the Spiritual World to
2. Becoming one of separativeness, exteriorly focused and materially driven by the outer World

He began to lose innersightedness and thus the ability to glimpse the Puzzle Box Cover of the grand design. In other words, he suffered a gradual loss of the whole or 'bigger picture'.

In his increasingly narrowing focus, he came to see separateness more and more among the puzzle pieces. He saw himself as separate from other created beings. Changes already abrew in the African/Black 3rd Root Race would be starkly registered during the later part of the Semitic 4th Root Race, where the balance would be tipped before their deepest registration within the Aryan/European 5th Root Race. The quality of consciousness would gradually shift from being Unitive to Separative. Not only would man lose sight of how to arrange or put back the puzzle pieces. Equally important, an increasing perception of separation between *all* entities would diminish the cohering, vitalizing power of *L-o-v-e* that holds all in unity and sees *all things as new.* In the cycles to come Might would win over Right.

Today we are working to restore our 1st eye in order to avert World catastrophe.

KaAbBa   Building The Lighted Temple
The Spiritual B(ARK)

As African Root Race man and woman you were like apprentices

Our story continues…

Movement within Ba consciousness

•In the Divine workshop of the mind of God.
•You were witness to the *Divinely intended archetypal* design
•Like a Puzzle Box Cover
•That was yet unbroken into its separate puzzle pieces
•Your 1st eye interior sightedness as – Ego enabled you to see and behold
•The whole moving Geometrical Arrangement
•You beheld, as well as vibrated with the Divine archetypal design and
•The Divine ideation called the Khus by the Kemetians
•With your consciousness in seamless Unity of the One
•You were at play with the *simultaneity* of *All-at-once-ness* and *One-at-a-time-ness*

•With your individualization in consciousness and gradual involutionary descent down the Tree of life
•You became the Manes, as called by the Kemetians, or the Son of Mind, as called by the Esotericists.
•Manes or mind is the specific building material and tools needed to play the seeming game of *Go Out*
•You acquire the use of mind, thought, and imagination –
•In your descent down the Tree of Life
•From a more Spiritual consciousness into a material consciousness
•You move from the subjective to the objective World-
•You are **Master** at the dual action of *Going Out – Yet – Remaining within*
•The unbroken, seamless unity of the One
•You became co-creative apprentice
•You set out to work to fashion a World you beheld but now must co-create
•Perched here in your awareness
•All you built in the material World reflected the Spiritual
•You affirm:
•I *Know*
•*And*
•*All This is That*

Movement within Ab consciousness

•Yet cycles pass and the descent in consciousness down the Tree of Life begins
•As the game of *Go Out* further ensues
•You take long, long, loving looks at the Puzzle Box Cover
•To see if you can re-member the pattern of re-construction in the Grand Design
•In the early AfricanSemitic Root Race consciousness cycle
•You are interiorly and Spiritually focused
•You express qualities of harmonizing, reconciling opposites, and holding the dualizing forces in nature (duality) in balance
•In your co-creative play you reference
•The Above with the *now sensed* Below and the DARK with the *now sensed* Light
•As you hold all in delicate balance you affirm:
• *I Know That I Know*
•And
•*This and That*

•Yet cycles continue to pass
•In the later AfricanSemitic Root Race cycles
•You are gradually *Outed* in consciousness deeper into the World of physicality and materiality
•Your *Going out* upon the limited thought of lower mind would last longer and longer
•You became less and less focused on your ages long, ritual practice which
• Kept the circle in consciousness unbroken
•As you became more and more preoccupied with the play-thing-ness of thought in your awakening Mental Soul body – Het-Heru – sphere 7, (Higher Abstract Mind) and Sebek - sphere 8, (Lower Concrete Mind)
•Each thought is connected with an emotion in your awakening emotional Soul body – Auset - sphere 9
•Which would register as sensation of pleasure or pain in your awakening physical Soul body – Geb – sphere 10
•The connection was made in your circuitry to desire pleasure and avoid pain
•And the will to assert the lower self for what it wanted *grew*
•You became more dualized in consciousness and
•Less willing to reconcile seeming opposites and find harmony and balance
•As you dualized in consciousness this registered in your brain matter
 •As you became more right brain hemisphere or left brain hemisphere focused
•You became less concerned about the bridging of 'This and That'
•And would now affirm:
• *This or That*

KaAbBa Building The Lighted Temple
The Spiritual B(ARK)

Movement within Ka (Ka-Ra-acter) consciousness

•And cycles continue to pass
•Knowing the Divine archetypal design gave you play with
•The seeming Puzzle pieces against
•The backdrop of the seamless Unity and cohering, loving power of the ONE
•You could think:
•Separativeness, Multiplicity, Particularization, Division, Diversity, and
• Analyze it all
•As your desire grew you 'hung out' more and more and longer and longer in the play-thing-ness of lower
  mind, emotion and bodily sensation
•Your awareness became more and more trapped in your lower mental, emotional and physical Soul bodies
•These three lower bodies that you had been constructing over eons of time
•Were *just* to be your equipment, the instrument for the
• Higher Soul to do its work in the World
•They were *just* to be used as your tools for Building the Lighted Temple
•For the glory of the God indwelling you and
•To radiate Heaven on Earth and
•To reflect the Unity in all the manifest diversity in God's creation which is The Self
•So that you could affirm:
•*I Know the One and the same Self in all the seeming self appearances*
• *Approximating Ka is/as Spirit Ka*
•*I Know the One in the Many*
•*KaAbBa - I have come full circle*

•When you are as Auset you are ceaseless in your devotion
•To gather all the seemingly broken (puzzle) pieces of your beloved husband Ausar
•Into the seamless unity of the One
•You are the clear crystalline and luminous surface upon which
•The One True Self is reflected
•You are the Lighted Temple

• *Instead*
•The descent into a de-Spiritualizing cycle down the Tree of Life
•Takes you *headlong* into a more dense, materialization of consciousness
•You became encased and entombed in these lower bodies
•That became more dense and materialized upon the physical plane
•You now dangle, like a *particle* from the Higher Spiritual realms
•Through *thinking* – you *thought* – your self into less and less
• You became a part-I-cularization in your own consciousness

•And identified as/with a lesser self, that small part that you could still see
•Now that your eye has been torn out and torn into pieces by Set
•Gradually through the involutionary cycle
•Your citizenship within the Higher realms became a distant memory
•No longer seeking the treasure house of the Soul in Seket-Aarnru
•Your Heavenly Abode among the Gods and Goddesses and Place of Peace – Hotep
• Forgetting the abode of God indwelling
•You thought a lot about this lesser self and you thought you were 'it'
•Your citizenship upon the physical Earthly plane and the
•Seeming acquisition of all therein
•Became the treasured goal

• In your game of *Go Out* - like any game –
•There came the enthusiastic, yet wanton and childlike breaking up of the puzzle pieces
•So it is in your later AfricanSemitcAryan Root Race consciousness cycle that you cry out, '*I
  can do it on my own, unaided, I need not reference or guide*'
•You are left to your own devices
•As the self is sensed more and more as separate from every other self
•You came to believe that you can *improve* upon God's design
•That you can take *some of the pieces* and *some of the laws* and put a thing called *Heaven on
  Earth* together
•Or was it Hell that you were intending as you fashioned
•Your own *designer and personalized World* creation
•And so it is with Man and Woman whose freedom it is to choose – *not to even* glimpse –
•The Puzzle Box Cover

•Who in blinded ignorance of the Divinely intended architectural design and
•Bereft of the cohering power of Love
•Boldly affirms:
•*This not That* and *That not This*
•Thus does mind become the *slayer of the Real* – The One True Self – Ausar
•Cut into fourteen pieces and cast apart

KaAbBa   Building The Lighted Temple
The Spiritual B(ARK)

Our story continues…

It is at first titillating to see the self as separate. It is a self that can take action, feel, think and use the will as power to acquire what it desires. Later, it becomes *frightful* to feel so 'seemingly' alone and isolated. How will you, 'Do it on your own' – that is, create Heaven on Earth? Or have we been creating our own Hell collectively as 3rd, 4th and 5th Root Race conscious humanity who is: 3-4-5 AfricanSemiticAryan Жonsciousness Admixture ASA/KA.

As the Aryan Root Race consciousness has prevailed within a downspiraling materialization cycle, our Puzzle Box Cover would be replaced by Public Broad-casting System of TV, Radio, and so called News. Instead of gaining our reference interiorly from the Puzzle Box Cover the (PBC) of the Great Architect of Creation, our reference comes from the Public Broad-casting System of TV media (PBS). Today, we get our Khus or Divine ideation that guides our actions from the Newstand. This is an exteriorization of an inner Spiritual process.

What images lurk on TV? Do we see images of wholeness here?

Let's dispell the word News:

#7. Oracle Metaphysical Dis-spelling Key: Look up definition (dictionary, glossary, reference texts, etc.)

Definition:

News- Information about recent events or happenings, especially as reported by newspapers, periodicals, radio, or television.

#11. Oracle Metaphysical Dis-spelling Key: What does the word sound like? Say the word out loud and then silently in a meditative state.

Derived Word List:

Nu, Nus – The waters of space. This is the Kemetic Neter and the infinite Spirit-Matter continuum from which creation arises.

#8. Oracle Metaphysical Dis-spelling Key: Meaning. See the relationship and oracle or story of the Neteru – Put word list together to tell a story.

Meaning:

News dispelled is Nus. The Ancients called the primal waters of space Nu (latent) and Nut (active). It is the unified field out of which all creation arises. To gain solutions to life's challenges, we must *go out in consciousness* equipped with the 'Nu' (s) or news. This is tapping into the *Source*. The Nu is called by various names which include: Energy-Matter, the Fount of All Possibility, and the Unified Field. When the impulse for our work in the World arises within the Fount of all Possibility, then all is made *Nu*.

It is in our separative consciousness that we bring the eye and ear to be *TV guided* by the PBS – the Public Broad-casting System. It is out of the news that we look for guidance on how to create the World. This is turning on the media or me-dia (L) to get a glimpse at how to build in accord with 'self' interest. Instead, we should attune to the PBC – Puzzle Box

Cover of Tehuti to see how All coheres in loving unity. We keep channel surfing trying to bring a 'fuller picture' to the eye and ear. Yet every channel is full of violence which assaults the mind and Spirit. Don't look here for your Image and Likeness of God. You will not find it here. The Hollywood Stars bring you no comfort or solace. There is nothing 'Holy' in Hollywood. It is a tree whose wood is dry, brittle and lifeless. It is bereft of the fires of Ra. The so called Stars are perpetrators of the Divine symbol of advanced initiation which is the Heru Amsu. The Me-dia(l) contributes to our brokeness in consciousness. The Me-dia(l) and the Stars who delight at shooting and blowing things up must get on board in helping in the reconstruction process. They have literally become 'shooting Stars' as each channel flashes gunbarrel after gunbarrel.

It is evident that in order to develop the tools for Psychological and Spiritual transformational practices we must develop a New vocabulary with Neteru that are exacting to what is intended. Towards this effort I offer the word *Nu-stand-ing* which will be used in this text. You gain Nu-standing by attuning to your inner Spiritual equipment. If we dispell the word 'attune' we see Nu and Nut within this word.

The mirror reflection of the word 'Nu' is the word 'UN' which is the acronym for the United Nations. In *principle*, this is a global body out of which humanity tries to draw forth:
• The most enlightened men and women who express
• The livingness of the highest ideation which reveals
• The interconnection and underlying unity within the Divine architectural design and plan

It is out of this local Planetary group of Nations – called the UN – that a reflection of the Nu may be glimpsed as - *'All things are made brand new'* -.

Let's dispell the word Nation:

 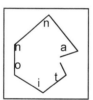

Derived Word List:
Anoint
At-On(e) – 'E' is the 'I' that has been made *wise*. It is the eye that arises as the serpent on the forehead called the Uraei by the Kemetians. It is how three eyes become the One All seeing eye which is:

#8. Oracle Metaphysical Dis-spelling Key: Meaning. See the relationship and oracle or story of the Neteru – Put word list together to tell a story.
Meaning: To Anoint is to make sacred or blest, to bring back into a state of purity.

KaAbBa   Building The Lighted Temple
The Spiritual B(ARK)

One of the many levels of At-One-ing is to align with the Divine intelligence of the Lord of the World, who is personified as our Planetary God – Ausar. Planetary Ausar Ba is our 'local' center of consciousness, reflecting the Supreme Intelligence of Universal Ba. This is further explained later.

We return to an earlier quote:

> …King Unas stood at the head of the Khu, i.e., he was the chief of all the Khu; and when the souls of the gods transferred themselves from their own spirit-bodies to Unas, their Khu were before Unas. The god received the king as a brother and placed him among the "imperishable Khu"…the Khu were beings of light, comparable to the stars, and the evidence of other passages supports this view, and indicates that the Khu of a man was the intangible, ethereal, transparent portion of his immaterial economy to which modern nations have given the name of "spirit".

We return to an earlier

> **Metaphysical Key To:**
> The Law of Correspondence
> "As above, so below; as below, so above."

• Just as King Unas (as Nu) stands as head or chief of all the Khus who stand in Heaven
• So too do those Sons and Daughters drawn from every Nation/Anoint-ing, who have become Godlike
• Come forth to stand before the Council General of the UN and
• Together they work as a 1st eye that sees within the Mind of God and intuits
• How the pieces/Peace come together to prevail on Earth

Fortunately, even with man's later destructiveness, the Earth itself is belching up the Neteru in signs and symbols that are revealing the things of this World. It is through their oracle that we have a way to dispell and reconstruct our way back – *HOME.* The Neteru will not be silenced. According to: *Rosicrucian Cosmo-Conception,* p. 283-284.

> Their [the Lemurian- African] consciousness was directed inward. They perceived physical things in a spiritual way, as we perceive them in a dream-at which time all that we see is within ourselves. When "their eyes were opened" and their consciousness was directed outward towards the facts of the physical world, conditions were altered.

Conditions have certainly been altered!

The Ausarianization of Consciousness Series 1
Metaphysical Keys To the Tree of Life & Oracle Keys to Dis-spelling Illusion
The Spiritual Journey in Unfolding Consciousness

172

Chapter 13
What's The Matter With Our Lives?

What's the matter with our lives is our density, coarseness, and lower vibration. You will overcome your descent into matter and begin your re-ascent into Spirit by clearing up the matter(s) within your own vehicles. In Ausarian Spiritual Transformation and Resurrection you are striving to be resurrected in Ausarian Consciousness – ASTR. Within this acronym is another which is AST. AST is the another name for Auset. Ast and Ausar are synonymous with Ka and Ba. Likewise, Ast and Ausar and Ka and Ba are inseparable. ASTR is doing the work to raise your vibration by transmuting (changing) the sub-stance of your vehicles from a more dense, coarse material nature which has a lower vibration, into a more refined and luminous solar substance of a higher vibration. When someone is told that they have a Ka-Ra-acter or Ka-erecter that 'stinks' or is 'lousy' they are being told that they are reflecting a more 'materialized' Ka-Ra-acter which falls short in its approximation to the in-Spiriting Ka, the true Image and Likeness of God in which we are made. As the Disciple moves through the Halls of Amenta he or she beseeches the Gods that his/her name is not made to 'stink'. This is expressed accordingly: E.A. Wallis Budge. *The Prt Em Hru. (The Egyptian Book Of The Dead)*, p. 258, Chapter xxxb.

> Ausar, the scribe Ani, saith: "My heart my mother, my heart my mother, my heart my coming into being! May there be nothing to resist me at [my] judgment; may there be no opposition to me from the Tchatcha. May there be no parting of thee from me in the presence of him who keepeth the scales! **Thou art my Ka within my body [which] knitteth** and stengtheneth my limbs. Mayest thou come forth to the place of happiness to which I am advancing. **May the Shenit not cause my name to stink**, and may no lies be spoken against me in the presence of the god. Good is it for thee to hear.

Let's dispell the word Shenit:
 # 1. Oracle Metaphysical Dis-spelling Key:
Put letters of word or words together in a circle, like a serpent putting its tail in its mouth. Coming full Circle.
#2. Oracle Metaphysical Dis-spelling Key: Read letters, putting together words, going forwards, backwards and in zig-zag patterns.
#3. Oracle Metaphysical Dis-spelling Key: You may crossover in order to use a letter more than once. Place re-used letter in parenthesis ( ).
#4. Oracle Metaphysical Dis-spelling Key: You may add a letter to complete a word. Place added letter in parenthesis ( ).
#5. Oracle Metaphysical Dis-spelling Key: Letter substitution-you may substitute a letter. Place substituted letter in parenthesis ( ).
#6. Oracle Metaphysical Dis-spelling Key: Make a list of derived words. Try to make the longest continuous unbroken word or string of words.

#7. Oracle Metaphysical Dis-spelling Key: Look up definition (dictionary, glossary, reference texts, etc.)

#8. Oracle Metaphysical Dis-spelling Key: Meaning. See the relationship and oracle or story of the Neteru – Put word list together to tell a story.

 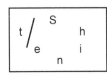

Derived word list:

Shenit -.

> **Definition:**
>
> Shenit –
>
> A class of Divine beings. E. A. Wallis Budge. *Prt Em Hru. (The Egyptian Book of The Dead)*, p. 258. May the Shenit, who make men to stand fast… Ibid. p. 309
>
> Special ministers to the king, officials of the Court of Ausar. (*Osiris and the Egyptian Resurrection,* V.1), p. 333.

Shine

Neshi –

> **Definition:** Wallis Budge. *An Egyptian Hieroglyphic Dictionary. V. II.* P. 386
>
> Neshi – He of the Sudan. Negro.

Meaning: The Neshi (Negro) are the shining ones, the shining stars. See *ACTS 2*.

Let's dispell the word lousy:

#11. Oracle Metaphysical Dis-spelling Key: What does the word sound like? Say the word out loud and then silently in a meditative state.

Sounds Like:

Low see (low seeing)

Lousy –

> **Definition:** infested with lice. 2. Extremely contemptible; nasty; 3. Very painful or unpleasant; 4. Inferior or worthless

Louse –

> **Definition:** Any of numerous small flat-bodies, wingless biting or sucking insects of the orders Mallophaga or anoplura, many of which are external parasites on various animals, including human beings. 2. A mean or despicable person..

Meaning: - Not seeing the higher aspects of our Spiritual nature can make us extremely contemptible. It is how we make the Heru within blind by tearing our eye into pieces. Ultimately, the approximating Ka or Ka-erect-er will become the Lighted Temple, the luminous reflection of the Image and Likeness of God.

Let's dispell the word stink:

Derived Word List:

Skin – As in, 'the skin we are in'.

Knits, knit, K(a) nit

Definition:

To make a fabric or garment by intertwining yard or thread in a series of connected loops either by hand with knitting needles or on a machine. 2.To become securely joined or mended together closely.

Nits, nit,

Definition:

Nit 1 – The egg or young of a parasitic insect, such as a louse.

Nit 2 – A unit of illuminative brightness equal to one candle per square meter, measured perpendicular to the rays of the source. [From Latin *nitor,* brightness, from *nitere*, to shine.] Please take note here of the Latin word *Nitere* and how this word dispelled reveals the word Neteri, Neter.

Nit, or Neith

Definition: E.A. Wallis Budge. *The Gods of the Egyptians, V.I,* p. 462.

Nit, or Neith is considered a 'Great Mother' and is synonymous with the Neteru Auset, Het-Heru and Nun. She is pictured with a bow, 2 arrows, a shield, a sceptre and a shuttel which are her tools. Her name means to 'to knit or weave.' She is associated with: the power of protection, the power to conceive and bring forth the new Sun god daily, the feast of Lamps, and the power of the eye of Heru. Accordingly:

> … and an ancient legend declared that she arrayed Ausar in the apparel which had been specially woven for him by the two rekhti goddesses, i.e., Auset and Nephtys. And because of the part which she had taken in arraying Ausar in his graveclothes Net, Nit was made to preside over the "good house," i.e., the chamber in which the dead were embalmed and swathed in linen, and over the chambers of the temples in which the unguents which were employed in public worship were compounded. **The unguents which she mixed for Ausar proved to be the means by which the body of the god was preserved from destruction and made young again,** and happy were the dead who were able to secure the ministrations of Net, Nit.

Meaning:

On a higher turn of the spiral, you are K(a) – Nit-ing together the garment of God. These Lighted 'Nits' are the many *sightings* of the 'self' now *seamlessly strung together* and realized as the *One*

KaAbBa   Building The Lighted Temple
The Spiritual B(ARK)

and Only SELF. On a lower turn of the spiral these are the 'nits' that we become encapsulated
and strangulated within as we see and falsely identify *self (and others)* as separate. This can leave us bereft of the fire, life and blood of Ra, and relying on the blood of others. As we Build The Lighted Temple, we chose whether we radiate Light or louse. The Kemetic Goddess/Neter Nit (K-nit)/Auset weaves the threads of

Light which are the garment of God. The cohering power of her love holds the garment together and her unguents make it 'sweet smelling' lest it fall apart, decay, be full of darkness, become extremely offensive and 'stink'. This brings us to our next

---

Metaphysical Key to:
Ausarian Spiritual Transformation & Resurrection ASTR

You may recount the words in the Disney movie which are: *'Mirror, mirror on the wall am I the fairest of them all?* Here the question reflects the concern with the outer physical body. The question instead should be: ***'Mirror, Mirror on the wall am I nearest to the All?'*** This brings us to the next

---

Metaphysical Key To:
The 7 Ka-resting Steps/Stairs/Arits to become ASTR or a STAR
The 7 Christ-ing Steps

As a self-reflective consciousness, Ego, Soul or Manes you can *choose* not to see right

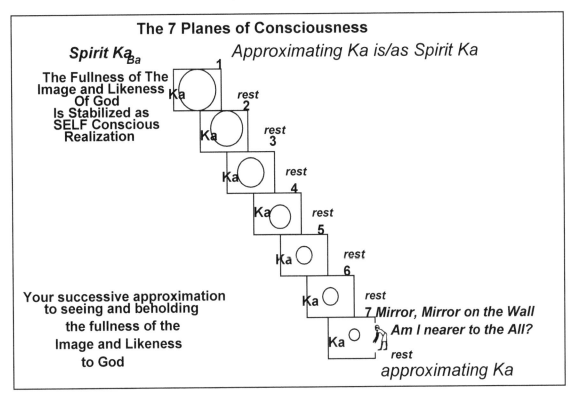

The Ausarianization of Consciousness Series 1
Metaphysical Keys To the Tree of Life & Oracle Keys to Dis-spelling Illusion
The Spiritual Journey in Unfolding Consciousness

176

relationship between Spirit and matter as a Christ/Karest Son or Daughter sees. You may see very materially. This is your choice. You may see an unspiritualized World; this is your view as long as your sight is exteriorly focused. As you climb the ladder of Life, which is the Tree of Life in your re-ascent, you must ask the same question upon each of the 7 stairs or Arits. *'Mirror, Mirror on the wall am I nearest to the All'?*

As you begin at the most material step, which is 7, you look in the mirror with a consciousness that sees your approximating Ka – what you have attained up to now. The Approximating Ka is your successive approximation to seeing and beholding the fullness of the Image and Likeness of God that you already are and have always been – but have properly forgotten. At each of the 7 Steps or 7 planes of consciousness your approximating Ka must come to reflect the Spirit Ka in greater fullness in order to pass on to the next step. This is Initiation. Ka is imaged at every step along the way. Each step is a Ka-Rest – a step upon which Ka finds rest.

There is a Ka-rest-ing or Christing at each of the 7 steps or stages of initiation. It is the successive Ka-rest-ing of consciousness that leads to Ausarian Resurrection. What is imaged is to see Mother-Father *KaBA* as inseparable. You are the Son/Daughter trying to see in full consciousness the Self as both Spirit-Matter, Mother-Father in harmony and balance. The full Self Conscious measure of this relationship is – Ausar Ba. Because we occupy both physical body and Spiritual body, Ka reminds the Manes of its One True Face throughout its long pilgrimage in form. This brings us to the next

---

Metaphysical Key To:
The 7 Stages of Initiations

These are listed below: Further explanation is given in *ACTS*. These are listed and briefly described as follows:

The 7 Stages of Initiations

Degree to:	Stage	Initiate is attaining/has attained
▲7th Degree Initiation	Resurrection	
▲6th Degree initiation	Decision	
▲5th Degree Initiation	Revelation	
▲4th Degree Initiation	Renunciation/ Crucifixion	Mastery over At-Onement with Souls (All Souls are One)
▲3rd Degree Initiation	Transfiguration	Mastery of the Mental Body
▲2nd Degree Initiation-	Baptism	Mastery of the Emotional Body
▲1st Degree Initiation	Birth	Mastery of the Physical Body

KaAbBa   Building The Lighted Temple
The Spiritual B(ARK)

> **Metaphysical Key To:**
> The Overlay of
>   The 7 Stages of Initiations

Refer to the *Big Map* on p. 111 of this text to see the 7 Initiations revealed in the Tree of Life.

The Kemetic Spiritual system[*] was predicated upon a total of 7 Souls or bodies with each growing successively more refined and Spiritualized. Each rung in consciousness upon the ladder or steps of re-ascent corresponds with 1 of the 7 Soul divisions as indicated in the diagram at right:

Each of these 7 Ka-rest-ing or stations likewise corresponds to the 7 Ka-Ra-acters or 7 personalities. This brings us to the next

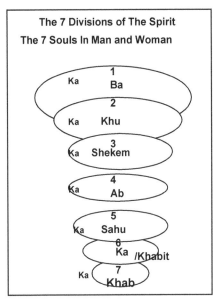

> **Metaphysical Key To:**
> The 7 Ka-Ra-acter Types

This are listed as:
1. KaBa
2. KaKhu
3. KaSekhem
4. KaAb
5. KaSahu
6. KaKhaibit
7. KaKhab

We again see the movement of Ka along the Spirit-Matter continuum. This continuum reveals that which is both *Spiritual and Material* or *Divine and Human* within the constitution of Man and Woman. We refer now to a previous quote where this is expressed accordingly: E. A. Budge, *The Prt Em Hru (Egyptian Book Of The Dead)*, p.lxi.

> And in addition to the natural and spiritual bodies, man also had an abstract individuality or **personality** endowed with all his **characteristic** attributes. This abstract personality had an absolutely independent existence. It could move freely from place to place, separating itself from, or uniting itself to, the body at will, and also enjoying life with the gods in heaven. This was the Ka, …The Ka dwelt in the man's statue just as the Ka of a god inhabited the statue of the god.

---

[*] **Understanding Your 14 - Fold Kemetic Energy Makeup** is included in **Appendix A** of this book.

The Spiritual body in which the dead is said to first arise is the Sahu Soul body. The Ka accompanies man and woman at each Soul stationing in which the consciousness is focused. This is expressed in the following accordingly: Alvin Boyd Kuhn. *The Lost Light,* p. 577.

> The Ka always accompanies the soul through its incarnations and returns. Thou hast come and thy Ka with thee" is the welcome greeting on the soul's return. The Manes passes from the state of a shade to that of a Ka when he is said to have completed his investiture. Then as a Sahu he is reincorporated in a spiritual body, and as a Khu he is invested with the robe of light and glory. No healthy child was believed to be born without this Ka, the soul of animate life; and in their pictures of it they made it resemble the physical body. They looked upon it as the "double" of the body. It did not die with the body.

You can see from this passage that the Spirit Ka accompanies you through your many incarnations but is Itself beyond encapsulation in the physical body. You continue to be reborn upon the wheel of birth and death until your ultimate rebirth in the first Soul body that transcends the grave and does not die – the Sahu Soul body. We have no life beyond the grave until we become Ab and Ba Soul conscious. Ka returns to whatever Soul body it is last stationed within. For example: At death if you are *Ka-rest-ed* in your Khab Soul body, which is 'upon' the 1st step of re-ascent up the Tree of Life, then Spirit Ka returns to finish the work of raising your consciousness to the Ka/Khaibit Soul Body, which is 'upon' the 2nd step of re-ascent and so on up the Stairs of re-ascent.

Through many incarnations over eons of time; the 'substance' which has built the Temple (3rd aspect triangle) and reflects the less than or distorted image of Ka is transmuted from a lower, coarse vibration of elemental or Lunar-moon material, into a higher Spiritual vibration of Solar or light essence (2nd and 1st aspect triangle). This is the raising of matter 'back into' Spirit. Thus Ka and Ba are At-Oned. You build your Spiritual Ark or Lighted Temple out of the 'substance' within your being. The Lighted Temple is realized through the hard won efforts of the disciple or pilgrim on the path trying to make her/his way 'Home'. This is expressed accordingly: *Ancient Egypt The Light of the World, V.I,* p. 488.

> In the vignettes to chapter 25 of the Ritual (Naville, Todt. Kap. Ed, vol I, p. 36) the deceased is shown his Ka, which is with him in the passage of Amenta, not left behind him in the tomb, that he may not forget himself (as we might say), or, as he says, that he may not suffer, loss of identity by forgetting his name. Showing the Ka to him enables the Manes to recall his name in the great house, and especially in the crucible of the house of flame. When the deceased is far advanced on his journey through Amenta, his Ka is still accompanying him, and it is described as being the food of his life in spirit world, even as it had been his spiritual food in the human life. "Thou art come, Osiris; thy Ka is with thee".

> The deceased in the Ritual is seen ascending the mount with the supporting rod or staff in his hand the Psalmist says, "He restoreth my soul", the speaker in the Ritual says rejoicingly, "My soul is with me". This in Egyptian is the Ka that was ultimately attained in the garden of peace. The Ka is the final form of the soul restored to the departed when they are

KaAbBa Building The Lighted Temple
The Spiritual B(ARK)

perfected in the assembly or, congregation on the mount. The speaker in Hetep says, "There is given to me the abundance which belongeth to the Ka and to the glorified.

Let's take for closer examination the words, 'the Ka is the final form of the Soul restored to the departed when they are perfected in the assembly or, congregation on the mount'. These words again reinforce that: it is Ka as Spirit in the beginningless beginning and Ka as Spirit in the endless ending. This brings us to the next

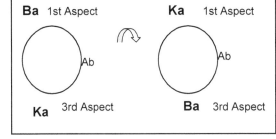

Metaphysical Key To:
The 3rd aspect re-becomes the
1st aspect

We see in the diagram at right that:
1. As God's will is made manifest it is reflected in Mother-Matter.
2. The approximating Ka now reflects in fullness the Spiritual Ka.
3. The 3rd aspect becomes the 1st aspect and the 1st aspect becomes the 3rd as the creative process *comes full circle.*
4. As Ka 'transcends' Ba it takes on a 1st aspect function of initiating the new, like the initiating breath of Ba.
5. During this incarnation, by the nature of how your Ka is qualified and Ka-Ra-acterized, it attracts the form- substance for your next body of manifestation.
6. By your ID Ka-rd, you stand in line and receive the sub-stance for the building of your future bodies of manifestation.
7. As you can see, you begin where you left off in building your Lighted Temple.
8. The word Ka is revealed within the word Karma. Through Ka-erect-er and Ka-Ra-acter we reap what we sew lifetime after lifetime.

If we dispell the word 'sew' we see that it reveals the word 'saw'. We reap what we last saw in the last lifetime and we sew a garment that reflects what we saw. It is quite a sew-saw journey getting this thing of unfolding consciousness just right, before the Scales of Maat. This is expressed accordingly: Alvin Boyd Kuhn. *The Lost Light,* p. 550-1.

He is no longer bound to the Khab [read here: dense physical body] at the gate of Amenta. Clad in bright new vesture, his Easter morning finery, he prepares to take passage on board the boat of the sun. "Behold me," he exclaims; "I have come to you and have carried off and put together my form." Perfected in his unified septenary nature he is ready to ascend to the Father in his original glory. For he has prayed that the Father may give unto him that glory which he had with him from the creation of the world. He has been told that he may behold his Ka. This was that soul that came forth from the hand of God at the beginning of his individual career, was in attendance on him all life through as a genius or daemon, and reabsorbed the lower personality to itself at the dissolution of the various elements. When honors were paid to a Pharaoh, offerings were made to his Ka, not to his mortal self, which could not be permanent.

Let's take for closer examination the words, 'He has been told that he may behold his Ka. This was that soul that came forth from the hand of God at the beginning...' These words are near and dear to my heart. They reveal that:

1. Ka is Spirit from the beginning even as it becomes immersed and expresses itself as an approximating Ka – in-form/matter.
2. We see that the 3rd aspect Neter Auset is the 1st aspect, the Divine Mother from which all creation arises. She is the Waters of Space, the Nu and she is at the beginning.

We now return to an earlier diagram:

Moving from left to right in the diagrams below, we see man and woman expressing as an individualized consciousness which knows itself as God in form on its own plane of manifestation. In the diagram at right, we now see man/woman as an entity (or entification) with a vertical line drawn through it symbolizing the spinal column. This is the Kemetic djed, tet or the backbone in man and woman. It is along the spine that the Divine fire of Ra makes its vertical ascent back to its source as Absolute, Pure Spirit. The dynamic movement of Ka along the djed symbolizes the Ka-erect-ing function at work within your Spiritual equipment. To be spineless is to lack Ka-erect-er or character.

The Ka returns to the Soul to continue its work of assisting man and woman towards full Self Conscious Realization. In our return we become freer from our long series of encapsulations as lesser self-identifications. In this diagram we may further see that:

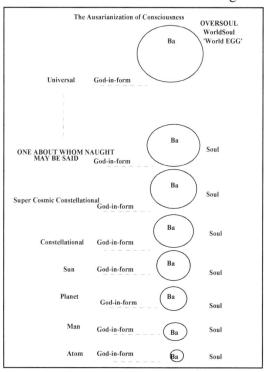

Ka is like the full computer program of the Divine Image and Likeness of God that can be reflected at any level of Ba.

1. Ka-Ra-acter or Character is how we reach Ra by continuing to erect the Image and Likeness of God. Thus, according to how we live our life we are a Ka-erect-er.
2. Your ASTR meditation practice and use of words of power called Hekau by the Kemetian and mantras in Eastern traditions are invocations raising the fire of Ra and aiding your re-ascent.

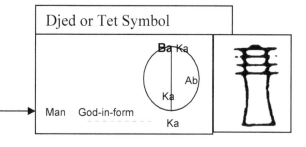

KaAbBa   Building The Lighted Temple
The Spiritual B(ARK)

These concepts are conveyed to us through the Ancient wisdom teachings and are symbolically expressed and pictured in the scene at right accordingly: E. A. Wallis Budge. *Prt Em Hru. (Egyptian Book of the Dead), Papyrus of Hunefer.* P. 280.

In this scene we see the Great Cat who is emblematic of the Sun or Ra himself. The Cat lived
near the Persea tree in Heliopolis. We also see the serpent of darkness Apepi who is emblematic of the enemies of Ra. Here the Cat is cutting off the head of the serpent of darkness which is symbolic of the triumph of Law, Order and Goodness over Chaos, wrong and Evil. (See also Budge. *Amulets and Superstitions*, p. 145).

Let's dispell the word Cat:
#10. Oracle Metaphysical Dis-spelling Key: Letter replacement. Here we have replaced the 'k' which had been substituted by the letter 'c.'
<u>Derived Word List:</u>
<u>Kat</u>

#8. Oracle Metaphysical Dis-spelling Key: Meaning. See the relationship and oracle or story of the Neteru – Put word list together to tell a story.
<u>Meaning:</u>
The Ancient wisdom teaches that the cat or the ka-t was sacred to Auset. This word contains the word Ka with the letter or neter 'T' added on. The letter 'T' is made of the horizontal crossbar which is matter, and the vertical axis, which is Spirit. It is the symbol of the creative process in which we see both: (a) the female genitalia or ovaries represented by the crossbar and (b) the male genitalia or penis represented by the vertical axis. The 'T' is the 20th letter in the alphabet and these two digits (2 + 0) sum to the number 2 – symbolizing duality or the dual forces – masculine/feminine – at work in the creative process.

Let's dispell the word Persea:

<u>Derived Word List:</u>
<u>Reaps</u>

Let's dispell the word Apepi:
#11. Oracle Metaphysical Dis-spelling Key: What does the word sound like? Say the word out loud and then silently in a meditative state.
<u>Sounds Like:</u>
<u>A pe(e)p</u>

The Ausarianization of Consciousness Series 1
Metaphysical Keys To the Tree of Life & Oracle Keys to Dis-spelling Illusion
The Spiritual Journey in Unfolding Consciousness

182

#7. Oracle Metaphysical Dis-spelling Key: Look up definition (dictionary, glossary, reference texts, etc.)

Definition:

Peep – A slight sound or utterance. To peek furtively; steal a quick; To peer through a small aperture or from behind something.

Meaning:

The encircling serpent is our current space/time bound encapsulation in which we 'come full circle' and 'reap' of the Tree of Life. We recognize that what we beheld is but 'A Peep' of who we are. We are ready now to expand passed our 'ring pass not' of limited self identification into the next greater expanse of Self conscious Identity. We undergo the symbolic 'cutting' action by the Ka-T which releases our 'growing eye's' hold upon yet another now seen, approximating Ka. Thus we learn to behold the myriad manifestations without becoming enamored by these temporary form appearances. We recognize that *'ever in back of these form appearances'*, the Image and Likeness of/as the *same* God is seen manifesting. The Spirit Ka, is remembered. How fully we see with the eye of Heru determines Ausar Ba consciousness, the One True Self Identification. When we, 'Let the Ka-t out of the Ba-g', we know the secret which is that the mini 'g'(od) we saw as the self was part of an even greater 'G'(od). Let Ka out of Ba and know the mystery of the SELF.

Chapter 14
The Transmigration Of The Soul

In the transmigration of the Soul we have had many incarnations upon the wheel of birth and death. Within each we have been gaining mastery in working with the laws of Maat. Maat must be held in delicate balance with its opposite sphere 5 – Herukhuti. Imagine the might required to assert yourself to your fullest potential, vibrating and manifesting the total sound of the grand archetypal design of your being. Herukhuti is the admonition to Live – Maat is the admonition to Let live. The delicate balance must be maintained between War and Peace, Might and Right, Mars and Jupiter, self-centeredness and Altruism, selfishness and Benevolence. This brings us to the next

> **Metaphysical Key To:**
> Transmigration of the Soul
> The Law of Rebirth
> Death, Birth, Transformation

There is no death. There is only the transmigration of the Soul from life into greater Life. Death is the seeming discontinuity of consciousness – a cutting into pieces of the ALL Consciousness – Ausar. At each 'death' the disciple appears again and again within the Hall of Amenta, that his heart may be weighed and thereby tested. Each time his heart has fallen short of being as light as the feather of Maat, he has to mount again the wheel of birth and death and fall back into the material realm.

•Your Soul seeks circumstance again and again upon the wheel of birth
•Until you appear before the scale and at last the scale is held in balance
•With the scale now balanced the arrow on the scale is straight
• Neither tipping left nor right
•Like St. Paul the 'scales' are falling from in front of your eyes
•As turn upon turn of the wheel you stand before
•Scale after scale until your sight is fully restored
•This is the restoration of the eye of Heru within the Ancient Egyptian Mystery System

As you undergo the Initiatory process, higher states of consciousness are achieved – until the state of God Conscious is the Realization. This cycle repeats itself until you, the disciple, finally stand within the Hall of Amenta and are *found Maa Kheru*. Thus, you are justified as living in truth, morally and in total equilibrium with the laws of God.

The Ausarianization of Consciousness Series 1   184
Metaphysical Keys To the Tree of Life & Oracle Keys to Dis-spelling Illusion
The Spiritual Journey in Unfolding Consciousness

Further Defining – What is the Sahu Body?

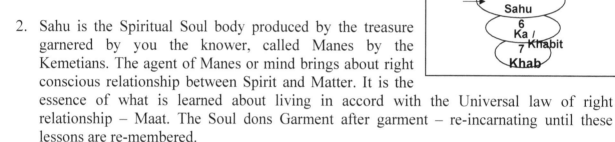

1. A well coordinated Ka-erect-er/Temple may not be guided and infused by the Ab and Ba Soul. We must seek to understand how the Ka-erect-er/Temple becomes the luminous Temple. This lighted vehicle is evolved through the process of Ab Soul and Ba Soul infusion. You are learning to re-polarize your consciousness in the higher Ab Soul and Ba Soul while disciplining and directing awareness within the lower physical, emotional and mental Soul vehicles. The resultant Lighted body or Soul body is called the Sahu. As Ka-erect-er is becoming infused with Ab and Ba through stages of initiatory development, the Sahu or Soul body is developed. Thus do you have a Lighted Temple as an instrument of service to the higher Ab and Ba Souls.

    The 7 Divisions of The Spirit
    The 7 Souls In Man and Woman
    1 Ba
    2 Khu
    3 Sekhem
    4 Ab
    5 Sahu
    6 Ka /
    7 Khabit
    Khab

2. Sahu is the Spiritual Soul body produced by the treasure garnered by you the knower, called Manes by the Kemetians. The agent of Manes or mind brings about right conscious relationship between Spirit and Matter. It is the essence of what is learned about living in accord with the Universal law of right relationship – Maat. The Soul dons Garment after garment – re-incarnating until these lessons are re-membered.

3. When Manes or mind does not reflect right relationship between Spirit and matter then man and woman are born into a new cycle and physical body to continue their quest.

4. In the quarries of life we are fashioning a fit instrument that reflects our Divinity and allows us to be of greater service on Earth. The Sahu body is the Glorious body of Light to the Kemetians. This is known as the Causal or the Egoic body in Esoteric Psychology.

Let's dispell the word Causal:
 # 1. Oracle Metaphysical Dis-spelling Key: Put letters of word or words together in a circle, like a serpent putting its tail in its mouth. Coming full Circle.
#2. Oracle Metaphysical Dis-spelling Key: Read letters, putting together words, going forwards, backwards and in zig-zag patterns.
#3. Oracle Metaphysical Dis-spelling Key: You may crossover in order to use a letter more than once. Place re-used letter in parenthesis ( ).
#4. Oracle Metaphysical Dis-spelling Key: You may add a letter to complete a word. Place added letter in parenthesis ( ).
#5. Oracle Metaphysical Dis-spelling Key: Letter substitution-you may substitute a letter. Place substituted letter in parenthesis ( ).

KaAbBa Building The Lighted Temple
The Spiritual B(ARK)

#6. Oracle Metaphysical Dis-spelling Key: Make a list of derived words. Try to make the longest continuous unbroken word or string of words.
#7. Oracle Metaphysical Dis-spelling Key: Look up definition (dictionary, glossary, reference texts, etc.)
#10. Oracle Metaphysical Dis-spelling Key: Letter replacement. Here we have replaced the 'k' which had been substituted by the letter 'c.' (or c replaces k)

This brings us to a new Oracle Metaphysical Dis-spelling Keys:
 # 13. Oracle Metaphysical Dis-spelling Key: You may abrade a letter so that it is changed to another letter as in 'h' to 'n'. Notice the loping off of the top of the 'h' to make 'n'.

> **Definition:** Dictionary
>
> Abrade – 1. To wear down or rub away by friction; erode. See synonyms at chafe. 2. To make weary through constant irritation; wear down spiritually. (Latin abradere, to scrape of: ab-, away);

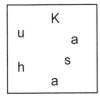 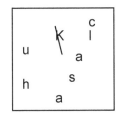

Derived Word List:

Causal –
> **Definition:**
> 1.a. The producer of an effect, result, or consequence. B. The one, such as a person, an event, or a condition, that is responsible for an action or a result. 3. A goal or principle served with dedication and zeal: 4. The interests of a person or group engaged in a struggle: 5. Law.

Cause –
> **Definition:**
> Of, involving, or constituting a cause.

#8. Metaphysical Dis-spelling Key: Meaning. See the relationship and oracle or story of the Neteru – Put word list together to tell a story.
Meaning
Here we see that the so called Esoteric 'Causal Body' is the Kemetic 'Ka Sahu' Soul body. The 'K' has been abraided into an 'l' and 'C'. Even though the spelling has been changed you can still *hear* 'ka sahu(l)' when you sound this word out and meditate upon it. The word *Cause* and Causal are derivatives of this word. When you stand more within the Ka Sahu or Causal Soul body you operate from the realm of cause, above reactivity and fluctuating circumstances.

5. The Sahu Soul body in the diagram on the previous page is pictured on the 5ᵗʰ plane of consciousness. The Sahu is the Soul body through which you may know transcendence and life beyond the grave. The Sahu body is like an *out pocketing* body in which the garnered treasure of each lifetime is stored. Thus the 'essence' of conscious life in form is garnered and stored here. It is not necessarily all the details of a lifetime, but what has been extracted and learned about right living in accord with the Universal law of right relationship – Maat. If the Sahu body 'contains' enough garnered treasure, one then passes onto the next expanse in consciousness – the Ab Soul, and is no longer constricted in the outer dense lower bodies of the physical, emotional and mental realms but may come and go between the physical and Spiritual realms. The treasure spoken of here is not the lower spiral of the Astrological sign Taurus the Bull, which is about Earthly accumulation and material possession, but it is the higher aspect of the sign of the Bull which is the eye of illumination and wisdom. It is Biblically your, 'treasure laid up in heaven beyond corrosion and theft'.

6. Sa-hu is the work of blending wisdom and fire. It is the fire of higher mind that is burnishing the Gem that is central in the lotus flower of the Ab Soul. The Sahu body is the body of Light in which man arises to live and take form again after he appeared dead in the grave. This is expressed accordingly: Gerald Massey. *Ancient Egypt The Light of the World, V.I,* p. 319.

> …The constellation of Horus [read here: Heru] as Orion was the ship of the Sahu, and ark of salvation configurated in the celestial waters as a boat that saved the souls from an eternal shipwreck. This was the sign of spiritual resurrection for the completed Manes. In another text the speaker prays that his soul may shine as a Sahu in the stars of Orion or Heru. It is said of Heru in the 'hymn to Osiris [read here: Ausar] the whole earth glorifies him, when his holiness proceeds (on the vault of the sky) "he is a Sahu illustrious amongst the Sahus", that is among the spirits glorified. The Sahu is a glorified form in which the soul of the deceased is re-incorporated for the life hereafter; this was represented by Orion the conqueror of death and darkness in the phase of eschatology.

This quote contains the ingredients necessary for Building the Lighted Temple – the Spiritual B-ARK. *It is your own Spiritual B-Ark that must rise, stay afloat and meet the great Spiritual Tides in the Perfect Storm.*

And Likewise: Ibid. p. 479.

> When the mortal entered Amenta, it was in the likeness of Ausar, who had been bodily dismembered in his death, and who had to be reconstituted to rise again as the spirit that never died. The mortal on earth was made up of seven constituent parts. The Ausar in Amenta had seven souls, which were collected, put together, and unified to become the ever-living one. The deceased in the image of the Ba soul asks that he may be given his new heart to rest in him Rit. Ch. 26). He becomes a sahu, or glorified body (ch. 47). He pleads that the way may be made for his soul, his khu (glory), his shade, and his ka (chs. 91 and 92). These

KaAbBa Building The Lighted Temple
The Spiritual B(ARK)

have to be united in the likeness of the typical Divine soul which was personalized as Heru the son of Ra, in whose image the spirits of the just made perfect finally became the children of God. When the deceased enumerates his souls, he is a manes in Amenta…

Ibid. p. 781.

He is now invested with the glory of the father…As a mystery of Amenta this investiture took place when the deceased became a Sahu and put on the Divine vesture of a spiritual body, or the soul of Heru. The Sahu signifies the invested, and it is identical with the Karest or the Christ, the risen Amsu-Heru.

Let's dispell the word investiture:

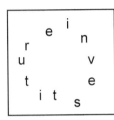 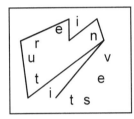 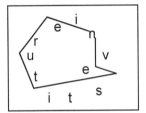

Investiture
Definition:
The act or formal ceremony of conferring the authority and symbols of a high office. 2. An adornment or a cover. From Latin invesitire, to clothe.

Vest (ed)
Definition:
1000 Law. Settled, fixed, or absolute; being without contingency; a vested right. 2. Dressed or clothed, especially in ecclesiastical vestments.

Invest
Definition: To commit (money or capital) in order to gain a financial return; To devote morally or psychologically, as to a purpose; commit:

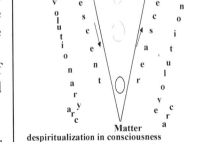

Retu(r)n I vest - As a 'return (ing) I' that is 'vest (ed)' you are what your eye has come to behold as you have Built the Lighted Temple, your garment of God, at each rung of the ladder of ascent.
Neteru I vest – The 'Neteru I vest' is the clothe or clothing of the Neteru, the Divine qualities of God. This is the Word made flesh.

Neteru V Sit, Neteru V Sit(e) – We return to an earlier diagram to assist in our dis-spelling.
•As THE WORD that is with God and has then *gone out* to become
•The Word made flesh
•You are sounding a Word

The Ausarianization of Consciousness Series 1
Metaphysical Keys To the Tree of Life & Oracle Keys to Dis-spelling Illusion
The Spiritual Journey in Unfolding Consciousness

188

•According to your vibration
•That is approximating the fullest measure of the WORD

Your Temple of manifestation is the WORD/Word made flesh. The involutional descent has carried THE WORD into matter, the evolutional ascent will carry THE WORD into Spirit. Along the 'V' are all the Neteru sit(ing)s, site-(ings) of the One, and the Same, True Self. In a World materially driven, it is hard to see that our greatest 'investment' comes from the treasure laid up in Heaven – the re-depositing of the self in our Higher Spiritual faculty. Thus does our worth '$'grow as we raise the serpent fire of Ra along the Djed pillar (spinal column) and make our re-ascent along the Spirit-Matter continuum in consciousness, while doing our work in the World.

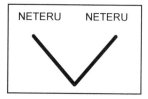

We return to a previous

> **Metaphysical Key To:**
> The Law of Correspondence
> "As above, so below; as below, so above."

After an Interlude of Seeming Death

7. Just as the baby's head crowns from the womb at birth into physical manifestation, so too there is a crowning of the head in the Sahu body in the tomb which leads to Spiritual birth, or re-birth. When you become invested, you have earned that which cannot be taken away. Kuhn calls the Spirit-Matter continuum the "opposite nodes of primal energy". It is within the Sahu body and through transmigration formulas that you are incorporated into a new Spiritual being who has rebirth, which is: *Sa/ Spirit - Fired Wisdom - Hu/matter.* The Sahu is the womb in which you are re-birthed in the Spiritual realm. It is here you are gestating and growing in full conscious Sonship as a Karest. This is expressed accordingly: Alvin Boyd Kuhn. *The Lost Light*, p. 578.

> The soul, ba, and the spirit, Khu, which were usually represented as a hawk and a heron in the hieroglyphics, partook of heavenly food and became one with the gods, and in time became united with the glorified body or heavenly frame, so that the soul, spirit, power, shade, double and name of the deceased were all collected in the one heavenly body, known as the Sahu, which may be described as the spiritual body. It was considered to grow out of the dead body, and its existence became possible through the magic ceremonies performed and the words of power spoken by the priests during the burial service. When the material body had been brought to the tomb for burial it acquired the power of sending forth from itself a body called the Sahu, which was able to ascend to heaven and dwell with the gods there.

KaAbBa   Building The Lighted Temple
The Spiritual B(ARK)

As your personality or Ka-erect-er undergoes Ab-Soul infusion, your Temple is radiated producing the Glorified body – Lighted Temple or Sahu. Sahu is the growing Egoic or self reflective consciousness. As Soul is relating Spirit and Matter in right relationship the essence of these life experiences is garnered in the treasure of the Soul, which for now is the Sahu body.

After an *interlude of seeming death* you begin where you left off in building vehicles of finer and more luminous substance that God may indwell. This is the process of transmutation. As you transmute, you transcend to higher planes of consciousness in the Ab and Ba triangles. As you undergo successive stages of initiation, you are transfigured from the conscious dwelling in your lower body into a conscious dwelling in your higher body.

The Temple is becoming Lighted as:

a.   It is becoming more Ab and Ba Soul infused

b.   The approximating Ka is reflecting more fully the in-Spirit-ing Ka

c.   You are gestating and birthing more in the womb of the Sahu Body, the glorious body you will fully adorn.

This is expressed accordingly:

> The ardent wish of the deceased in Amenta to attain the power of appearing once more on the earth is expressed again and again in the Ritual as the desire to become a soul or spirit that has the power to reproduce itself in apparition, or as the double of the former self, which was imaged in the Ka; the desire for continual duration after death, or in other words for everlasting life, also with the power to reappear upon the earth among the living.

The more Ab and Ba soul infused, the greater the power to appear both on the inner and outer plane.

Chapter 15
What Is – The Ab Soul and Ba Soul Infusing Process - Further Defining *BKA*? The Transmigration of the Soul Continued

What is called by the Esotericist the Soul and Spirit Infusing Process, was long before called BKA in the Kemetic or Egyptian Mystery system. This is the process of impregnating the female. In the Ausarianization of Consciousness, which is your re-ascent into sacredness, you are in this ongoing impregnation process within yourself. The following pictures both seek to illustrate this *dynamic* Ausarian Spiritual Transformation and Resurrection or ASTR process that is occurring within you:

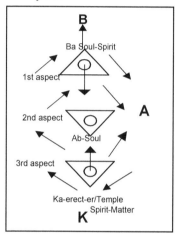
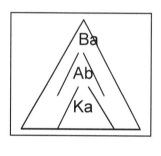

As you journey along a Spiritual path you move through stages of initiation, which are graduated expansions in consciousness. Through these stages of initiation you gain conscious experience of the Divine Father interacting with the Divine Mother throughout all levels of manifestation. Ausarian Resurrection is the conscious livingness of the marriage union of the Divine Father and Mother within your very being.

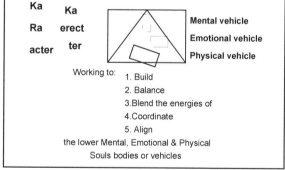

We return to a previous diagram seen at right:
You will recall that in earlier stages of the ASTR practice, the Ka-erect-er showed misalignment, lack of coordination with its vehicles and little 'contact' or appropriation with the higher Ab Soul.

KaAbBa Building The Lighted Temple
The Spiritual B(ARK)

Ab-Soul Infusion

1. With steadfast ASTR practice, as seen in the new diagram at right, the work of Ka-Ra-acter building has been balancing, blending, and coordinating the energies of the physical, emotional and mental Soul bodies which renders a fit instrument. Through this disciplined activity the Temple is becoming increasingly more illuminated, responsive, aligned and under the grip of the Ab Soul program.

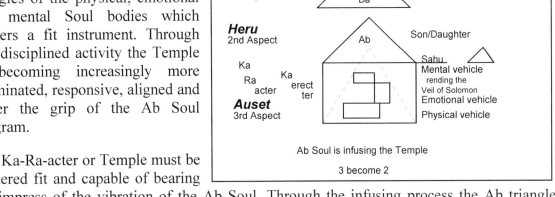

2. The Ka-Ra-acter or Temple must be rendered fit and capable of bearing the impress of the vibration of the Ab Soul. Through the infusing process the Ab triangle seeks to grip these lower Soul bodies or vehicles, taking command so that this Temple becomes a pure channel through which the Ab can effectively work in the World.

3. Through Stages of Initiation the Ka-Ra-acter becomes the Lighted Temple so that ones' higher Soul purpose may be expressed and not just the personal ambitions of the Ka-erect-er. With increasing Ab and Ba Soul comes increasing access to power. This personality must come under the subordination of the Higher Soul program or this increased access to power can be used to feed personality ambition. The Personality instrument is brought into alignment and becomes obedient and capable of bearing the light and higher vibration of the Soul. The Spiritual qualities exhibited by you will solely depend on the extent to which Ab Soul is influencing the Temple.

4. Rending the Veil of Solomon is to break through that which seemingly separates Spirit-Matter. There is tremendous power that is gained when the Ka and Ba are brought into relationship by the Ab Soul consciousness. A premature rending of this veil, without learned and disciplined access to higher Ab and Ba Soul consciousness, would bring in power that would only serve to strengthen the limited Personality focus without the Spiritual enlightenment guiding action in the outer World. Like in the story of Auset, we must learn how to pass ourselves through the purificatory fire which burns off the dross, restores our immortality and makes us pure Gold, as radiant as the Sun. As Solomon or Sun of Man, we learn much about the process of transmigration by observing Salmon who must swim upstream to spawn and give birth anew.

5. The Ab Soul is the consciousness and will used to live a life in alignment, and in accord with Divine Will to build a vessel which is your Temple or instrument for service in the World. The Ab and Ba Soul work through this Temple. It is the directive of the Ab Soul to creatively and intelligently build a Temple, an environment and a World that is in accord with the Divine Archetypal Design.

Ba-Soul Infusion

6. An important hint is giving in the following source of the Ancient wisdom which says accordingly: The Tibetan. *Esoteric Psychology, V.II*, p. 287.

> After the third initiation, the disciple begins to work with, and to understand the significance of Spirit and his consciousness shifts gradually out of the Soul [read here Ab Soul] into that of the Monad [Read here: Ba] in the same way as the consciousness of the personality shifted out of the lower awareness [read here: Ka triangle] into that of the soul. [Read here: Ab].

I digress here momentarily to note with you the reader that even though these reference sources have been 'custodians' of the Ancient wisdom they have 'garbled' it. Like mining through sand to find the gold treasure that lay hidden – it takes utmost discernment to even de-code it. What is key here in this quote is the concept that, 'after the third initiation the disciple comes *gradually* under the influence of the Ba triangle'. If we think about this, the 3rd Initiation is a very high initiation for humanity today. This quote provides a reference point and guards against overestimation about where we *think* we may be on the path.

7. The Ab-Soul triangle serves as link between Ba Soul and the material instrument – the Ka-erect-er/Temple – through which it functions. Thus, God's presence is sensed by all around you. The work of the Ab and Ba infusing process is seen in the diagram at right. The more Ka-Ra-acter development there is, the more Solarized and lighted the substance of your physical, emotional and mental vehicles become. As the process of Ab and Ba Soul infusion (BKA) ensues, the more your Temple becomes radiated by Light and the more you radiate Light out into the World.

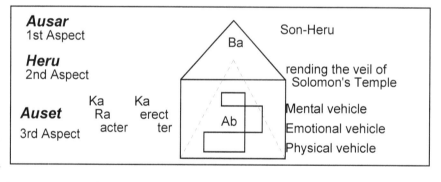

8. Ka-Ra-acter is to see Ra the Sun (Son) of God in action upon the stage of life expressing itself in who you are and who you are becoming. As you develop Ka-erect-er and Ka-Ra-acter *and Build The Lighted Temple* which is your *Spiritual B-Ark,* you *Come Forth* to hear the words spoken by God Ausar to you Heru the Karest/Christ, *'This is my Son/Daugther in whom I am proud'.*

It is through individualized Ba in man that he may grow to have the conscious experience of Universal Ba. Ultimately, the Universal Ba, also called the Oversoul, is the consciousness of Ba as Soul at all levels of immersion in the manifested Universe. In our essential nature as Spirit – all are equal. However individual humans experience:

KaAbBa Building The Lighted Temple
The Spiritual B(ARK)

1. Differing levels of growing conscious awareness – Ab
2. Different levels of coarseness and refinement in their body of manifestation – Ka
3. Differing levels of Self conscious realization of the One True Self - Ausar Ba.

Again we return to a previous Metaphysical Key as the next Metaphysical Key is introduced:

Metaphysical Key To:	**Metaphysical Key To:**
The Law of Correspondence "As above, so below; as below, so above."	Ka Ab Ba as seen Cosmically in the Sun - Earth -Moon cycles

These shifting events may be observed cosmically in the night sky as they play themselves out in the New and Full Sun/Moon cycles. In the following diagrams the Sun symbolizes Ba, the Moon is Ka and the Earth is Ab.

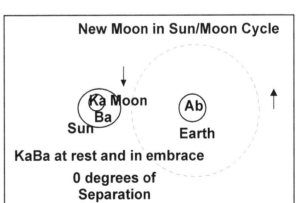

What we seek to understand in the first diagram is that:

1. As Ab Son/Daughter you are in the process of 'seeing', at the Full Moon cycle culmination, how much in fullness you behold the relationship between Ba and Ka, Father/Mother.
a. The Sun and Moon are in opposition or they are exact opposites. This means that they are in 180 degrees of separation.
b. To be Ab Heru, in the middle of Ba Ausar and Ka Auset causes us to have dual, or double vision.
c. As Ab Heru, your 1st eye is developing the ability to: simultaneously *hold and see,* all self reflections or particularizations, that seemingly appear, as Ka in relationship to Ba.
d. If Ausar the Father in you is seen as broken into pieces and strewn in many directions, then Auset, the Mother in you is quite busy in the re-gathering and re-member-ing process in consciousness. Her aspiration for the One True Self leads her to be quite desirous; with many attachments to the seeming selves, the lesser self ID-identifications, along the way.

What we seek to understand in the second diagram is that:

2. KaBa as Father/Mother in embrace are 'seeding' at the New Moon cycle that which will give you Son/Daughter expanded self awareness as Ab Heru.
a. The Sun and Moon are in conjunction. This means that they are together with 0 degrees of separation.

b. When Ka and Ba are At-Oned, as *KaBa*, your 1st eye is restored.

c. KaBa At-Oned is the EYE that sees ITSELF

d. If Ausar the Father is seen as whole, then Auset the Mother is at rest.

This brings us to the next

Metaphysical Key To:
    A   U   M
  Sun - Earth - Moon
  Ba   Ab   Ka

As Heru, you are the Word, that re-becomes THE WORD in your long pilgrimage to reconstruct the broken body of Ausar. Through the sounding of this powerful Hekau, Word of Power, the 'U' which saw duality, comes to see as One and affirms: 'I AM'.

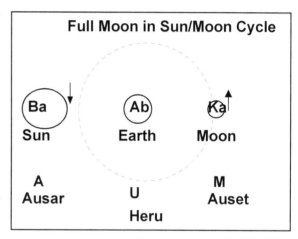

Metaphysical Key To:
The Overlay of Ka Ab Ba as seen Cosmically
Sun - Earth - Moon
A   U   M
Ba   Ab   Ka

Refer to the *Big Map* on p. 111 of this text to see Ka Ab Ba, revealed in the Tree of Life:

1. Cosmically in the *Sun – Earth – Moon* cycles, and

2. Vibrationally in the Divine sound *AUM*

This brings us to the next

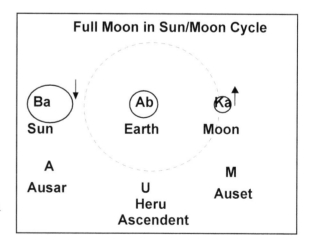

Metaphysical Key To:
Understanding Astrological Qualities of
The Kemetic Energy Formula
Sun - Ascendent - Moon

The Sun as Ausar, the Ascendent as Heru, and the Moon as Auset are pictured at right and described on the page that follows:

KaAbBa Building The Lighted Temple
The Spiritual B(ARK)

Ba
Ausar

The Sun Astrologically – What you easily radiate. If you look at the Sun, Ra, in the sky it 'just is'. It is the line of least resistance for a particular life cycle. You express the energy of the sign that the Sun is in. It is the quality of energy you use to express your One True Self Identification. It is vitality, identity, the 7 – Fold Ka-Ra-acter reconstructed. It is a starting point, and how things orbit around you. It is the expression of alignment with Divine Will, once personal will has been brought under the grip of the higher Soul program.

Ka
Auset

The Moon Astrologically – Represents your ceaseless, persevering devotion to reconstruct the broken body of Ausar, so that the Image and Likeness of God is reflected without distortion. It likewise represents the past, subconscious, automatic, habitual, and the residual that inhibit progress. The repetitive rhythm or Ka/Khaibit or habit, must be broken if psychologically transformative progress is to be made. The Moon is the temporary reflector of the lesser self identification(s). There is a tendency to fall back on the Moon during crisis. It is a comfort zone for lesser self identification which must be relinquished, to open to wider identification, until the One True Self is Realized. In other words, releasing 'snapshots' which ID you as *less than*. The Moon reflects the fullness of the light of the Sun (Soul). It is the quality of energy used to be *habituated* on the Fullness of the One True Self, which is our nurturance – the only thing that truly satisfies need and desire.

Ab
Heru

The Ascendent Astrologically – Brings the Ka-erect-er/personal life (personality/temple) into alignment with the will of the Ab and Ba Soul Bodies. The energy of the sign is an indicator of your Soul's work in this incarnation. It is the purpose of incarnation, lessons to learn, goals to achieve, Soul qualities to aim for. It is the method that the Soul will use to achieve its purpose. It is the key to the design which the Ab Soul intends to actualize through the personal life or otherwise stated – It is the key to the design by which the Soul will grip its instrument, its temple for service in this lifetime. It is how the Heru or Karest/Christ has an office within you. It is the quality of energy used to operate this office of inner government and administration, making choices and managing the affairs of daily living, so that your Soul program is fulfilled. It is the point on the horizon – the Apta in the Kemetic system. Thus, it is the point of emergence, and *Coming Forth by Day as Heru.* It is the energy used by you as Heru to gain ascendency in the resurrection of Ausar.

Refer to the *Big Map* on p. 111 of this text to understand Astrological Qualities of, The Kemetic Energy Formula: Sun – Ascendant – Moon, as revealed in the Tree of Life. This brings us to the next

The Ausarianization of Consciousness Series 1
Metaphysical Keys To the Tree of Life & Oracle Keys to Dis-spelling Illusion
The Spiritual Journey in Unfolding Consciousness

196

> **Metaphysical Key To:**
> Maa Kheru Symbol (front cover)

In coming toward the end of this book these symbols are seen again and hopefully now – more deeply understood.

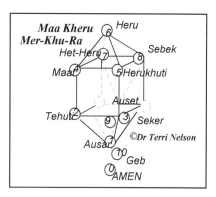

Maa Kheru Symbol:

There is no death. There is only the transmigration of the Soul from life into greater Life. Death is the seeming discontinuity of consciousness – a cutting into pieces of the ALL Consciousness. This is symbolized as the broken body of Ausar, cut into fourteen parts. At each 'death' the disciple appears again and again within the Hall of Amenta, that his heart may be weighed and thereby tested. Each time his heart has fallen short of being as light as the feather of Maat, he has to mount again the wheel of birth and death and fall back into the material realm. This cycle repeats itself as we undergo the Initiatory process. Higher states of consciousness are achieved – until the state of God Conscious is the stabilized Realization. The disciple, finally stands within the Hall of Amenta and is *found* *Maa Kheru*. Thus, you are justified as living in truth, morally and in total equilibrium with the laws of God.

AUM

As Heru sphere 6 in the Tree of Life, you are the Word, that re-becomes THE WORD in your long pilgrimage to reconstruct the broken body of Ausar. Through the sounding of this powerful Hekau, (word of Power), the 'U' which saw duality, comes to see as One and affirms: 'I AM', the Divine marriage between Ausar-sphere 1 and Auset – sphere 9, Father/Mother, Spirit/Matter.

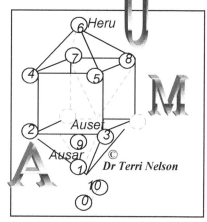

KaAbBa, MerKaBa, Chariot, Symbols:

If we dispell the word <u>Chariot</u> (see Metaphysical Keys to Dispelling Illusion) it reveals the 'Rota(ating) eye or 'I'of Hrakti 'O' (Herukti) that sees full circle. It is the eye of Heru on the double Hori(zon). Perched within the whole moving geometry within the mind of God:

1. You hold and see all within your Ab – heart.
2. *You Mer (Mirror) the Image and Likeness of Father/Mother God – KaBa.*
3. You become the Chariot of God
4. You are now *impulsed from an effortless stream wherein the Will of God is known and* your co-creative Son/Daughter Sun-Ship is made manifest – *The Lighted Temple is Built.*

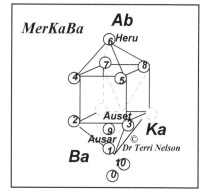

KaAbBa Building The Lighted Temple
The Spiritual B(ARK)

Let's dispell the word Earth:

Derived Word List:
Heart

Meaning:
The Ab Soul or Heart in man and woman together make up the Ab Soul of the Earth. When we dispell the word Earth we see that it reveals the word Heart. Not only is our individual heart weighed upon the scales of Maat but also our collective heart as one Human family is likewise weighed. As we stand before the scales the question is: Are we as: 3-4-5 AfricanSemiticAryan Konsciousness Admixture – ASA/KA, tipping towards the balance of Justice? This brings us to the next

Metaphysical Key To: The 7 Souls (Sun) Dial

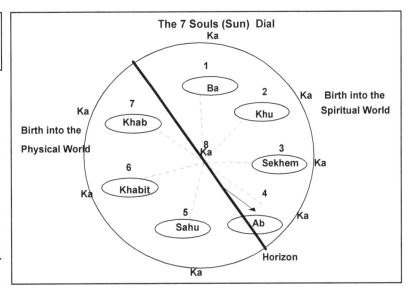

What is The 7 Souls (Sun) Dial?
In the diagram at right, the 7 Souls are pictured on a dial. The hand may be pointed to and focused upon one area of Soul development versus another. In this diagram the arrow is pointing to the Ab – Soul indicating that the disciple (in our example) has attained to the 4th degree of Initiation which is Renunciation and has crossed over into the Higher World of Spirit. S/He:

1. Has Mastered the Sahu body and is now resident in the Ab Soul body
2. May choose to come and go between the Spiritual and material realms
3. Is breaking the bondage of being on the wheel of birth and death
4. Is overcoming all desire of the Earthly physical plane
5. The disciple may take on a refined and Solarized body, called a 'Mayavirupa' by the Esotericists; in which to manifest, in order to perform and fulfill some expressed Planetary purpose. This is a Spiritual body drawn from the etherialized sub-stance of the higher realms and not the dense physical body we don through the 'normal' birth process.

The Ausarianization of Consciousness Series 1
Metaphysical Keys To the Tree of Life & Oracle Keys to Dis-spelling Illusion
The Spiritual Journey in Unfolding Consciousness

198

This is the lesson in At-One-ing in consciousness. The Kemetians call this Ba or Ausar. This is the evolutionary path. We must cleanse and purify the Mother – Auset within us of any distortions – in order that the Mother may behold the Father – the One True Self. *What time is it* has to do with where you are upon the Soul/Sun dial. In other words, how much of the matters within yourself have been Ka-rested (Christed). The question becomes: Where are you on the Ka-dia(l)? This brings us to our next

> **Metaphysical Key To**:
> What is Africa or the African?

Let's dispell the word Africa:

#10. Oracle Metaphysical Dis-spelling Key: Letter replacement. Here we have replaced the 'k' which had been substituted by the letter 'c.'

#11. Oracle Metaphysical Dis-spelling Key: What does the word sound like? Say the word out loud and then silently in a meditative state.

Derived Word List:

A Free Ka

A Fri Ka

A Freak Ka

> **Definition:**
> Freak – 1. A thing or occurrence that is markedly unusual or irregular.

We revisit a previous Metaphysical Key in order to continue our Dis-spelling.

> **Metaphysical Key To**:
> Restoration of The 1st Eye
> *Overcoming impediment # 2*
>   Blindness

#8. Oracle Metaphysical Dis-spelling Key: Meaning. See the relationship and oracle or story of the Neteru – Put word list together to tell a story.

Meaning:

Africa, or Afrika dispelled is A free Ka, a free Spirit – this is the return to the Mother Continent. The word Continent dispelled is contentment – which is Ba – peace, hotep. 'A-Fre(I)e-Ka' is a state of consciousness as well as a geographical land mass. When the approximating Ka is united with Ba, - *KaBa* – then it is *free and unfettered* in reflecting Spirit Ka – the Image and Likeness of God – *without flaw or distortion.* When we live out of accord with the Divinely intended design and purpose for our lives, we look in the mirror and see 'A Freak Ka' – an image full of distortion. When the two eyes represented by 'ee' in the word Free are made One, which is the single or 1st eye then we may affirm, I am 'A Fri Ka'. This is biblically expressed: 'If thine eye is made single then thy whole body is full of Light.' This is further expressed accordingly: Albert Churchward. *Signs and Symbols of Primordial Man,* p. 211.

KaAbBa Building The Lighted Temple
The Spiritual B(ARK)

The Ka or spirit after death separated from the Ba or soul and went before the Divine Creator to be judged, and, if justified, then returned to the Soul and could travel after throughout the universe.

This brings us to the next

> **Metaphysical Key To**:
> What is America?

Let's dispell the word America:
Derived Word List:
A mer I Ka -

#8. Oracle Metaphysical Dis-spelling Key: Meaning. See the relationship and oracle or story of the Neteru – Put word list together to tell a story.

Meaning – America has become the continent upon which the consciousness of the 3 major Root Races in the Human family can be glimpsed. As such, America is 'A mer I Ka' or 'A mirror I Ka'. It is an 'I' that can look in the 'mer' and see its (approximating) 'Ka'. Amerika is where the principles of freedom, justice and equality must truly ring forth for all Humanity who come to its shores. It is one of the major centers where the Divine Intelligence who is guiding our Planet, called Planetary Ausar Ba, gets a 'read' on how we are doing as a Human Family.

•We must bend over backwards to become anew
•*Anu* being as our Kemetic practice teaches
•We must bend over backwards such that head touches toes
• In the conscious union of Spirit and Matter
•Reuniting the Father and Mother –The Primal Couple within
• In perfect balance and equipoise
•Then the heart of the full blazing resurrected Sun – Son/Daughter stands revealed
•Dressed in the finest raiment from Head *to* Heart *to* Toe   *Ba Ab Ka*
•As the Diamond – no longer in the rough
•But the highly burnished gem
•The Lighted Temple
•*KaBa*

The Ausarianization of Consciousness Series 1
Metaphysical Keys To the Tree of Life & Oracle Keys to Dis-spelling Illusion
The Spiritual Journey in Unfolding Consciousness

200

Chapter 16
Re-claim-ation Of Our History – Know Thyself
Re-claim-ation Of Our Ability To Tell Time

Our story Continues…
In order to look at what has occurred in the day and subsequently the night of Earth history, we need to continue to reclaim the Metaphysical Keys. As descendants of African people, the original people, we are now living in a very significant time of Earth history.

If you could but realize:
•The timing of your incarnation in this moment in human evolution
•The Spiritual potency that impresses us and empowers us
•And the opportunity that beckons us
•You would be overcome with joy and awe that you have chosen to be here on Earth – *Now*

The next Metaphysical Key enables you to overcome Impediment #3. It is to be re-membered and re-claimed if your way Home in Ausarian resurrection is to be unobstructed. It is as follows:

Metaphysical Key To:
Knowing How to Tell Time
Overcoming Impediment #3
Loss of The Ability to Tell Time and
To Know What Time It Is

As African and Diaspora, we have lost the ability to 'tell time' as our Ancient Ancestors did. We have been out of touch with the concept of larger cycles of time. Time is what keeps everything from happening at once. Accordingly: The Tibetan. *Discipleship in the New Age, V.II*, p. 252.

> You must ever bear in mind that that which is revealed is eternally present…All that is revealed upon the Path of Discipleship and of Initiation is forever there, but that which can perceive, reach out and include has developed with the ages.

What are these ages?
What are some of the factors that prevent us from examining a larger time scale in which to place our Spiritual journey?
When I teach classes folks are able to recite the following:
7 days equals one week
52 weeks equals one year
10 years equal one decade
100 years equals one century
1000 years equals one millennium

KaAbBa Building The Lighted Temple
The Spiritual B(ARK)

As we now witness the close of one millennium and the beginning of a new, our awareness is heightened in appreciating the millennium *as* a cycle of time. Yet many people are unaware of time cycles beyond this. Thus, they are unable to 'tell time' beyond these limiting time frames of reference. It is also of interest to note that in a World where the consciousness is 'materially' driven, most folks can name denominations of huge sums of money. If I ask how many zeros follow the number 1 to make up a million dollars or even a billion dollars, the answer is readily available! Yet, how come we don't often know time beyond the three zeros of a millennium?

How did this happen? Especially when our Ancestors could not only tell great cycles of time both *forwards and backwards* but they also knew the energetic quality that would characterize events to come and events long past! They knew that each cycle would run its course over time, eons long. This is noted accordingly: Albert Churward, *Origin and Evolution of The Human Race,* p. 10-11.

> The old Egyptian Wise Men kept the time, and marked down every stage. They have left records of the same, for at least ten Glacial Epochs...and the Egyptians recorded time and the revolution of these for over 250,000 years, during the period of the Stellar Mythos, and they have left the fact recorded.

How did we as Afri-kan people forget the Art and Science of, 'Knowing What Time It Is'? This has been both:
1. Deliberate through our being manipulated as well as
2. The result of the qualifying energy of the time cycle in which we have been living and are only just now stirring from our deep sleep

We revisit again the next Metaphysical Key which enables us to overcome Impediment #1. It is to be re-membered and re-claimed if our way Home in Ausarian resurrection is to be unobstructed. Again, it is as follows:

Metaphysical Key To:
Know Thyself
Overcoming Impediment #1
Not Knowing Our History
Not Knowing Our Way Home
Not Taking Responsibility for Knowing, Seeking, Finding
Being All Spooked Up

It is important to note that African descended people and others have become 'spooked up' about Astrological and Astronomical events. Have you ever wondered why it is that Europeans flock all over the World to learn the very Arts and Sciences of *our* Ancient ancestry that so many in the African community reject? These include: Tree of Life (KaAbBa/KaBaLa), Oracle/Prophesy,

Tarot, Herbal Medicine, Numerology, Energy Balancing, Sacred Geometry, Astrology, Breath-work, Yoga, Meditation, Power and Qualities of Neteru, Ra (Kundalini) and Chakra work, Faith Healing, and Ritual, just to name a few.

This is in large measure attributable to the Biblical verse Deuteronomy 18:10-12. 14 which is accordingly:

> 10: There shall not be found among you any one that maketh his son or his daughter to pass through the fire, or that useth divination, or an observer of times, or an enchanter, or a witch.
> 11: Or a charmer, or a consulter with familiar spirits, or a wizard or a necromancer.
> 12: For all that do these things are an abomination unto the Lord: and because of these abominations the Lord thy God doth drive them out from before thee.
> 14: For these nations, which thou shalt possess, hearkened unto observers of times, and unto Diviners: but as for thee, the Lord thy God hath not suffered thee so to do.

Let's take for closer examination the specific reference to, 'observing the times'. If we knew, 'What time it is,' we would come into great power of understanding and directing our course. If we do not understand what time it is, we will continue to grope in the dark.

Note here the specific reference to the word, Witch. Have you noticed that there is no word in the Western World, a World patriarchally driven, that describes a woman with power? The two most commonly used words to describe a woman who exhibits any power are, 'Witch or Bitch', Even in a World where she may have been called Priestess, she is denied priesthood in one of the foremost institutions - The Catholic Church. Now, how can it be that one half of the World's population is denied its power to assert the fullness of the ONE TRUE SELF? This systemic Religious posture has exuded to every corner of our Planet - Geb - sphere 10.

Note here the specific reference to 'one that maketh his son or his daughter to pass through the fire'. Recall in Our Story how Auset, who was hired as nurse to the son of the Queen of Byblos, caused him 'to pass through the fire' in order to purify his mortal parts and restore him to immortality. We can see here that our Neter and Divine Mother - Auset would be branded a Witch by Christian definition. Her teaching may be Metaphysically understood to mean that we must all: hold our own 'feet to the fire', be Self disciplined, work in accord with Divine will, purify our mortal parts and be restored to immortality.

As God conscious beings, the Ancients walked the Earth as God Kings. It was only in the later cycles of time that the Ancient Arts and Sciences would become debased and abused by those who would come in the descending cycles of time and carry the World into deeper materialization in consciousness.

Events in the consciousness of humanity across the unfolding cycles of time have contributed to:

KaAbBa Building The Lighted Temple
The Spiritual B(ARK)

a. The fragmentation or splintering in the presentation of the wisdom in the Ancient Arts and Sciences which would render their power for good less effective and thereby make suspect their curative ability.

b. The loss of understanding of the twin forces in nature, in that all has its thesis and antithesis and can be used for good or ill. The power of discernment and discrimination for making choices in the use of the Arts and Sciences would thus be impaired.

c. Loss of God conscience and consciousness, as well as the ability to intuit the grand archetypal design in creation. Unlike the Ancestors, guided by the 1st eye, this would leave those who use Ancient Arts and Sciences without a discernible blueprint to guide them or, no Puzzle Box Cover (PBC). Thus actions would be fraught with many 'wrong turns'.

d. These abuses of the wisdom would evoke fear from the masses of that which is powerful, manipulated for ill, and misunderstood.

This brings us to the next

Metaphysical Key To:
To Understanding Energy
Energy is Energy
Energy may be used:
1. Positively at a higher turn of the spiral at its optimal and Divine level of expression or
2. Negatively at a lower turn of the spiral at its despiritualized and debased level of expression

---

Yet when it comes to being able to 'Tell Time', we must reclaim the conscious awareness that Astrological and Astronomical events inform us of:
1. What cycle of time we are in or simply, What Time it is
2. The quality of energy occurring within a time cycle
3. How to co-creatively work within the great Divine plan for creating Heaven on Earth, given the time and qualifying energies available

For example:
If a farmer goes out and plants his seeds in the dead of Winter he will not have a favorable outcome. His seeds will fall to the frozen ground and die. But if the farmer goes out to plant his seeds in the early Spring, he is choosing a more propitious or favorable cycle of time both:
a. Astronomically according to the position and phase of the Sun and Moon
b. Astrologically according to the energies coming through the sign of Aries (tropically considered) signaling the start of Spring which ensures a better crop outcome.

Here the farmer's wisdom enables him to use the Astrological qualities that are operative in the cycle of Spring and the Astronomical qualities due to the position of the Sun.

The Ausarianization of Consciousness Series 1
Metaphysical Keys To the Tree of Life & Oracle Keys to Dis-spelling Illusion
The Spiritual Journey in Unfolding Consciousness

204

Did Christopher Columbus have access to our Ancient Arts and Science?
The short answer is, Yes. Some African descended people may want to quickly assign Christopher Columbus to the heap of someone who did not 'do much' or even 'know' much. After all, it is said he did not 'discover' a new World, a World that was already 'here and inhabited'. When we look at large cycles of time and World events, it becomes clear that there are many that can be named as 'destined' to make significant changes in World consciousness and events, 'in their time'. Humanity will later deem whether their actions and energy upon the World stage were used for good or for ill. Nevertheless, it may be said that Christopher Columbus was one of the foremost 'pioneers' that the Aryan-European World has had in contributing to the Christianization, Imperialization, and Capitalization of 'the Planet' or what is commonly called, the 'New World'.

At that time, parts of the so called 'Old World', which then included Europe, were steeped in 'the dark ages' due to the suppression and destruction of the Ancient Wisdom Arts and Sciences by earlier pioneers of the Aryan-European World, which included Alexander The Great, etc. (See *Stolen Legacy, Isis Unveiled*). Disconnected from the Ancient Kemetic Arts and Sciences, 'they had come to believe' the World was flat. Nicolaus Copernicus was a Polish Astronomer who lived from 1473-1543. He was condemned for his theory that the Earth was round and rotates daily on its axis and revolves around the Sun with the other Planets in the Solar system.

Likewise, Christopher Columbus, an Italian explorer 1451-1506, in the service of Spain is 'credited' with knowing (believing) that the Earth was a round sphere and for having the strong conviction that he could sail West from Europe to find a new route to the East, thereby bumping into or 'discovering' America in 1492. Christopher Columbus was knowledgeable in Astronomy and Astrology. He studied the works of Ptolemy who lived in the 2nd century A.C.E. and was foremost in the fields of Astrology and Astronomy. He was not so disconnected from the Kemetic Ancient Wisdom as seen in the following: Accordingly: *National Council For Geocosmic Research, 93 edition,* p.12.

> Christopher Columbus, a master mariner from Genoa, had first appeared at the Spanish court in 1486. Columbus had studied the writings of Ptolemy and also those of the astronomer Abraham Zacuto.

Christopher Columbus kept a journal of his voyages. What we learn from these is that he used the wisdom of the Ancient Arts and Science to 'tell of events to come' i.e. - 'tell time' - so that his voyages would be guided and made safe. This is expressed accordingly: Ibid. p.18 -19:

> Why was Columbus so concerned with the planets? Specifically, why did he want to remain in a safe harbor to await "the Sun in opposition to Jupiter, which is the cause of strong winds?" We have discovered a source for this statement in a preface added by the publisher of the 1481 edition of the Ephemerides. The section on predictions of the weather, written by Bartholomeus Mariensuess, states that "Jupiter and the Sun makes strong winds either in the aspects of quartile [90 degree separation] or opposition [180 degree separation]." This new

evidence supports the ideas that Columbus carried the 1481 edition of Regiomontanus Ephemerides on his historic first voyage.

We see here that Columbus was an 'observer' who looked at relationships between Planetary bodies, Constellations and the quality of their energies in order to 'tell the most propitious time' for action in the outer World.

And Continuing: Ibid.

> Columbus took such astronomical warnings seriously. On Christmas Day of 1502, during his fourth voyage, Columbus was sailing along the coast of what is now Panama. His *Letera rarissima* [read here: journal] contains the following description: "Once more I put into the harbor, since I did not dare to await the opposition of Saturn with Mars, so tossed about on a dangerous coast, since that generally brings tempests or heavy weather.

1. Perhaps it would have been a bit awkward for much to be said about Christopher's reliance upon Astrology and Astronomy, when he ultimately was commissioned to establish colonies for the Christian World under the rule of King Ferdinand and Queen Isabella, a marriage which combined both Spain and Portugal.

2. Christopher Columbus availed himself of the Ancient wisdom, which assisted his voyage. Ultimately, these voyages contributed to the enslavement of African people, who ended up chained in the bottom of slaves ships, bound for the Americas.

3. Countless numbers of times has the Ancient Wisdom contributed in building this so called, 'New World'.

4. Nothing built in this so called 'New World' surpasses that which was built by the Ancients. All of the 'new' is dwarfed by the magnificence of the Old. This is expressed accordingly: Albert Churchward, *Origin and Evolution of The Human Race,* p. 67 - 68.

> The Middle Ages, so called, were retrograde in the advancement of real knowledge and learning. From the time of the fall of the Old Egyptian Empire not much advancement was made in true knowledge for many hundred years. There was a set back. The Greeks and Romans although better known to the present generation than the old Egyptians [read here: Kemetian], because scholars have been able to read their literature, were no advancement on the old Egyptians in science-how much in art it is difficult to say; they have been much overrated. ...The Greeks and Romans copied and gained most of their knowledge from the Egyptians, did not improve upon it, but perverted much of the truth, and the Roman Church has done more than anything else to keep the people down in a dark and degenerate age. ...

5. As African descendants, if we continue to remain 'spooked up' and do not avail ourselves of our Ancient wisdom; we will continue to grapple in the darkness, as helpless as a ship without a rudder or as helpless chattel in the bowel of the slave ship, as has already been - a part of Our story.

What has further contributed to our loss of ability to Tell Time?
The short answer is lack of knowledge and systems of education that teach us how, according to the Kemetic adage, *To Know Thyself.*
We return to a previous

Metaphysical Key To:
The Law of Correspondence
 As above, so below; as below, so above

This is the law of Correspondence. (Kemetic Law of Tehuti - See *The Kybalion*). It guides you to examine from the level or plane that you do know, to that which you do not as yet, know that you know. By knowing the individual 'self' as a micro universe, you will know the Self as a macro Universe. The micro and macro or individual and Universal are likewise called Ba by the Kemetians, which means Soul.

As we enter the new millennium it may seem daunting enough to move the mind to capture what has taken place in our Earth history even during the last 2000 years. Many who have attended a public school system have been introduced to a linear time line that perhaps went back to 800 B.C. in a study of Greek and Roman History and forward to look at American and European history. Many, both black and white saw time lines in history classes that looked like the diagram below:

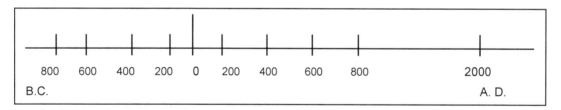

```
        |   |   |   |   |   |   |   |   |           |
   800  600 400 200  0  200 400 600 800         2000
   B.C.                                          A. D.
```

You can see here that so called 'Human history' would lack any focus upon events happening prior to 800 B.C. Such a 'time line' gravely truncates our view of ourselves, the World, the Solar System, the Galaxies, the Supercosmic Galaxies and ultimately the Universe in total. As an Ancient people, our story extends into the night of time. Accordingly: *Isis Unveiled,* p. 522.

> But, even then, the merciless hands of time had left its traces upon their structures, and some of them whose very memory would be lost were it not for the Books of Hermes, [read here: - Books of Tehuti, Kemetic Books] had been swept away into the oblivion of the ages. King after king, and dynasty after dynasty had passed in a glittering pageant before the eyes of succeeding generations and their renown had filled the habitable globe. The same pall of forgetfulness had fallen upon them and their monuments alike, before the first of our historical authorities, Herodotus, preserved for posterity the remembrance of that wonder of the world, the great Labyrinth.

KaAbBa Building The Lighted Temple
The Spiritual B(ARK)

> The long-accepted Biblical chronology has so cramped the minds of not only the clergy, but even our scarce-unfettered scientists, that in treating of prehistoric remains in different parts of the world, a constant fear is manifested on their part to trespass beyond the **period of 6,000 years, hitherto allowed by theology as the age of the world.**

In this limiting time-space awareness and divorced from Our Story, our sense of who we are becomes collapsed within these flesh, bones and blood frames we call bodies. Living an Americanized and Westernized lifestyle gives these bodies duration of about 55 - 65 years. This is a very narrow view indeed of who we really are. Our education in America has tricked many of us into the belief that time is linear. This is literally a 'grave' distortion of a Metaphysical Key and our resultant loss of the ability to Tell Time heralds death.

We are the well trained adult elephant who, as a baby, had one leg tied by a short rope, to a stake in the ground. In our restricted movement of going 'round and round' in a small circle, we circumscribed our brain, we circumscribed our mind, we circumscribed our consciousness. Today, so obedient is the adult elephant, and so confident are his masters in training him, that he no longer needs to be tied to the stake, for he will not roam. The only visible evidence of his confinement is the now cut, short rope that still dangles from the same leg, the reminder that keeps him afraid to brave that which is beyond the circus 'ring pass not'. This brings us to the next important Metaphysical Key, which is that we must understand Our Story:

> **Metaphysical Key To:**
> Understanding Our History

We cannot divorce history from our understanding of cycles of time. If we are *to wrap the consciousness around* our remote history then we must likewise be able to transcend limiting conceptions of what time is and move within greater cycles of time. It is beyond the scope of this book to give the reader dimensions any greater than the dot '•' on this page that could capture the breath and depth of manipulation and destruction of African descended people. The following gives mere reflection. Accordingly: Hassan-El, Kashif Malik. *The Wilie Lynch Letter and The Making of a Slave. Let's Make a Slave*, p. 7 (16).

> Earlier, we talked about the non-economic good of the horse and the nigger in their wild or natural state; we talked out the principle of breaking and tying them together for orderly production; furthermore, we talked about paying particular attention to the female savage and her offspring for orderly future planning; then, more recently we state that, **by reversing the positions of the male and the female savages, [read here: - creating a strong female, weak male]** we had created an orbiting cycle that turns on its own axis forever, unless phenomenon occurred and reshifted the positions of the male and the female savages.

Let's take for closer examination the words: 'and reversing the positions of the male and female.' These words bring us to the next

> **Metaphysical Key To:**
> The Kemetic Law of Gender

The Ausarianization of Consciousness Series 1
Metaphysical Keys To the Tree of Life & Oracle Keys to Dis-spelling Illusion
The Spiritual Journey in Unfolding Consciousness

208

The Kemetic Law - The Law of Tehuti (called Hermetic Law by the Greeks) is expressed accordingly: *The Kybalion,* p. 39

> Gender is in everything; everything has its Masculine and Feminine Principles; Gender manifests on all planes.

We are able to see that our own Ancient wisdom was inverted for misuse by our captors.

And continuing, Lynch goes on to say -

> Our experts warned us about the possibility of this phenomenon occurring, for they say that **the mind has a strong drive to correct** and re-correct itself over a period of time if it can touch some substantial **original historical base**; and they advised us that the best way to deal with this phenomenon is to shave off the brute's mental history and create a multiplicity of phenomenon of illusions, so that each illusion will twirl in its own orbit, something similar to floating balls in a vacuum. The creation of a multiplicity of phenomenon or illusions entails the principles of cross-breeding the nigger and the horse as we stated above, the purpose of which is to create a diversified division of labor thereby connecting level of labor, **the result of which is the severance of the points of original beginnings for each sphere illusion.** Since we feel that the subject matter may get more complicated as we proceed in laying down our economic plan concerning the purpose, reason, and effect of cross-breeding horses and niggers, we shall lay down the following terms for future generations.

Let's take for closer examination the words: 'the mind has a strong drive to correct and re-correct itself over a period of time if it can touch some substantial original historical base'. It is through our reconnection with our history or Our Story that we have a re-awakening, re-membering, and re-ascension. Thereby, do we overcome actions against the Black Race to sever the points of our 'original beginnings'.

The Prt Em Hru - The Book of Coming Forth by Day - was a Book of guidance for the Ancients. It has been improperly named The Egyptian Book of the Dead. To the contrary, it is a book that gives guidance to the Manes in this life, life hereafter and life everlasting. This is expressed accordingly: Gerald Massey. *Ancient Egypt The Light of The World,* p.195-196.

> It was indeed the book of life and salvation, because it contained the things to be done in the life here and hereafter to ensure eternal continuity (Rit, ch. 15, hymm 3)... The Ritual was pre-eminently a book of knowledge or of wisdom, because it contained the gnosis of the mysteries. Knowledge was all-important. The Manes make their passage through Amenta by means of what they know...The Egyptians had no vicarious atonement, no imputed righteousness, no second-hand salvation. No initiate in the Osirian [read here: Ausarian] mysteries could possibly have rested his hope of reaching heaven on the Galilean line to glory.

KaAbBa Building The Lighted Temple
The Spiritual B(ARK)

The above quote informs us that we possess the Book of Knowledge which gives us the power: 'to go in and out by day ...', to penetrate our dwelling place and also make our way to the fields of peace and plenty called Seket-Aarnru, to find our way back *Home* and thus be restored in our Ausarian consciousness. Events in the later part of Our Story would include 400 years of slavery and 100 years of post slavery. But even within this 500 year time span in our conscious memory, many African descendents can not even retrace their footsteps back to the villages from which they came from on our Mother Continent, Africa. Our language, which would connect us, seems lost. With some exceptions, like Alex Haley, whose family retained a few words and trace memories of his African village, the pathway for many of the African Diaspora back to their native village home has grown cold. It has been obscured by our captors, who went to great extremes to destroy all traces of reconnection. Fortunately, present day DNA research on the skeletal remains from African burial grounds offers great promise for descendants in this retracing process.* However, it must be borne in mind that those who have obscured the way of return to our Earthly homes (village) are one and the same as those who claim to have our salvation by guiding us along the return pathway to our Heavenly Home. Is this a story as dubious as the belief in Santa Claus?

Why has the way been obscured?
There is no one answer to this question although much in this text seeks to reveal some indications. Some will make a Pilgrimage to Kemet, to find *Our Story*. This is all necessary, well and good. We must see the Great monuments and that which is inscribed in stone. Yet the 'stuff' of *our story* is likewise in the British and other museums, strewn among various Masonic and religious orders, and personal archives. In summary, lots of folks have our 'stuff'. The stuff of our story is likewise buried underground in the Earth, in caves, submerged underwater and elsewhere. It is also stored within the akashic records, available for those with subtle enough sight to read and 'download'. Much of our stuff has been consumed by the fires of those who would see it destroyed.

We must all prevail in sifting through the treasured splinters of the Ancient Wisdom, wherever they are found in the re-claim-ation process - that we may trace our way - *back to the source*. If we are patient, holding the reactivity of the emotional body quiet which is Auset - sphere 9, the Divine Mother aspect of our Spiritual nature, we will behold Ausar - sphere 1, the Divine Father, upon her clear, limpid surface. To re-trace your footsteps back to your Earthly Home and your Heavenly Home will require *Knowledge* and great discernment. It all goes back to Black, the source, and the deep. We have been given the Knowledge we need. This is expressed again in the discourse between Auset and her son Heru as she speaks accordingly: Virgin of the World, *The Sacred Books of Tehuti* (See G.R.S Mead, *Thrice Greatest Hermes;* Dr. Muata Ashby, *Ausarian Resurrection*).

> Such was all-knowing Tehuti, who saw all things, and seeing understood, and understanding had the power both to disclose and to give explanation. For what he knew, he engraved on stone; yet though he engraved them onto stone he hid them mostly, keeping sure silence

---

* See article by Saeed Shabazz. Staff Writer/Final Call. *Howard University Scientists Make Historic DNA Breakthrough.*. www.finalcall.com/national/dna1-4-200.htm.

though in speech, that every younger age of cosmic time might seek for them. And thus, with charge unto his kinsmen of the gods to keep sure watch, he mounted to the stars

Tehuti returned to Heaven and invoked a spell on them, and spoke these words: 'O holy book, who has been made by my immortal hands, by incorruption's magic spells…free from decay throughout eternity, remain untouched and incorrupt from time! Become un-seeable, un-findable, for every one whose foot shall tread the plains of this land, until old Heaven does bring forth the proper instruments for you, whom the Creator shall call souls.

Thus, O my son Heru, Tehuti brought the teachings of wisdom which were given to him by the God of All, and they are hidden in nature until the time when those who are ready to seek for their essential nature, those with true aspiration, seek with honesty and reverence.

Fortunately, many African descendants have embarked in studies (independently and in study groups) pushing further back in time, covering the Egyptian/Kemetic Dynasties, beginning with the First Dynasty and rulership of King Narmer (Menes) - 3150 B.C. E. through to Pre-Dynastic Kemet - 4236 B.C.E - 10,000 B.C.E and earlier. Yet our history goes back even further into the night of time. In understanding how to tell time, we must become familiar and at ease with the use of even larger Astronomical and Astrological time cycles as we explore the vastness of the Universe in which we live.

Just as a cycle known as a Millennium is a period of 1000 years, a cycle of 2,160 years is called an Age, and an even larger cycle of 25,920 years called a Great Age and so on. Like our Ancient Ancestors, many are pushing the time line backwards and forwards thousands and even millions of years. So in trying to grasp an understanding of 'what time it is' and 'where we are' in our Spiritual Journey in Ausarian consciousness, we come and *re-awaken* to the next Metaphysical Key that *Time is Spiral:*

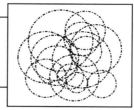

Metaphysical Key To:
Time Cycles - Time is Spiral

The diagram above seeks to illustrate that there are smaller cycles of time within even larger cycles of time and larger cycles of time within even vaster cycles of time. Time cycles are like wheels, within wheels, within wheels. These wheels turn upon one another, like gears in a vast time machine; the time that they 'tell' forms a backdrop behind events unfolding in human history. *Time is what keeps everything from happening all at once in consciousness.* It is the illusion of Time, which gives us the Story *to tell* in The Journey of Unfolding Consciousness. The energy each cycle brings qualifies and conditions what happens in our ongoing space-time living. The story Humanity tells is about whether we were able to:

KaAbBa   Building The Lighted Temple
The Spiritual B(ARK)

1. Spiral the qualities (Neteru) of energy available in a cycle of time <u>upwards</u> so that their optimal, Divine expression is made manifest
2. Spiral the qualities (Neteru) of energy available in a cycle of time <u>downwards</u> so that their debased, de-spiritualized expression is made manifest

There are numerous cycles, which can help us glimpse insight into the great question, 'What Time is it? These Time cycles are described in *The Ausarianization of Consciousness Tablet Series 2 **ACTS 2** - The Metaphysical Keys to The Tree Of Life with Oracle Keys to Dis-spelling Illusion.*

For now we note that many have received an erroneous mis-education. Largely absent from the educational system has been:
1. Knowledge of events dating back further into the Ancient History and
2. Acknowledgment of the *Greatness* of African people and their contribution to this 'World period' and evolutionary cycle

The Ausarianization of Consciousness Series 1
Metaphysical Keys To the Tree of Life & Oracle Keys to Dis-spelling Illusion
The Spiritual Journey in Unfolding Consciousness

212

Chapter 17
The Spiritual Implications Of The Perfect Storm
Where are we today?

In the diagram at right, the vertex in the letter 'V' illustrates how Spirit has made its deepest descent into matter. As greater descent is reached in the involutionary time cycle, man's consciousness has become more materialized. Along the way humanity has gradually lost sight of the interconnecting webwork and interdependence between all kingdoms of life. Individualism reigns as man and woman have come to see themselves as a self separated from all other 'selves'.

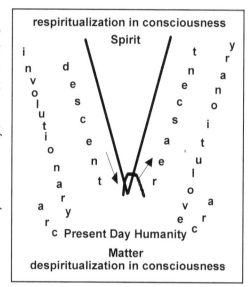

1. Today humanity sits perched within the vertex of the 'V' having reached the greatest point of materialization and darkness in consciousness.

2. It is now well into its struggle to start turning the corner in the vertex, thus in its uphill climb toward the re-spiritualization in consciousness.

3. The Spiritual Waters are rising and meet with the contending Material forces. *The Spiritual Tides and the Material Tides Clash.*

4. Present day humanity has been sitting with the fullness of its use of 'free will' to choose whether to build according to Universal Laws or out of accord. These Laws were known to the Ancients as the Laws of Maat and the Law of Tehuti. These laws govern right relationship throughout manifested creation and how karma is dispensed for having chosen to build in alignment or in violation of these Laws.

5. Consequently, man and woman are today now sitting squarely with the Karmic consequence of their actions. It is likewise the time when bad deed or wrongs are quickly *outed*. You will not get 'down the street' before your deeds are known. Likewise, it is the time when good deeds, acts of heroism and selfless service are seen. It is the time when one is in receipt of the just and accumulated Karma of good deeds, favor, miraculous happenings and bestowal of blessings. These miraculous happenings I call Unexpected Sudden Goodness (USG) or Expected Sudden Goodness (ESG). If you are not expecting Sudden Goodness or good fortune then when it comes it is unexpected.

KaAbBa Building The Lighted Temple
The Spiritual B(ARK)

Likewise, it is the time when one is in receipt of bad Karmic accumulation and the fear, destruction and peril wrought from these just fruits. The Karmic debt must be paid. This brings us to a previous

---

Metaphysical Key To:
The Kemetic Law of Rhythm

---

6. These events are occurring upon the backdrop of various time cycles which are all converging to create 'The Perfect Storm'.

7. Our involutional descent into materialism has provided us with many so called 'technological advances' but has left us Spiritually bereft and empty. Increasingly humanity is steeping more and more within the consequences and the impact of how it has been building a World *askew* to the Divinely intended design. In humanity's game of 'particularization' we have come to sit squarely in this 'broken consciousness'.

8. Although man is in a physical-ized and material-ized form his Ausarian Resurrection comes from his re-identification in *Consciousness as Spirit*. This is the awareness of the *Self* as co-eternal with the Undifferentiated, Condition-less, Form-less, Bound-less, Infinite All. This is the identification of the One True Self as the Image and Like-ness of God in which each man and woman is made. Today, upon our Planet Earth, we are operating under the rulership of separative consciousness. This separative consciousness has been choosing to build out of accord with the Divine plan and Universal law.

9. In the 3-4-5 AfricanSemiticAryan Konsciousness Admixture ASA-KA - we are now sitting squarely in the vertex of the 'V' with the fullness of our Karmic load of wrong thought, word and deed. The karmic consequence of our collective actions in Earth History have come due. Humanity is steeping within the impactful consequences of building a World out of accord and askew to the Divinely intended design. The Earth reels under the mismanagement, and collectively we have great pains and suffering.

• In our unbroken Ausarian consciousness we knew the underlying unity guiding
• The seamless relationship between all beings in creation.
• In humanity's 'game of particularization'
• We have come to sit squarely in this 'broken consciousness'
• We are like the beached Whale
• Whales are Wheels and Time is up
• Time to return back Home.
• We are Grinding our wheels in the Vertex
• Trying to round the corner so we can get out of the spin and the grind

We are perched within the vertex of the 'V', in between the shifting and overlapping of Great Time Cycles, as one set is closing out and another set is beginning. What should our viewpoint be?

We must hold simultaneously the dual view point that we now teeter both:
1. Perilously at the tail end of a despiritualizing, materializing, downspiraling cycle of time with its attendant destructive and disastrous effects and
2. Propitiously at the doorway of this re-spiritualizing, upspiraling cycle of time in which humanity and the Earth will know unimagined Spiritual heights of peace and well being.
3. Seeing clearly through both eyes moves you interiorly in consciousness to see through your *1ˢᵗ eye, which* guides you through *The Perfect Storm.*

Why are we all called to be *Noah* at this time?
When Noah built the ARK- also called here the B-ARK - he had read certain signs of the times, which told him to make preparations for the rising waters. Your B-ARK is the Tree of Life, which is your Spiritual equipment. We are now being impressed by an inflow of Spiritual waters or energies at this time in our Earth's history and evolution. Like Noah, we are *all* now charged with building an Ark for the rising Spiritual waters.

•In this Perfect Storm
•The Spiritual Waters are rising
•At this great vertex in time
•Cycles are converging to create the *Perfect Storm*
•In the midst of these great convergences, cataclysms are occurring
•We must know our direction or alignment given all the signs of the rising *Spiritual tide*
•We must focus on how to prepare a Spirit *worthy vehicle*
•One that can bear the great Spiritual impress
•After emerging from a long dry spell of material darkness
•This convergence will feel like a *Spiritual tidal wave*
•Washing over Spirit depleted humanity
•Waters battering our physical, emotional and mental equipment
•To be sat down and forcefully fed and made to drink
•At a brimming Spiritual banquet table
•After one has known starvation and thirst, this may produce strange, even discomforting symptoms.
•In short, *the waves from this Spiritual infusion will batter the vessels of humanity, testing them in their*
Spirit worthiness

Let's dispell the word Noah:
#11. Oracle Metaphysical Dis-spelling Key: What does the word sound like? Say the word out loud and then silently in a meditative state.

KaAbBa Building The Lighted Temple
The Spiritual B(ARK)

Sounds Like:

Noah is Knower

#8. Oracle Metaphysical Dis-spelling Key: Meaning. See the relationship and oracle or story of the Neteru - Put word list together to tell a story.

Meaning: To be Noah is to be a Knower. A Knower is to be poised within the Ba or 1ˢᵗ aspect triangle of your Spiritual faculty. It is to be in Ba or Ausarian consciousness. It is to be At-Oned with God.

Should such knowledge of the rising oceanic tides lead you to create a 'sea worthy' vessel and other fortified shelters to shield you from the respective elements?

This may seem like the obvious question to ask but it *is not* what this book seeks to address. You may build whatever *outer* structures you deem necessary. The Sea worthy Vessel that *The Ausarianization in Consciousness Tablet Series* seeks to address is to be found in the building of your own Lighted Temple. Then and only then will you ride out the rising Spiritual Waters in the midst of the Perfect Storm.

As Knower (Noah) we are each called to address the following questions:

Where do I stand in regard to these converging cycles?

1. What are some of the signs of preparedness?
2. What is the urgency for making rapid preparation?
3. What is my Soul Purpose and Soul Ra(y) Energy?
4. Where am I going on my Spiritual journey? What is my intention, course direction and destination through this Spiritual Storm? What is the map or pathwork to Spiritual ascent or Ausarian Resurrection
5. How am I building a Spiritual B-Ark or vehicle for the rising Spiritual tides and the Perfect Storm? What is my Spiritual B-Ark or Temple? How is my Spiritual B-Ark navigating and bearing the impress of these Spiritual waters? How might the rising Spiritual tides be advantageous in my journey?
6. What are some of the cycles that inform the question, What time is it?
7. Where do I stand in regard to these converging cycles?

How can I stand in a place and time that is both propitious and perilous?

It is a propitious time for those who know that they are co-workers in the great Divine plan and stand in alignment with their Soul purpose of aiding humanity, Earth, and her inhabitants. The energies now favor the full expression and manifestation of your benevolent, innovative and creative ways of being which will heal and awaken the true meaning of Humanhood.

It is a perilous time in this turning point because material consciousness, at its lowest vibration has grown the *most* crystallized, solidified, coarse and dense. Thus the grip of this consciousness and the forms it has produced are made strong. At the same time its degree of concretization has made it the most brittle and subsequently most fragile. This consciousness - with its outworn lifeless forms - ever nearer to shattering and unable to contain the indwelling life - now seeks new forms of expression and viability.

The Ausarianization of Consciousness Series 1
Metaphysical Keys To the Tree of Life & Oracle Keys to Dis-spelling Illusion
The Spiritual Journey in Unfolding Consciousness

216

Those who have come to Earth at this time to do the healing work are perched at the turning point in this vertex. They are the heralders and the bringers of the dawn. They have the work of building the New World in the midst of the contending forces which will work with *ferocity and treachery* to hang onto the old. Those contending forces will wax and wane in strength during the Earth's transition out of its de-Spiritualizing cycle into its re-Spiritualization cycle.

Facing the contending forces will be like facing a massive and grotesque fire-breathing dragon that is writhing and agonizing as it takes its last gasping breaths. *It is most dangerous.* Even as it gasps you must watch out for the mighty tail as it thrashes and whips around to strike and destroy those in its midst, as it *too* is destroyed. Those helpers and healers called now from all Races and all nations must build in the midst of devastation and destruction of the old. They must keep their alignment and focus. Knowing we are perched both perilously and propitiously allows us to be *both cautious while optimistic* in our approach to living and serving Earth and her inhabitants at this time.

Massive Planetary disturbances are occurring worldwide. What does this all mean? It means rising waters, raging fires, twister winds and shifting Earth beneath our feet. We have the literal threat of floods with the melting of the Polar ice caps. There are a number of changing time cycles that are affecting what is happening now on our Planet. These are described in a later chapter. For now it is important to know that these cycles are converging to create the *'Perfect Storm'*.

What Are Some Of The Signs Of Preparedness?
You recognize that:
1. You have chosen to incarnate at a very significant time in Earth's history. Many lifetimes have prepared you for this incarnation of service.
2. You are being impressed more and more by the in-flowing Spiritual energies of this Age.
3. You have been following a Spiritual path and the 4 pillars of Disciplic Living are part of your Daily ASTR practice: This brings us to the next

> **Metaphysical Key To:**
> The 4 Pillars Of Disciplic Living

Prayer/Meditation   Study/Reflection

Service/Purpose   Practice/Discipline

4. You have come into this incarnation with a strong sense of Soul purpose. You feel compelled to hold your alignment with the Divine will and plan in order to play your part in the

KaAbBa Building The Lighted Temple
The Spiritual B(ARK)

sacredization of Earth. As a co-worker in the Divine plan you work to fulfill your Soul purpose.

5. You feel the pulse of the Earth and her heartbeat. You are awakening more and more to her pain and suffering and your mission of saving and serving. Your heart opens to assist Earth and her inhabitants through the travails. Your own pain and suffering is being transmuted into the luminous healing balm of loving understanding that you now use to salve, serve and save. Through your own impacts you know the roadwork from the inside out and show others the way. This *balm* must run more tenaciously ahead of the manmade *bombs*.

6. Given the difficulty and enormity of the work you may have doubts, think you are crazy and even fear your own death if you heed what Spirit is impelling you to do. Yet, you likewise know that something in your Spirit won't rest and will even die if you fail to do what you have come to do. This somehow brings you back to the Spiritual urgency inside you that must see your vision fulfilled.

7. You are recalling past lives where you have been witness to great human tragedy. Fear of physical death recedes as you remember that you have experienced many deaths of the body over many lifetimes. Perched more and more in a continuity of consciousness you are seeing more that death is but a transition from one life into the next. You have been in rehearsal for this moment over many lifetimes. The moment has now arrived to be of greatest Earth service. By reviewing your past lifetimes with stillness and calmness you are able to download the healing wisdom of the Ancient Arts and Sciences.

8. You are attending school at night within the Halls of Wisdom, on the inner plane, where you are being rapidly taught by the Inner Teachers. You download from the Akashic Records outlines of past, present and future events.

9. You attune to your own inner wisdom, the Master within you for guidance. Your own inner wisdom brings you into resonance with the Planetary center of Divine will and intelligence that is outworking on the Planet. This is the inner council chamber of the Most High God - Ausar, - *The One In Whom We Live and Move and Have Our Being, Lord of All the Worlds*. As you align your will with Divine will you glimpse ever more the outlines of the Divinely intended archetypal design that seeks to be made manifest. You seek to build a World more and more in accord with the Divinely intended design and purpose for our Planet.

10. You experience ever increasing contact with the 'inner plane helping agency' of Elder Teachers, which is guiding the Planet and her inhabitants into sacredization. You no longer fall under the sway of operating from the reactive level of battling and disillusionment over the agenda of your 'employment' on the outer plane. You easily and clearly see where these outer plane 'work' agendas are lacking innovative ideas and are powerless to truly heal and transform humanity, Earth and her inhabitants. Instead, you attune to the Agenda of this inner Spiritual agency for guidance, Divine ideation and direction. You find balance between the

'bread n butter' demands of the material World and the call of your Soul. You are coming more under the grip of your Soul program.

11. Working now from the level of cause, you become a co-worker and co-creator in the Great Divine Plan and a causative agent in the outer World. You seek to make changes in your outer plane agency knowing your true inner plane 'employment' in a Higher Agency. You have a sense of being *worked on* from the inner Spiritual realm. You are being aided to bear the impress and higher Spiritual vibration of the inflowing Spiritual energies. Your vehicles are being *keyed* up to bear the impress of Spirit. You feel a great sense of expectancy as though something wonderful is about to occur even if the details are not clearly revealed. You disdain sleep – seeing it as opportunity lost to Earth service - yet submit for the sake of preserving the mental, emotional and physical vehicles or bodies for maximum performance and for inner plane contact, renewal and revelation.

12. You know that in many instances the Elder Teachers on the inner plane view with amusement the very resumes, letters of recommendations, educational degrees and other documentation used as *proof* of your qualifications when making application for employment in the outer plane. As you are called to subjectively stand before the Elder teachers for an interview on the inner realm- *know that you are qualified, tested and true.* Be assured that you have awaited this moment for Eons long and even if you have residual doubts and fears, you are *prepared, protected and empowered* now for this moment in our Earth's history of re-ascent into sacredness.

What Is The Urgency For Making Rapid Preparation?
To answer these questions each person must understand the equipment that they have been evolving over time, which is both human and Divine. This Spiritual impress will find some with a fit vessel and even more without. Before looking at how you direct your course or the suitability of your vessel or instrument let us look at the urgency to make rapid preparation. We must face some of the harsh realities for how we have been building our vessel or B-ARK over time. There are three identifiable groups in humanity who are now being impacted by the rising Spiritual tide:

1. The first group will be of those who have been following a Spiritual path. They will be buoyed by the rising Spiritual tides. Already luminous and lighted their vessel will be lifted by the tidal waves. Cresting magnificent Spiritual peaks, they will express a profusion in their creative ability. They will outpour their Spiritual gifts in a tremendous demonstration of service to humanity.

2. The second group with their partially and ill prepared vessel will scramble last minute to build and refine the equipment while simultaneously attending to the Spiritual Storm. This will be tedious. Getting the vessel to bear a vibration it is unaccustomed to while navigating the storm may cause a shattering or shipwreck in the equipment.

3. The third group will consist of those who have made little or no preparation. They will simply be drowned if not rescued and offered sanctuary by the first and second group. They will likewise offer those in the first and second group their biggest test in the Aquarian principles of Brotherhood/Sisterhood, Universal Love and Service.

Chapter 18
Ausar Ba Planetary
Ba, as God indwelling in the garment of our Planet Earth

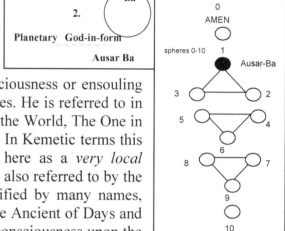

Our story continues...
Sphere 1, in the Tree of Life
Ausar Ba –Planetary

Ausar Ba -Planetary, the Great Being having consciousness or ensouling our *very local* Planet Earth is known by many names. He is referred to in the Ancient wisdom and the Bible as, 'The Lord of the World, The One in Whom We Move And Live And Have Our Being'. In Kemetic terms this Being called Planetary God may be referred to here as a *very local* Nebercher or Lord of The World. This Great Life is also referred to by the Esotericists as the Planetary Logos and is personified by many names, which include: Kumara, Sanat Kumara, Ausara, The Ancient of Days and Melchizedek. What we call 'God' depends on our consciousness upon the myriad levels of Ba, as Ba finds stationing upon the ascending rungs of the evolutionary ladder, up to and including the Universal Ba in total.

This sphere, or World or God in whom we live and move and have our being is our *current domain* for Spiritual evolution. Earth is a focus of our Spiritual Journey at this time. Why? Because on a physical level it is our dwelling place. On a consciousness level, Earth is our current school for Cosmic evolution and conscious unfoldment. When we learn the lessons of the Soul here on our tiny planet Earth, then we will go on to other realms in Cosmos for advancing Spiritual unfoldment. Learning to be 'in this World but not of it' is the path of Ausarian Resurrection.

Let us remember that the Spiritual faculty of man and woman is both Divine and human, both Spiritual and material. As such, your Spiritual faculty has been built from the 'top down' and from the 'bottom up.'

We return again to a previous key

Metaphysical Key To:
The Number 7
7 Kingdoms in Nature
The Sepentary Nature of Man and Creation

KaAbBa Building The Lighted Temple
The Spiritual B(ARK)

The Law of the Septenary 7 is expressed in the divisioning of the 7 Kingdoms of Nature. Accordingly: The Tibetan, *Esoteric Psychology. V, 1,* p. 216.

1. **The Kingdom of Solar Lives**
2. **The Kingdom of Planetary Lives**
3. **The Kingdom of Souls**
4. **The Human Kingdom**
5. **The Vegetable Kingdom**
6. **The Animal Kingdom**
7. **The Mineral Kingdom**

This brings us to the next

Metaphysical Key To:
Overlay of the 7 Kingdoms in the Tree of Life

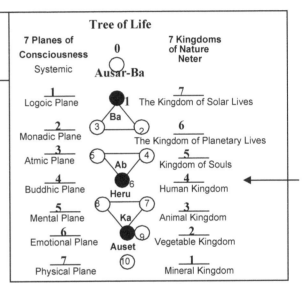

The 7 Kingdoms are revealed with the Tree of Life in the diagram at right:

As indicated by the arrow, Humanity is in the 'middle' with 3 Kingdoms above and 3 Kingdoms below. Man and woman are members of the 4th or Human Kingdom of nature. They have been building the more dense, material vehicles of their Spiritual constitution from the 3 lower Kingdoms in Nature, which are the Mineral, Vegetable and Animal Kingdoms. This is the Earthly or physical realm.

And Likewise -

Man and woman have been building the more subtle and refined vehicles of their Spiritual constitution - the Divine - from the 3 higher Kingdoms in Nature which are the Kingdoms of Souls, Planetary and Solar Lives. This is the invisible, Spiritual realm.

Man and woman build their Spiritual Faculty - the Divine - from the *top down* - from the realm of Spirit to the realm of matter. This is expressed in the following Ancient wisdom Yoga Sutra accordingly:

> Having pervaded the Universe with a fragment of myself, I remain.

And Likewise -

Man and woman have been building their Spiritual Faculty - the Human - from the *bottom up* - from the realm of matter to the realm of Spirit. This is expressed in the following Ancient wisdom saying accordingly: *Secret Doctrine.*

>A rock becomes a plant, a plant becomes and animal, an animal becomes a man, a man becomes a God.

On a lower turn of the spiral when it comes to awakening consciousness even though some men and women walk around 'donning a garment of Human form' they have *barely exited* the Animal Kingdom. The long list that straddle between the Animal and Human Kingdoms would include those among us who make the daily news for serial killing, sexually assaulting, torturing, maiming and destroying other members of the human family. They likewise bring destruction to the animal, vegetable and mineral kingdoms. The Animal Kingdom, which is instinctually driven to meet survival needs for food and reproduction, may seem brute. Yet we don't see these atrocities committed on the same scale in the Animal Kingdom that we see in the Human Kingdom (i.e. bombing, chemical warfare, pollution, Racial Holocausts, impoverization, etc.). This is the result of manes or mind operating in conjunction with untamed brute force and instinctual animal nature.

On a higher turn of the spiral there are those initiates of advanced degree who are among us on the Planet who have entered the 5th Kingdom, the Kingdom of Souls. Some walk among us, many are in retreat in mountains away from the coarse vibration of average humanity. As more of us enter the 5th Kingdom through ASTR (STAR), we will once again tip the balance whereby high initiates and God Kings will walk the Earth. This brings us to our next

---

Metaphysical Key To:
Ausar Lord of The World
Planetary Ba

We return to an earlier quote in which Ausar Ba is revealed accordingly:

Nebertcher Saith,

>I am the creator of what hath come into being, and I myself came into being under the form of the god Khepera, and I came into being in primeval time. I came into being in the form of Khepera, and I was the creator of what came into being, that is to say, I formed myself out of the primeval matter, and I formed myself in the primeval matter. My name is Ausares, who is the primeval matter of primeval matter. I have done all my will in this earth, I have spread abroad therein, and I have made strong (or, lifted up) my hand. {He is described as the pautet pautti}. I was alone, for they (i.e., the gods) were not born, and I had emitted from myself neither Shu nor Tefnut. I brought my name into my own mouth, that is to say [I uttered it as] a word of power *hekau,* and I forthwith came into being under the form of things which were created and under the form of Khepera.

KaAbBa   Building The Lighted Temple
The Spiritual B(ARK)

Let's take for further examination the words, 'My name is Ausares, who is the primeval matter of primeval matter.' We see here that from the stirring within the primeval matter/water Creator/Creation set in motion.

And likewise expressed in the following accordingly: The Tibetan. *Cosmic Fire,* p. 748. From the Archives of the Lodge.

> The Asuras veil their faces, and the pit of maya reeleth to the foundation. The stars of the eternal Lhas vibrate to that sound, the WORD uttered with sevenfold intensity. Greater the chaos becometh; the major centre with all the seven circulating spheres rock with the echoes of disintegration. The fumes of utter blackness mount upwards in dissipation. The noise discordant of the warring elements greets the oncoming One, and deters Him not. The strife and cries of the fourth great Hierarchy, blending with the softer note of the Builders of the fifth and sixth, meet His approach. Yet He passeth on His way, sweeping the circle of the spheres, and sounding forth the WORD.

Let's take for closer examination the name, 'Asuras', and the phrase, 'He passeth on His way, sweeping the circle of the spheres, and sounding forth the WORD.' This name, dis-spelled is Ausar. Ausar sounds the Word or vibration that we must all measure up to in our Planetary sphere, Earth, that is the 'World in which we live and move and have our being'. Ausar is plural here because at this level it speaks to the God indwelling the Planets in our Solar system.

Do not become confused here, lest it be said that the Kemetians believed in many Gods. The Ancients knew that there is but One GOD. Yet he is a GOD with many *Outfits* whose total wardrobe makes up the body of His manifest expression - i.e. Universal Ausar Ba. Remember that it is in garment(s) that we do see the reflection of God revealed - thus do we become GOD conscious of the One True Self.

Let's Dispell the word Asuras:
#6. Oracle Metaphysical Dis-spelling Key: Make a list of derived words. Try to make the longest continuous unbroken word or string of words.
<u>Derived Word List:</u>
<u>Ausar, Ausars</u>
<u>AU(M)</u>

#7. Oracle Metaphysical Dis-spelling Key: Look up definition (dictionary, glossary, reference texts, etc.)
<u>Definition:</u> H.P. Blavatsky, *Theosophical Glossary,* p. 40.
<u>Asuras -</u> ...in the most ancient portions of the *Rig Veda*, the term is used for the Supreme Spirit, and therefore the Asuras are spiritual and Divine. Asu means breath, and it is with his breath that Prajapiti (Brahama) creates the Asuras.
#8. Oracle Metaphysical Dis-spelling Key: Meaning. See the relationship and oracle or story of the Neteru - Put word list together to tell a story.
<u>Meaning:</u>

So we see here that: Ba and Asu both mean 'breath'. Ba = Asu. Thus do we say Ausar Ba throughout this text. AUM - Is the Most sacred word (See also, Aung, and OM) which is sounded by various religious traditions to most approximate the Great Divine Breath 'Au', and the vibration that hurls and keeps the Universe and all created beings within in manifestation. Ausar is sounding the perfecting sound of AUM, drawing all within its 'ring-pass-not' to be At-Oned within the Universal Ba - the return of Spirit to Spirit. Again, *That* which arises from the 'stirring' within AMEN and is called Ba is also called Ausar, Monad, Khepera, Kether, World Egg, World Soul, Ra, and so on. The One Universal Ba or World Egg expresses as a multiplicity of worlds or eggs within Itself. Ba is the immutable, indivisible, eternal, immortal, individualized Spiritual principle in manifestation which expresses itself along the scale of creation. Each World Egg, or entity of ensouling consciousness is properly called - Ba.

Our Solar System consists of our Sun, Moon and orbiting Planets shown in the following chart: [4]

Planetary Ba	Kemetic Name
Sun	Ra
Mercury	Sebku
Venus	Bennu-Asar
Earth	Geb
Moon	Khensu
Mars	Heru-Khuti
Jupiter	Heru-Ap-Sheta-Taui
Saturn	Heru-Ka-Pet (Heru, Bull of heaven)
Trans Saturnian Planets (beyond Saturn)	
Uranus	'veiled' until 1781
Neptune	'veiled ' until 1846
Pluto	'veiled' until 1930

The Ancients gave reverence to the Great Being having consciousness and ensouling the Sun, Ra. Our Sun is our nearest star in our local Galaxy. The Sun is Solar Ba, Neter or God. The Ancients also gave great reverence to 'nearby' Constellations. Constellations are clusters of Suns or Great Stellar Neteru. Along with the 12 Astrological Constellations these also include: Sept (Sirius, Sophis), The bull, Meskheti (Great Bear), Sahu (Orion) and the Pleides. These are also Ba, i.e., Sirius Ba, Great Bear Ba, and Pleiades Ba. The Ancients recognized the One indwelling God expressing ITSELF in the garment of Universe.

---

[4] There are many planets as yet 'unidentified' in our Solar System.

KaAbBa   Building The Lighted Temple
The Spiritual B(ARK)

There are 12 zodiacal signs or constellations. Each Zodiacal sign is ruled by a Planet. The 12 Zodiacal signs or constellations and their ruling Planets bring us to our next Metaphysical key and are listed below and then seen as an overlay in the Tree of Life diagram:

> **Metaphysical Key To:**
> The Astrological Constellations/Signs and Planetary Rulers

Neter:	Planet:	Sign:
Sphere 1 Ausar	Uranus (Pluto)	Aquarius
Sphere 2 Tehuti	Neptune (Jupiter)	Pisces (Sagittarius)
Sphere 3 Seker	Saturn	Capricorn (Aquarius)
Sphere 4 Maat	Jupiter	Sagittarius (Pisces)
Sphere 5 Herukhuti	Mars/Pluto	Aries, Scorpio
Sphere 6 Heru	Sun	Leo
Sphere 7 Het-Heru	Venus	Taurus, Libra
Sphere 8 Sebek	Mercury	Geminii, Virgo
Sphere 9 Auset	Moon	Cancer
Sphere 10 Geb	Earth	--------

The Ausarianization of Consciousness Series 1
Metaphysical Keys To the Tree of Life & Oracle Keys to Dis-spelling Illusion
The Spiritual Journey in Unfolding Consciousness

226

Metaphysical Key To:
The Overlay of the Astrological
Constellations/Signs and Planetary Rulers

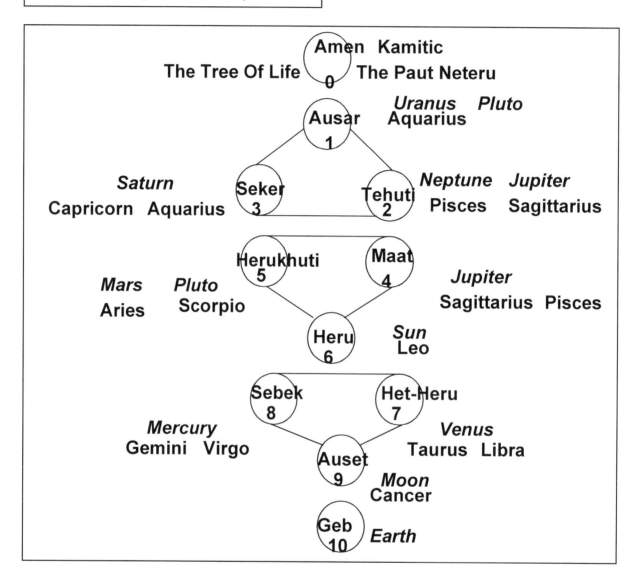

The qualities that each of the 12 Zodiacal Signs and the Planets bring are given in the, Understanding Kemetic Energy/Appendix A. Through the study of Astrology and Astronomy the Ancients were conscious beyond just our Earth Globe. Each of the spheres in the Tree of Life is under the rulership of Planetary and Constellational energy. Our Ancient Ancestors were conscious beyond the ring-pass-not of the Earth. To be more Cosmically or Universally conscious is to become more God conscious.

KaAbBa   Building The Lighted Temple
The Spiritual B(ARK)

And continuing with the previous quote, The Tibetan. *A Treatise On Cosmic Fire.* -

> From the nadir to the zenith, from eve unto the Day be with us, from the circle of manifestation to the centre of pralayic peace, is seen the enveloping blue, lost in the flame of achievement. Up from the pit of maya back to the portals of gold, forth from the gloom and darkness back to the splendour of day, rideth the Manifested One, the Avatar, **bearing the shattered Cross.** Naught can arrest His return, none can impede His Path, for He passeth along the upper way, bearing His people with Him.
>
> Cometh the dissolution of pain, cometh the end of strife, cometh the merging of the spheres and the blending of the hierarchies. All then is re-absorbed within the orb, the circle of manifestation. The forms that exist in maya, and the flame that devoureth all, are garnered by the One Who rideth the Heavens and entereth into the timeless Aeon.

Why is the cross finally shattered?
It has served as a pole vault back into the heavens, the Spiritual realm, the Dreamtime of Unitive consciousness, wholeness. Thus, as Ausar Ba, do we see the Spiritual Journey of Unfolding Consciousness. Movement from the Individualized Ba of Man to the Universal Ba is thus indicated accordingly: The Tibetan, *Initiation Human and Solar,* p. 7-8.

> As the human being develops, the faculty of awareness extends first of all beyond the circumscribing walls that confine it within the lower kingdoms of nature (the mineral, vegetable and animal) to the three Worlds of the evolving personality [read here: the Physical (Khab), Emotional/Astral (Ka/Khaibit) and Mental (Sahu) Soul bodies of the Ka-erect-er] to the planet whereon he plays his part, to the system wherein that planet revolves, until it finally escapes from the solar system itself and becomes universal [read here: Universal Ba].

Many incarnations are spent as man and woman are developing consciousness. After becoming fully human you next move to become a member of the Kingdom of Souls the 5th Kingdom. It is through the practice of meditation that your consciousness becomes unbounded. This is the breaking of the mummy bandages that bind Ausar. Holders of the Ancient wisdom often veil the journey of unfolding consciousness under other terms. This is expressed in the following quote. The Kemetic terms are placed in brackets here by me - that as Ausar Ba you may realize accordingly: Ibid.

> That the development of the human being is but the passing from one state of consciousness to another. It is a succession of expansion, a growth of that faculty of awareness that constitutes the predominant characteristic of the indwelling Thinker. It is the progressing from consciousness polarized in the personality, lower self, or body, [read here: Ka-erector] to that polarised in the higher self, ego or soul, [read here: - Ab], thence to a polarisation in the Monad or Spirit, [read here: -Ba] till the consciousness eventually is Divine.

Instead of knowing the Self as boundless we came to identify as a limited self collapsed and encapsulated within a space/time boundaried experience. Ausarian Resurrection is the putting back together into the 1 of Ba. In your return ascent you become freed from your long series of lesser self-identifications. For humanity this is our first lesson and rehearsal in **AT-ONE-ING** and thus do we re-become **Ausar Ba.** Rehearsal is an interesting word.

Let's Dispell the word rehearsal:

#6. Oracle Metaphysical Dis-spelling Key: Make a list of derived words. Try to make the longest continuous unbroken word or string of words.

#5. Oracle Metaphysical Dis-spelling Key: Letter substitution-you may substitute a letter. Place substituted letter in parenthesis ( ).

#11. Oracle Metaphysical Dis-spelling Key: What does the word sound like? Say the word out loud and then silently in a meditative state.

Derived Word List/Sounds Like List:

Re hear s(o)l

#8. Oracle Metaphysical Dis-spelling Key: Meaning. See the relationship and oracle or story of the Neteru - Put word list together to tell a story.

Meaning:

If we dispell this word we get re-hear-sol. Sol is the Sun, as in Solar. In our journey we have come to treasure a little self or ego which we have shrouded in layers of lesser identifications. In order to embrace the Higher EGO - One True Self Identification as Ausar Ba we must re-hear or attune to the vibration of the Sun. - called Ra by the Kemetians, Sol by the Greeks.

The 7 Systemic Planes of Consciousness previously described, concern themselves within the 'ring-pass-not' of our Solar System comprised of our Sun (called Ra by the Kemetians) and the Planets. The biblical phrase, *'There is nothing new under the Sun',* has much meaning here in your Ausarian Spiritual Transformation and Resurrection, ASTR. This brings us to the next

> **Metaphysical Key To:**
> The Path of At-One-Ment in
> The Ausarianization of Consciousness

1. First, on our long return journey *Home* during our evolutionary ascent and re-Spiritualziation in consciousness, every self individualization or 'self-particularization' must awaken to the seamless Oneness *it is* with every other 'self-particularization'. This is At-One-ing in consciousness and re-identification as the One True Self –Ausar Ba. Man and woman are attaining to be Ausar Ba which is to be conscious within the 'ring pass not' of the Planet - Ausar Ba Planet - Earth.

Thus we are attaining to be Self conscious Identification with/as Ausar Planetary Ba, the Great Intelligent Being Ensouling our Planet.

This is the Planetarization of consciousness.

KaAbBa   Building The Lighted Temple
The Spiritual B(ARK)

2. Next, Man and woman are attaining to extend consciousness within the 'ring pass not' of the Sun - Ausar Ba Sun. We are attaining to be conscious of everything 'under the Sun', which the Ancients called Ra. Through our identification as Ausar - the One True Self - we are able to access in consciousness 'everything under our Sun'.

Thus we are attaining to be Self conscious Identification with/as Ausar Solar Ba, the Great Intelligent Being Ensouling our Sun.
This is the Solarization of consciousness.

3. From this awareness, we will then attain to be conscious as the Great Beings ensouling multiple Star or Constellational systems beyond our Solar System 'ring pass not' are conscious.

Thus we are attaining to be Self conscious Identification with/as Ausar Constellational Ba, the Great Intelligent Being Ensouling our Constellations.
This is the Stellarization of consciousness.

4. The At-One-Ing Pathway is *open* to continue the process of attaining to be Self Conscious Identification with/as *Ba* - on up to, and including - Ba Universe in total.

Thus we are attaining to be Self conscious Identification with/as Ausar Universal Ba, the Great Intelligent Being Ensouling our Universe.
This is the Universalization of consciousness.

When we bring our consciousness to the Ba triangle within our Spiritual equipment we are entering that center of peace which has its correspondence in the etheric Planetary Center called *Sekhet Aanru* and *Sekhet Hetepu* by the Kemetians and Shamballa by later day Esotericists. In this 'place' we gather as One with the Gods and Goddesses. It is the center where the *Will of God is Known.* In this abode you are the word made Truth having sounded the fullest sound of the power of Seker. Or, as we shall see later, the power of the *seeker.*

The following terms are synonymous:

Kemetic	**Esoteric**
Sekhet-Aanru, Sekhet-Hetepu	Shamballa
Ba consciousness	Monadic consciousness:
	Elysian Fields

Let dispell the words Sekhet Aanru:

 # 1. Oracle Metaphysical Dis-spelling Key: Put letters of word or words together in a circle, like a serpent putting its tail in its mouth. Coming full Circle.

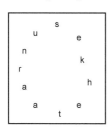 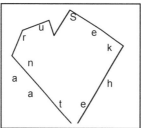

#2. Oracle Metaphysical Dis-spelling Key: Read letters, putting together words, going forwards, backwards and in zig-zag patterns.

#3. Oracle Metaphysical Dis-spelling Key: You may crossover in order to use a letter more than once. Place re-used letter in parenthesis ( ).

#4. Oracle Metaphysical Dis-spelling Key: You may add a letter to complete a word. Place added letter in parenthesis ( ).

#5. Oracle Metaphysical Dis-spelling Key: Letter substitution-you may substitute a letter. Place substituted letter in parenthesis ( ).

#6. Oracle Metaphysical Dis-spelling Key: Make a list of derived words. Try to make the longest continuous unbroken word or string of words.

Derived Word List:

Seek Return

#7. Oracle Metaphysical Dis-spelling Key: Look up definition (dictionary, glossary, reference texts, etc.)

Definition: E. A. Wallis Budge. *Prt Em Hru (Egyptian Book of the Dead),* cxxxvi.

Sekhet-Aarnru - The "Field of the Aanru plants," was a name originally given to the islands in the Delta where the souls of the dead were supposed to live. Here was the abode of the god Ausar, who bestowed estates in it upon those who had been his followers, and here the beatified dead led a new existence and regaled themselves upon food of every kind, which was given to them in abundance. According to the vignette of the cxth chapter of the Sekhet-Aanru is the third division of the Sekhet-hetepu, or "Fields of Peace, " which have been compared with the Elysian Fields of Greek mythology.

#8. Oracle Metaphysical Dis-spelling Key: Meaning. See the relationship and oracle or story of the Neteru - Put word list together to tell a story.

Meaning:

This word dispelled is *Seeker Returns.* Seek Return in Ausarian consciousness which is your conscious return to your Eternal Home.

KaAbBa Building The Lighted Temple
The Spiritual B(ARK)

Let's Dispell the words Elysian Fields:

Diagram 1   Diagram 2

   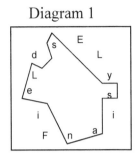   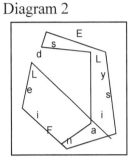

Derived Word List:

Fideli(t)y less(o)n   (Diagram 1)
fidelity
di sees finality
Finale Analysis   (Diagram 2)

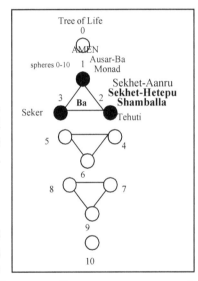

Meaning:

In the Final Analysis, the Lesson in Fidelity, loyalty, faithfulness, and devotion has been won. As Auset, you have been devoted and faithful in re-gathering the broken body of Ausar. The Finality of dual vision has come and the primal couple as Father-Mother is *in embrace* and *at rest - KaBa.*

Let's dispell the word Shamballa:

The Esotericists use the veiled word Shamballa to describe this highest aspect in your Spiritual faculty. There are 808 mentions of the word Shamballa in the 24 Tibetan books. Together they tell a whole story giving meaning to this term. You may check these out for your own research purposes. For our purpose here now - the derived definition from all these citings in short is:

Definition:

Shamballa - The Inner Counsel Chamber for the Most High God. The Planetary centre in which the Will of God is Known. It is all manifestation in the duration of the Planetary heartbeat. Furthermore, if we continue to dispell this word, we see that what these books derive is just a new spin on that which was derived by the Kemetians thousands of years before:

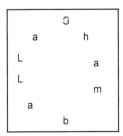   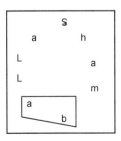

#5. Oracle Metaphysical Dis-spelling Key: Letter substitution-you may substitute a letter. Place substituted letter in parenthesis ( ).
Here, 'o' substitutes for 'a.'
Derived Word List:
Shal(o)m - Hebrew word for peace.
Ba

#8. Oracle Metaphysical Dis-spelling Key: Meaning. See the relationship and oracle or story of the Neteru - Put word list together to tell a story.
Meaning:
Shalom Ba - Place of peace, Presence - i.e., Ausar Ba or Ausarian Consciousness.
Shamballa = Hotep AusarBa. It is the etheric centre on Earth where all that are resident in this sphere of their Spiritual faculty meet in the inner Council Chamber *with and as* the Most High God. Shamballa is *local* Ba, on Earth. If you strive toward Spiritual *Home* while in your Earthly incarnation you will enter into Shamballa as symbolic *return to Home* of Universal Ba. Shamballa is called Sekhet-Aarnru by the Kemetians. It is the region in the Tuat where the Souls of the blessed dead live and serve with/as Ausar.

Let's turn the attention to focus within the 'SELF' in order to access all that is needed to bring Heaven to Earth.

Understanding Kemetic Energy/Appendix A

Oracle Metaphysical Dis-Spelling Keys

In using the Metaphysical Dis-spelling Keys along with many other Metaphysical Keys to the Tree of Life we will attempt to break the 'spell of illusion' in our re-ascent up the Tree of Life.

 # 1. Oracle Metaphysical Dis-spelling Key: Put letters of word or words together in a circle, like a serpent putting its tail in its mouth. Coming full Circle.

#2. Oracle Metaphysical Dis-spelling Key: Read letters, putting together words, going forwards, backwards and in zig-zag patterns.

#3. Oracle Metaphysical Dis-spelling Key: You may crossover in order to use a letter more than once. Place re-used letter in parenthesis ( ).

#4. Oracle Metaphysical Dis-spelling Key: You may add a letter to complete a word. Place added letter in parenthesis ( ).

#5. Oracle Metaphysical Dis-spelling Key: Letter substitution-you may substitute a letter. Place substituted letter in parenthesis ( ).

#6. Oracle Metaphysical Dis-spelling Key: Make a list of derived words. Try to make the longest continuous unbroken word or string of words.

#7. Oracle Metaphysical Dis-spelling Key: Look up definition (dictionary, glossary, reference texts, etc.)

#8. Oracle Metaphysical Dis-spelling Key: Meaning. See the relationship and oracle or story of the Neteru - Put word list together to tell a story.

#9. Oracle Metaphysical Dis-spelling Key: Take each letter one at a time or in combination with one or more letters and derive its meaning.

#10. Oracle Metaphysical Dis-spelling Key: Letter replacement. Here we have replaced the 'k' which had been substituted by the letter 'c.'

#11. Oracle Metaphysical Dis-spelling Key: What does the word sound like? Say the word out loud and then silently in a meditative state.

#12. Oracle Metaphysical Dispelling Key: Take out duplication of letters so that each letter appears only once.

#13. Oracle Metaphysical Dis-spelling Key: You may abrade a letter so that it is changed to another letter as in 'h' to 'n'. Notice the loping off of the top of the 'h' to make 'n'.

> **Definition:** Dictionary
>
> Abrade - 1. To wear down or rub away by friction; erode. See synonyms at chafe. 2. To make weary through constant irritation; wear down spiritually. (Latin abradere, to scrape of: ab-, away.

KEMETIC ENERGY LIFE PURPOSE FORMULA

The Story of Ausar, Auset and Heru and the Cosmic Energies in our Natal Chart

The story of Ausar, Auset and Heru connects us with the Cosmic Energies in our Natal Chart. The Natal Chart is a snapshot of the heavens at the time of our birth. This snapshot becomes the energy template which is with us throughout this incarnation. As we learn about this template we discover that we have more ease of access to our particular compliment of energies. We also discover that we may use these energies at their highest, most exalted, Divine level and strength or we may use these energies at their lowest, most debased, unrefined level and weakness. As Heru, we make choices, we decide.

Using your: 1) Sidereal Natal Chart 2) the Astrological, Planetary, and Neterological Energies found in this Appendix and 3) the Kemetic Energy Life Purpose Formula below, you will be able to see how the Story of Ausar, Auset and Heru is unfolding in your life and Spiritual journey. As you study and fill in the respective Astrological, Planetary and Neterological Energies corresponding to your Sun, Moon and Ascendent you are learning how to construct your Kemetic Energy Life Purpose Formula. You will need your birth date, place and time. Contact the Academy of Kemetic Education and Wellness, Inc. so that a Natal Chart may be prepared for you. Additionally, you can request a Kemetic Energy Life Purpose Formula Reading. A reading may also be requested using your Tropical Natal Chart.

Sidereal
Ka Moon/Lunar
As Auset with ceaseless persevering devotion, I express/utilize the qualities of (Astrological, Planetary, Neterological) in order to re-gather the broken body of my beloved Ausar.

Ab Ascendant
As Heru I harness personal will in accord with Divine will to achieve my Soul purpose in this incarnation. I express/utilize the qualities of (Astrological, Planetary, Neterological) in order to operate the office of the Karest within me and to gain ascendancy in the resurrection as Ausar.

Ba Sun/Solar
As Ausar using the power of least resistance, I express/utilize the qualities of (Astrological, Planetary, Neterological) in order to reconstruct and radiate the fullness of the One True Self Identification as Ausar.

The Ausarianization of Consciousness Series 1
Metaphysical Keys To the Tree of Life & Oracle Keys to Dis-spelling Illusion
The Spiritual Journey in Unfolding Consciousness

236

Metaphysical Key To:
Meditation
AUM
Ka Ab Ba

AUM
Ka Ab Ba
Meditation

1. Sitting quietly with:
a. Straight back, eyes closed
b. Hands upon lap
2. Rhythmic lower abdominal breathing
a. Inhale - expanding lower abdomen, extending stomach out in a 'Pot belly'
b. Exhale - contracting lower abdominal muscles one inch below navel
3. Become aware of your physical/etheric body - Khab - Geb - sphere 10. Allow yourself to experience relaxation in your physical body. Move your conscious awareness throughout your body. If you feel any tension anywhere, take a deep breath and breathe into that area and watch it relax.
a. Sound AUM as confirmation of stillness within physical body.
4. Become aware of your emotional/astral body - Auset - sphere 9. The emotional body can be like the tempest tossed sea.
a. As the observer - Heru - sphere 6, you can see how you could go out upon wave after wave of emotions. Each wave followed by another- rising to a peak then crashing.
b. As the observer - Heru- allow yourself to experience calmness, stillness and serenity within the emotional body - the Mother - Auset. See the water and water's surface as clear, still and pure. The ability to tame the emotional storms is the deeper Metaphysical meaning of the story of the Christ/Karest/Heru walking on water.
c. Sound AUM as confirmation of stillness within emotional body.
5. Become aware of your Mental body which includes: Sebek- Lower mind - sphere 8, and Het-Heru Higher Abstract mind - sphere 7. These are the thought form-making and imaginative spheres of your Spiritual equipment.

KaAbBa Building The Lighted Temple
The Spiritual B(ARK)

a. The thoughts and imaginings can be like stallions running wild in every direction kicking up dust and obscuring the Light of the Soul which illuminates the mind.

b. As the Observer - Engage the will to reign in the wild thoughts of the mind into Divine order and patterned beauty. Experience poise and mental clarity of the lower and higher aspects of the mental body.

c. Sound AUM as confirmation of stillness within mind.

6. Experience the alignment and coordination between your physical, emotional and mental vehicles. This is your personality, Ka or Ka-erect-or. It is the Lighted Temple you are building for/as the God Indwelling. It is the instrument used by your (Higher) Soul to do its work in the World.

7. Move your awareness to the Ab Triangle within your Spiritual equipment.

a. Hold and see all within your Ab – heart. Become aware of the growing conscience and consciousness within the heart. Hold personal will in alignment with Divine Will, governing in accord.

b. Become aware of your Soul's intent and purpose.

c. Experience your instantaneous Soul to Soul linking in Group conscious awareness within the Kingdom of Souls.

d. With your awareness poised within the Chariot of God – Ka Ab Ba.

e. You Mer (Mirror) the Image and Likeness of Father/Mother God.

f. Become aware of the Light of the Soul that radiates your Temple.

g. Sound AUM as confirmation of stillness within the Ab Triangle.

8. Move your awareness to the Ba Triangle within your Spiritual equipment. This is the center where the Will of God is Known.

a. Experience the presence, power, peace and omniscience of/as God indwelling - Hotep.

b. You are now - ***impulsed from an effortless stream wherein the Will of God is known***

a. You are Divinely guided, your co-creative Son/Daughter Sun-Ship is being made manifest and ***The Lighted Temple is be-ing Built.***

c. Sound AUM as confirmation of stillness within the Ba Triangle.

9. For five to ten minutes Chant AUM as you visualize the power of the Sun Ra, as a symbol.

10. For five to ten minutes Sound AUM silently within as you visualize the power of the Sun Ra, as a symbol.

The Ausarianization of Consciousness Series 1
Metaphysical Keys To the Tree of Life & Oracle Keys to Dis-spelling Illusion
The Spiritual Journey in Unfolding Consciousness

238

Metaphysical Key To:
The Kemetic 14 Fold - Spiritual Energy Formula

The Kemetic 14 Fold - Spiritual Energy Formula

The Kemetic 14 Fold - Spiritual Energy Formula is a tool for Ausarian Spiritual Transformation and Resurrection, ASTR (STAR). When we open our House which is our Spiritual Constitution, we see 14 major Energies at work: These include: 6 Rayological, 3 Astrological, 3 Neterological, 1 Name (Neter), and 1 Invokative of needed quality. **How to discern:** The source or 'knowingness' is what the Kemetians call the oracle of Tehuti speaking through us (sphere 2) and what the Christians call the Still Small Voice. Tap into this guidance now through your meditation prayer, reflection, and quietude.

The Ab Soul Ra(y)

The Ab Soul Ra(y) indicates your Life and Higher Soul purpose. It is this *sound* or *vibration* that guides you in knowing and fulfilling the work you have come to do in service to humanity and to the Planet. This is the Soul program and qualities of energy that are directing you in this incarnation. Attune to the inner wisdom within you for guidance in understanding your Ab Soul Ra(y) and purpose.

-See which Soul Ra(y) qualities of energy (strengths and weakness) you find resonance.

The Astrological Energies

-You must have the date, place and time of your birth to erect your Natal Chart and learn about your Astrological Energy.

-See which Astrological qualities of energy (strengths and weakness) are governing your:

Moon - Ka, Ascendent - Ab, and Sun - Ba.

The Neterological Energies of the Kemetic Neteru

-See which Kemetic Neter qualities (strengths and weakness) you find resonance.

Read and Meditate upon:

1. The Rayological, Astrological and Neterological Energies (See Appendix).
2. Try to discern in each instance which Energies you resonate with
3. Your Name (Neter) may or may not have revealed itself to you
4. Attune to which quality are you needing to invoke more of, into your life

Call 617-296-7797 *Academy of Kemetic Education, Right Relationship Maat, Inc.* For:

Astrological Charts and Full Readings

Complete Kemetic 14 Fold - Spiritual Energy Formula Reading

For more detail on the Kemetic Neteru see *ACTS 2*

KaAbBa Building The Lighted Temple
The Spiritual B(ARK)

The Kemetic 14-Fold Spiritual Energy Formula

A Tool For Ausarian Spiritual Transformation AST

When we open our House we see 14 major Energies: 6 Rayological, 3 Astrological, 3 Neterological, 1 Name (Neter), 1 Invokative of needed quality

Rayological Key:

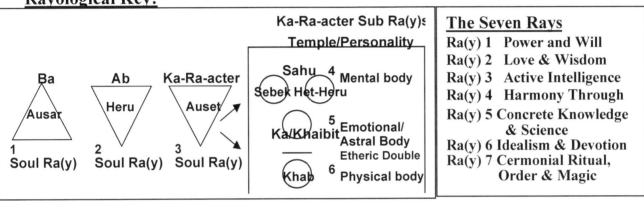

Astrological Key:

7. Sun   _____
8. Moon   _____
9. Ascendant   _____

Neterological Key:

10. Kemetic Neter (past):_____

Neter you have been working with in the past and feel some mastery in this faculty of Spirit.

11. Kemetic Neter (present):_____

Neter you are working with in the present.

12. Kemetic Neter (future):_____

Neter you see as ascending on the horizon, coming into view as a strongly influencing energy you will begin to embody more in the future.

13. EnergyInvoking more:_____

Ra(y)ological, Astrological)

14. Ren_____

   Inner Spiritual Name

Example:
The Kemetic 14-Fold Spiritual Energy Formula
A Tool For Ausarian Spiritual Transformation AST
14 major Energies: 6 Rayological, 3 Astrological, 3 Neterological, 1 Name (Neter), 1 Invokative of needed quality

Rayological Key:

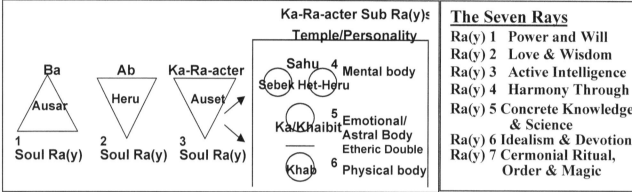

Example:
Ba Ra(y) 3 Ab Ra(y) 2 Ka-Ra-acter Ra(y) 6   Mental Soul Body Ra(y) 4
Emotional Soul Body Ra(y) 2
Physical Soul Body Ra(y) 7

Astrological Key:
   7. **Sun**   Leo
   8. **Moon**   Pisces
   9. **Ascendant** Sagittarius

Neterological Key:
10.Kemetic Neter (past):   Auset
Neter you have been working with in the past and feel some mastery in this faculty of Spirit.
11.Kemetic Neter (present): Tehuti
Neter you are working with in the present.
12.Kemetic Neter (future): Herukhuti
Neter you see as ascending on the horizon, coming into view as a strongly influencing energy you will begin to embody more in the future.
13.Energy Invoking more: 7th Ra(y) Order
Ra(y)ological, Astrological, Neterological)
14. Ren: Heru
   Inner Spiritual Name

KaAbBa   Building The Lighted Temple
The Spiritual B(ARK)

Metaphysical Key To:
Sphere 0 AMEN

No 'qualities' are assigned here because AMEN is INFINITE ALL *and EVERY-THING-NESS* and paradoxically NO-THING-NESS. It is NETER NETERU - ALL QUALITY which is inclusive of QUALITY of being UNQUALIFIED. However in our feeble human attempt to describe the indescribable the following may be proffered:

- INFINITE
- THE ALL IN ALL
- NETER NETERU
- FOUNT OF ALL POSSIBILITY
- THE ONE WITHOUT A SECOND
- SUPREME BE-NESS
- BOUNDLESS ALL
- LIMITLESS POTENTIAL (All Qualities)
- GOD
- SPIRIT
- THE ETERNAL
- THE CAUSELSS CAUSE
- THE UNCONDITIONED CONDITION
- IMMUTABLE (Changeless) ALL
- ABSOLUTE
- THE SUPREME
- BEGINNINGLESS BEGINNING
- THE ROOT CAUSELESS CAUSE
- THE UNCONDITIONED CONDITION
- THE EVERYTHING-NESS AND NO-THING-NESS
- THAT WITHOUT POINT OR CIRCUMFERENCE.

> **Metaphysical Key To:**
> Sphere 1 Ausar Neterological Energy

Planet(s): Uranus (Pluto)
Sign: Aquarius

+ Positive Qualities/ Skilled Use
•A Ray of the Absolute Spirit that penetrates into the dark depths of matter then raises and redeems every aspect of itself back into itself - Pure Spirit
•The One True Self Realized Being-ness
•The Drawer from the Fount of All Possibility
•The Drawer of All Power, All Wisdom, All Pervading Presence
•Unlimited Access to the Fount of All Possibility
•Unlimited and Unconditioned state of Being-ness in Conditioned state of Becoming
•The Eternal Witness within Infinite All in All-ness
•God Indwelling
•God as Creator and Created being
•God Essence in-form
•All Peace Hotep
•The Knower
•Is-ness of All Neteru within the to-be Circumscribed Field of Expression

- Negative Qualities/Unskilled Use
•Disconnection from All Power, All Wisdom, All Pervading Presence
•Diminished conscious livingness & experience of/as God actualizing in the physical World (Geb)

KaAbBa Building The Lighted Temple
The Spiritual B(ARK)

Metaphysical Key To:
Sphere 2 Tehuti Neterological Energy

Planets: Neptune (Jupiter)
Signs: Pisces (Sagittarius)

+ Positive Qualities/ Skilled Use
•Divine Ideation & archetypes In The Mind Of God, The Divine Khus
•Divine Wisdom
•Supreme Intelligence
•Divine Mind
•Divine Love
•Truth
•Unity Underlying Diversity
•The Whole Moving Geometrical Arrangement In The Mind Of God
•The Divine Box Cover Of The Multitudinous Piece Puzzle of Creation
•Knowledge Of Whole, Part And Perfect Relationship Between
•Unity As The Perfect Idea In The Mind Of God
•Intuition
•Divinely Intended Architectural Design And Plan for Manifestation - Pure And Perfect Without Distortion Or Flaw
•Light & Illumination
•Dissolver of Boundaries
•Omniscience
•Resolver of 'Seeming' Duality Into The One
•Synthesizing Power Of Love And Wisdom Cohering The Myriad Particularizations Or Pieces Of Created Forms Into The Seamless Unity Of The One
•Unity Underlying Diversity
•The Divine (oracle) Utterances That Bring Us To The Apex Of Any Triangle - A Point Of Resolution Into Light Supernal
•Expanse Into Wholeness, Oneness, and Unity With All Beings

- Negative Qualities/Unskilled Use
•Tapping into Limited Circumscribed Contents of Concrete Mind to Solve Life's Problems Without Reference with Divinely Intended Archetypal Design

The Ausarianization of Consciousness Series 1
Metaphysical Keys To the Tree of Life & Oracle Keys to Dis-spelling Illusion
The Spiritual Journey in Unfolding Consciousness

244

> **Metaphysical Key To:**
> Sphere 3 Seker Neterological Energy

Planet: Saturn
Signs: Capricorn (Aquarius)

+ Positive Qualities/ Skilled Use
•Creative Power & intelligence
•Vibrational drawing of the circle which contains the greatest good
•'Ring Pass Not' or Circumscribed Field of Experience in which Divine Purpose is to be Structured and Made Manifest.
•The Authoritative Demand for the Full Vibrational Sounding and Expression of the One True SELF in the to-be Manifested Form
•Creates Structure and Sets Limits within which Full Creative Potential is to be Expressed
•Exacting, Efficient, Effective, Capable, Fully Equipped, Achieving the Goal of the Archetypal Design
•Vibrational Sounding of the to-be Created Forms Fostering Evolutionary Process
•Infinite Potential in a Vibrationaly Drawn Boundaried Field of Expression
•Words of Power, Hekau,
•Alloter of the to-be 'Ringed' (boundaried) Space/time Cyclical Schedule
•The Power in Achieving One's Intended Purpose in Fullness Through Graduated 'Ring-Pass-Nots' of Boundaried Experiences

- Negative Qualities/Unskilled Use
•Harsh Over Demanding or, Weak Under Demanding Father, Authority
•Ineffectual, Impotent, Incompetent
•Unable to Set or Hold Structural Limits for Self Unfoldment and Manifestation
•Lack of Structure or Authority
•Rigidity or Crystallization of Structure
•Unbridled Power and Abuse
•Creates New Form or Destroys/Shatters Old Form Indiscriminately/Prematurely

KaAbBa   Building The Lighted Temple
The Spiritual B(ARK)

Metaphysical Key To:
Sphere 4 Maat Neterological Energy

Planets: Jupiter (Neptune)
Signs: Sagittarius (Pisces)

+ Positive Qualities/ Skilled Use
•Universal Law of Right Relationship
•Karma
•Truth, Beauty, Justice
•Peace, Peacemaker
•Right Working Together with Might (Love and Will)
•Mercy
•Philosophy that Embraces All
•Blind Justice Based on the Essential Self in All
•Right Regard, Spirit of Goodwill
•Honoring Web of Interdependence Between All Created Beings

- Negative Qualities/Unskilled Use
•Philosophy for the Few
•Blind Justice that Discriminates Based on Difference
•Incorrect Regard, Lack of Goodwill, Seeing Separation and Difference Between All Created Beings
•Injustice
•Denial of Liberty and Freedom
•Denying Self and/or Others the Right to Assert the One True Self Identity in Fullness
•Overindulgent
•Right vs. Might (Love Without the Balance of Will)
•Dishonoring Web of Interdependence Between All Created Beings

The Ausarianization of Consciousness Series 1
Metaphysical Keys To the Tree of Life & Oracle Keys to Dis-spelling Illusion
The Spiritual Journey in Unfolding Consciousness

246

Metaphysical Key To:
Sphere 5 Herukhuti Neterological Energy

Planet: Mars   (Pluto)
Signs: Aries and Scorpio

+ Positive Qualities/ Skilled Use
•Assertion
•Triumphant Disciple
•Defeator of Set
•Motion, initiator
•Strength
•Enforcer
•Might and Right (Will and Love) working together
•Courage
•Asserting the fullness of the One True Self
•Upholding the right of self and others to assert the One True Self Identity in fullness
•Defender, Warrior of the Right - *MaaKheru*

- Negative Qualities/Unskilled Use
•Aggression
•Cruelty
•Transgressor
•Cowardice
•Might vs Right, Will Without Balance of Love
•Domination, Repression, Control Over Others

KaAbBa Building The Lighted Temple
The Spiritual B(ARK)

Metaphysical Key To:
Sphere 6 Heru Neterological Energy

Planet Sun
Sign: Leo

+Positive Qualities/ Skilled Use
• Higher Will
• The Soul
• The Christ Principle Within
• Self Asserting
• Bending Personal Will, Ego into Alignment with Divine Will (Ego, The One True Self)
• Use of Will to Build in Accord with Divinely Intended Design
• Vitality Triumphant Over Set
• Growing, Unfolding Consciousness and Conscience
• Seat of the Soul
• Radiant heart
• Pure Self awareness
• Radiant Intelligent, Loving, Will
• The "I" in, I Arise and Go to My Father's Home (Ausar)
• The "I" in, I and My Father (Ausar) are One
• Glorified Son of Father Spirit and Mother Matter
• Skillful Use of Love, Will and Creative Intelligence
• Conscious Participation in the Divine Plan and Purpose
• Fullfiller of Life Purpose

- Negative Qualities/Unskilled Use
• Use of Will to Build Out of Accord with Divinely Intended Design
• Lack of Conscience, Conscious Awareness
• Unrelenting Intelligent Conscious Use of the Lower Will to Build Out of Accord with the Divinely
  Intended Design (Sociopath, Anti-Christ, Setian Living) Loss of Soul
• Alignment with Personal Will (Ego, the Myriad Lesser Selves)
• Devitalized - Easily Defeated by Set, Blinded, Heartless
• Unintelligent, Unconscious Self Seeking Personal Will
• Distorted Self Awareness
• Selfishness, "I," " Me," Centered
• Lack of Conscious Participation in Divine Plan and Purpose

> **Metaphysical Key To:**
> Sphere 7 Het-Heru Neterological Energy

Planet: Venus
Signs: Taurus and Libra

+ Positive Qualities/ Skilled Use
•Magnetic Attractive Power
•Higher, Abstract, Aspiring Mind
•Imagination
•Aspiring for Higher Ideal, Archetype
•What You Love and Attract
•Beauty, Refinement, Sociability, Good Taste
•Artistic, Creative
•Sensual, Pleasure Seeking
•Lofty Ideals
•Higher Aspiration for The One True Self
•Engages the Sexual Energy - Ra - to Ascend to Higher Chakras
•Glimpses Inner Archetypal Patterning of Greater Wholeness and Beauty
•Magnetically Attracts and Aspires Towards Archetypal Patterning of Greater Wholes
•Appreciation of Life's Pleasures on Earth, Aspiring to Spiritual Treasure in Heaven
•Bringer of Harmony in Relationships, Mediates Discordant Energies

- Negative Qualities/Unskilled Use
•Engages the Sexual Energy - Ra - to Descend to Lower Chakras
•Seductive
•Desirous Mind
•Obsessive
•Lustful
•Addicted to Lower Pleasures
•Addicted to Old Patterning
•Unwholesome Attraction
•Lower Desire for the Myriad Lesser Self Identifications (drugs, movie stardom, etc.)
•Base Preoccupations, Unrefined, Lacking Social Graces

KaAbBa Building The Lighted Temple
The Spiritual B(ARK)

Metaphysical Key To:
Sphere 8 Sebek Neterological Energy

Planet: Mercury
Signs: Gemini and Virgo

+ Positive Qualities/ Skilled Use
•Analytical
•Discriminating, Discerning
•Separating into Parts, Categorizing, Sorting
•Ability to Clothe Divine Ideation in Thought-Form
•Ability to Make Divine Ideation Tangible, Applicable & Practical in Real World
•Ability to Ground Higher Ideation and Ideals into Practical Life Solutions
•Segretive, Separative Mind, Dissects, Particularizes, Looks at Parts
•Concrete Mind
•Knowledge, Data, Information
•Communication
•Rationalizes
•Flexible, Adaptive Mind
•Methodological, Organizing Mind
•Critical Thinking, Problem Solving Mind

- Negative Qualities/Unskilled Use
•Flight of Ideas, Impractical, Ungrounded, Scatter and Chaos
•Rigid
•Prejudicial, Discrimination, Arrogance
•Mental Coldness
•Bigotry, Criticism
•Sees Part as Reality and Loses Sight of Underlying Wholeness as Reality
•Falsely Identifies Self as Contents of Mind
•Working on Limited/Circumscribed Contents of Mind without Reference to Infinite Wisdom (Tehuti)

> **Metaphysical Key To:**
> Sphere 9 Auset Neterological Energy

Planet: Moon
Sign: Cancer

+ Positive Qualities/ Skilled Use
•Receptive
•Reflection of the Divine Father
•The Marriage between the Divine Father and The Divine Mother within
•Reproduction, Generativity
•Mother
•Watery, Fluid, Elastic, Impressionable, Impregnable, Imagistic Nature
•Clear, Limpid, Reflective Water
•Subconscious, Memory
•Beholder of the Divine Archetypes
•Receiver of Higher Creative Impressions
•Devotion
•Desire, Feeling Nature, Emotions, Sensitivity
•Protective
•Receptivity to Positive Seeding for Future Birth in Form (Geb)
•Womb of The One True Self
•Luminous Mirror-Reflection of God

- Negative Qualities/Unskilled Use
•Holder of the 'Stuff' of Past (Repressed Memories)
•Old Patterns, Conditioning, 'Habits'
•Pollution
•Moody, Overemotional, Over Reactivity
•Smothering
•Unwholesome
•False Devotion
•Receptivity to Negative Seeding for Future Birth in Form (Geb)
•Tomb of Myriad Lesser, False Selves
•Distortion of the Divine Father Within
•Distorted, Darkened, unGodly Reflection
•Murky, Turbid Waters
•Falsely Identifies Self as Feelings

KaAbBa Building The Lighted Temple
The Spiritual B(ARK)

Metaphysical Key To:
Sphere 10 Geb Neterological Energy

Planet: Earth

+ Positive Qualities/ Skilled Use
•The Manifestation of God Indwelling and Divine Living on Earth
•The Manifestation of God Indwelling and the Livingness of God on Earth
•The Divinely Patterned World of Beauty Made Manifest
•Peaceful, Harmonious Living (Hotep), Life in Abundance
•Spirit Infusing Matter Visibly and Tangibly Expressed, Heaven on Earth
•Right Relationships Justice
•A World in Accord with the Laws of Maat, Lawful

- Negative Qualities/Unskilled Use
•The Manifestation of Evil or Setian Living on Earth
•The World of Sorrow and Suffering that Manifests when Building Out of Accord with the Divinely Intended Design.
•Dis-eased Body, Environment, Planet
•War, Aggression, Destruction, Death
•Falsely Identifies Self as Body, Physical Form - Khab
•A World Out of Accord with the Laws of Maat, Unlawful

The Ausarianization of Consciousness Series 1
Metaphysical Keys To the Tree of Life & Oracle Keys to Dis-spelling Illusion
The Spiritual Journey in Unfolding Consciousness

252

Metaphysical Key To:
Astrological Sign: Aries
Planet: Mars

1. Aries.

Sign: Aries
Symbol: The Ram
Rays: 1, 7
Cross: Cardinal
Element: Fire
Anatomy: head, face, brain, upper teeth.

Planetary Ruler: Mars
Assertive, impulsive, energy, excitement, aggressiveness, God of war, combative, effort, asserting the *lower* self or *Higher* Self. Triumph of Soul over personality. Right and might working together. Ray 6

Key phrase. *I Am. "Power to Begin." Activity*

Strengths:
initiative
pioneering spirit
adventurous
assertiveness
leadership
self-directed
dynamic energy
independent
quick
courageous
power to originate

Weaknesses:
domineering
rash
impulsive
impatient
aggressive
competition
unrealistic estimation
combative
lack of moderation
arrogant
lacks follow through

Keynote: *I come forth and from the plane of mind, I rule. Will*

KaAbBa Building The Lighted Temple
The Spiritual B(ARK)

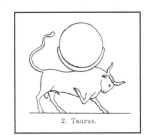

2. Taurus.

Metaphysical Key To:
Astrological Sign: Taurus
Planet: Venus

Sign: Taurus
Symbol: The Bull
Ray: 4
Cross: Fixed
Element: Earth
Anatomy: throat, neck, ears, vocal chords, thyroid, tongue, mouth, tonsils, lower teeth.

Planetary Ruler: Venus
Appreciation of beauty, what you love, what you value materially/spiritually, what you possess, color, artistry, refinement, subtle discernment of mental faculty, Goddess of love. Ray 5

Key phrase: *I Have. I Want.*
"Desire to Materialize"
Stability.

Strengths:
patience
stability
grounded-ness
practicality
endurance
strong sense of value
artistic
drive toward illumination
thorough
pleasure, sensual
building
persistent
reliable
loyal
possessions, power to acquire

Weaknesses:
stubborn
slow-moving
desires
stuck
self-indulgence
possessiveness
materialistic
argumentative

Keynote: *I see, and when the eye is opened, all is illumined. Aspiration. The Light of Love.*

The Ausarianization of Consciousness Series 1
Metaphysical Keys To the Tree of Life & Oracle Keys to Dis-spelling Illusion
The Spiritual Journey in Unfolding Consciousness

254

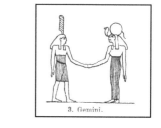

3. Gemini.

Metaphysical Key To:
Astrological Sign: Gemini
Planet: Mercury

Sign: Gemini,
Symbol: The Twins
Ray: 2
Cross: Mutable
Element: Air
Anatomy: lungs, collar bone,
hands, arms, shoulders,
nervous system.

Planetary Ruler: Mercury
Communication, information,
speaking, writing, thinking,
planning, reasoning, bridging,
field of knowledge, messenger
of the Gods, Mercury and the
Sun are One. Ray 4

Key phrase*: I think. I speak.*
I communicate. "Interplay
Between the Opposites."
Versatility

Strengths:
adaptable
flexibility
communication
speaking
writing
Intelligence
agility
awareness of duality
networking
busy
quick
witty
curious
relates soul and personality.

Weaknesses:
scattered
instability
poor follow through
restlessness,
inconsistency
manipulation
hyperactive
nervous
changeable
lacking concentration

Keynote: *I recognize my*
other self, and in the
waning of that self, I
grow and glow. Right
relation. I serve the
One.

KaAbBa   Building The Lighted Temple
The Spiritual B(ARK)

> **Metaphysical Key To:**
> **Astrological Sign: Cancer**
> **Planet: Moon**

4. Cancer.

Sign: Cancer,
Symbol: Khepera (Crab)
Rays: 3, 7
Cross: Cardinal
Element: Water
Anatomy: breast, stomach,
upper lobes of liver.

Planetary Ruler: Moon
Home, roots, foundation,
habits, memory, womb, tomb,
habit, subconscious, conditioning. Ray 4

Key phrase: *I feel.*
"Clothing the Spirit in
Form" Devotion.

Strengths:
nurturing
mothering
protective
feelings
emotions
receptivity
care-giving
domesticity
realization of wholeness
psychic, impressionable
belonging
sympathetic

Weaknesses:
over-sensitivity
moodiness
over protectiveness
clingy
fear
worry
retrogression
timidity
brooding
easily hurt

Keynote: *I build a*
lighted house and
therein dwell. The Whole
is seen as one.
Humanity.

The Ausarianization of Consciousness Series 1
Metaphysical Keys To the Tree of Life & Oracle Keys to Dis-spelling Illusion
The Spiritual Journey in Unfolding Consciousness

256

Metaphysical Key To:
Astrological Sign: Leo
Planet: Sun

Sign: Leo
Symbol: The Lion
Rays: 1, 5
Cross: Fixed
Element: Fire
Anatomy: heart, sides, upper back.
Planetary Ruler: Sun
The *lower* self or *Higher* Self as center, personal will in or out of alignment with Divine Will, vitality, leadership, radiance of Soul light and love, magnetic attractive power, Co-creative *Sun*-Son/Daughter-ship. Ray 2

Key phrase: *I will. I show. I create. "Expression of Individuality" Magnetism.*

Strengths:
assertion of will
self-expression
vitality
I-dentity
creativity
dramatic
life force
self-confidence
entertaining
power to rule inspire
center of attention
center of loving (romance)
purpose
play
dignity
royalty

Weaknesses:
arrogance
domination
show-offish
extravagance
lower self-centeredness
excessive pride
egotism
patronizing
vanity

Keynote: *I am that, and that am I. The One True Self.*

KaAbBa   Building The Lighted Temple
The Spiritual B(ARK)

6. Virgo.

Metaphysical Key To:
Astrological Sign: Virgo
Planet: Mercury

Sign: Virgo
Symbol: The Virgin
Rays: 2, 6
Cross: Mutable
Element: Earth
Anatomy: Intestines, liver, pancreas, gall bladder, lower plexus upper bowel.

Planetary Ruler: Mercury Linking principle of mind, Karest/Christ Consciousness in form, Christ-ing/Karest-ing of matter. (See Mercury under sign of Gemini). Ray 4

Key phrase: I analyze. I discriminate. "Purification of Form." Practicality.

Strengths:
perfector of forms
problem solving
power of analysis
manages detail
methodological
meticulous
service
capacity for hard work
ability to nurture inner light
purification and health
humility
careful
technique
skill

Weaknesses:
hypercritical
perfectionist
fastidiousness
pettiness
worrier

Keynote*: I am the mother and the child. I God, I, matter am.* "Christ in you the hope and glory." The Christ activity.

The Ausarianization of Consciousness Series 1   258
Metaphysical Keys To the Tree of Life & Oracle Keys to Dis-spelling Illusion
The Spiritual Journey in Unfolding Consciousness

Metaphysical Key To:
Astrological Sign: Libra
Planet: Venus

7. Libra.

Sign: Libra
Symbol: The Scales
Ray: 3
Cross: Cardinal
Element: Air
Anatomy: Kidneys, lower back, adrenal glands, appendix.

Planetary Ruler: Venus
Appreciation of beauty, what you love, what you value materially/spiritually, what you possess, color, artistry, refinement, subtle discernment of mental faculty, Goddess of love.
Ray 5

Key phrase: *I relate. I evaluate. I balance. "Relationship Leading to Union" Harmony.*
Strengths:
right relationship
justice
harmony
partnership
marriage
we
higher ideal
able to see both/all sides
cooperation
diplomacy
law
mediation
sociability
peace loving
artistic
refined
balance

Weaknesses:
indecision
over-reliance on partners
ambivalence
love of pleasure
a pleaser to avoid conflict
judgmental

Keynote: *I choose the way which leads between the two great lines of force. Balance attained. Divine love. Understanding*

8. Scorpio.

Metaphysical Key To:
Astrological Sign: Scorpio
Planet: Mars, Pluto

Sign: Scorpio
Symbol: The Scorpion
Anatomy: genitals, bladder, rectum, reproductive organs.
Ray 4
Cross: Fixed
Element: Water

Planetary Rulers:
Mars & Pluto
Mars - Assertive, impulsive, energy, excitement, aggressiveness, God of war, combative, effort, asserting the *lower* self or *Higher* Self. Triumph of Soul over personality. Right and might working together.
Ray 6

Pluto - Purging, birth, death, transformation, destruction, death of desire, death of personality to achieve final liberation, penetrating into form (matter), redeeming it into the light. Ray 1

Key phrase: *I desire. I share. I "Struggle with Darkness Leading to Victory." I Conquer.*

Strengths:
psychic
triumph
discipleship
intense, passionate
joint resources
penetrative insight
death, rebirth, transformative
regeneration
probing
investigative
mystery
sexuality
sexual organs

Weaknesses:
secretive
revengeful
manipulative
dependency
destructive
repressive
treacherous
obsession
jealous
the inner darkness
that which needs
redeeming

Keynote: *Warrior am I and from the battle I emerge triumphant."*
Higher unity achieved. The triumphant Disciple.

The Ausarianization of Consciousness Series 1
Metaphysical Keys To the Tree of Life & Oracle Keys to Dis-spelling Illusion
The Spiritual Journey in Unfolding Consciousness

260

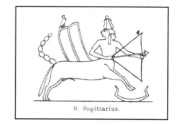

9. Sagittarius.

Metaphysical Key To:
Astrological Sign: Sagittarius
Planet: Jupiter

Sign: Sagittarius
Symbol: The Centaur
Rays 4, 5, 6
Cross: Mutable
Element: Fire
Anatomy: thighs, hips, upper leg

Planetary Ruler: Jupiter
Expansion, abundance, beneficent, evolutionary unfoldment, optimism, philosophy. Ray 2

Key phrase: I aspire. I seek. I foresee. I understand. "Envisioning the Goal." Visualization.

Strengths:
higher mind
philosophy
lofty idealism
rapid intuition
adventurous spirit
travel (inner and outer)
justice, just
goal directed
seeker of truth
expansiveness
optimism
teaching
higher wisdom
religion
freedom loving

Weakness:
exaggeration
blind optimism
tactlessness
recklessness
impatient
pushy
judgmental

Keynote: *I see the goal. I reach that goal and then I see another.*

KaAbBa Building The Lighted Temple
The Spiritual B(ARK)

10. Capricornus.

<table>
</table>

Metaphysical Key To:
Astrological Sign: Capricorn
Planet: Saturn

Sign: Capricorn
Symbol: The Goat
Rays 1, 3, 7
Cross: Cardinal
Element: Earth
Anatomy: knees, lower leg

Planetary Ruler: Saturn
Confinement, limitations, 'ring-pass-not', discipline required to lead the life of discipleship, promotes growth through opportunity. Ray 3

Key phrase: *I utilize. I attain. I use. I attain. "Climbing to the Peak of Achievement"*

Strengths:
discipline
achievement
responsibility
industriousness
creating structure
conforming to highest law and will
ambitious
authority
time
fathering

Weaknesses:
materiality
rigidity
suppression
callousness
pessimism
isolation
crystallization
fitting in

Keynote: *Lost am I in light supernal, yet on that light I turn my back. The Conqueror of Death.*

Metaphysical Key To:
Astrological Sign: Aquarius
Planet: Uranus, Saturn

Sign: Aquarius
Symbol: The Water Bearer
Ray: 5
Cross: Cardinal
Element: Air
Anatomy: ankles

Planetary Rulers: Uranus &
Saturn

Uranus - Innovative,
revolution, rebellion,
liberation, social reform,
independence, open minded,
unique, strange, sudden,
unexpected, lighting,
electricity, power to shatter
old idea bringing in new
archetypal ideation, Intuition,
power of creative, innovative
ideas. Ray 7

Saturn - Confinement,
limitations, 'ring-pass-not',
discipline required to lead the
life of discipleship, promotes
growth through opportunity.
Ray 3

Key phrase: *I know. I Share.
I Serve. Distribute.
"Distribution of Energy in
Service" Imagination.*

Strengths:
humanitarianism
spirit of sharing
universality
group conscious spirit
serving for the benefit of all
progressive
reformation
freedom
friendship
utopian
the future
impersonal
Inventive
scientific
altruistic

Weaknesses:
rebellious
aloof
eccentric
superficial
unpredictable
temperamental

Keynote: *Water of Life
am I, poured forth for
thirsty men. The Server
of all men. The burden of
the World.*

KaAbBa Building The Lighted Temple
The Spiritual B(ARK)

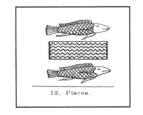

12. Pisces.

Metaphysical Key To:
Astrological Sign: Pisces
Planet: Jupiter, Neptune

Sign: Pisces
Symbol: The Fish
Rays 2, 6
Cross: Mutable
Element: Water
Anatomy: feet

Planetary Ruler:
Neptune & Jupiter

Neptune - Dissolver of
boundaries, universality,
imagination, intuition,
transcendent awareness,
transcendent, unity,
spirituality. Ray 6

Jupiter - Expansion,
abundance, beneficent,
evolutionary unfoldment,
optimism, philosophy. Ray
2

Key phrase: *I believe. I save.*
"Empathy with all Beings"

Strengths:
imagination
psychic ability
compassion
self-denial
inclusive
more courage than any other
sign
Oneness
essence
sacrifice
power to serve
non-material

Weaknesses:
escapism
nebulous, vague, evasive
dreamy
illusion, delusion
psychosis
martyr
substance abuse
pain, suffering
overwhelmed
helplessness
gullibility
hyper-sensitivity
sentimentality

Keynote: *I leave the*
Father's home, and
turning back I save.
Spiritual responsibility.
The Saviour.

Astrological Qualities of Kemetic Energy Formula

Ba
Ausar

The Sun Astrologically is what you easily radiate. If you look at the Sun, Ra, in the sky it 'just is'. It is the line of least resistance for a particular life cycle. You express the energy of the sign that the Sun is in. It is the quality of energy you use to express your One True Self Identification. It is vitality, identity, the 7 - Fold Ka-Ra-acter reconstructed. It is a starting point, and how things orbit around you. It is the expression of alignment with Divine Will once personal will has been brought under the grip of the higher Soul program.

Ka
Auset

The Moon Astrologically represents your ceaseless, persevering devotion to reconstruct the broken body of Ausar, so that the Image and Likeness of God is reflected without distortion. It likewise represents the past, subconscious, automatic, habitual, and the residual that inhibit progress. The repetitive rhythm or Ka/Khaibit or habit, must be broken if psychologically transformative progress is to be made. The Moon is the temporary reflector of the lesser self identification. There is a tendency to fall back on the Moon during crisis. It is a comfort zone for lesser self identification which must be relinquished, to open to wider identification, until the One True Self is Realized. In other words, releasing 'snapshots' which ID you as *less than*. The Moon reflects the fullness of the light of the Sun (Soul). It is the quality of energy used to be *habituated* on the Fullness of the One True Self, which is our nurturance – the only thing that truly satisfies need and desire.

Ab
Heru

The Ascendent Astrologically brings the Ka-erect-er/personal life (personality/temple) into alignment with the will of the Ab and Ba Soul Bodies. The energy of the sign is an indicator of your Soul's work in this incarnation. It is the purpose of incarnation, lessons to learn, goals to achieve, Soul qualities to aim for. It is the method that the Soul will use to achieve its purpose. It is the key to the design which the Ab Soul intends to actualize through the personal life or otherwise stated – It is the key to the design by which the Soul will grip its instrument, its temple for service in this lifetime. It is how the Heru or Christ has an office within you. It is the quality of energy used to operate this office of inner government and administration, making choices and managing the affairs of daily living, so that your Soul program is fulfilled. It is the point on the horizon - the Apta in the Kemetic system. Thus, it is the point of emergence, and *Coming Forth by Day as Heru*. It is the energy used by you as Heru to gain ascendency in the resurrection of Ausar.

> **Metaphysical Key To:**
> **The Rayological Energy**

RA(Y) 1
THE RA(Y) OF WILL AND POWER
Some Strengths Characteristic of Those Upon the First RA(Y) *

•Strength of will, courage, fearlessness
•Dynamic power to lead, govern, direct
•Leader, executive, administrative, diplomatic type
•Keen understanding of principles and priorities, power to synthesis, centralise
•Power of beneficent destruction, power to destroy
•Power to liberate
•Strong one-pointed focus
•Strong sense of purpose
•Detachment, independence
•Power to initiate, to begin
•Wisdom to establish, uphold or enforce the law
•Power to preserve and uphold values and principles, large mindedness
•Sacrifices self for greater causes
•Truthfulness arising from absolute fearlessness
•Demonstrates the power of love

Some Weaknesses Characteristic of Those Upon the First RA(Y)

•Egotism, Excessive pride
•Separateness, isolativeness
• Arrogance
•Willfulness
•Power-hungriness, demonstrates the love of power
•Anger, violence, hardness and cruelty
•Unrelenting ambition, obstinacy, impatience
•Inhibits, suppresses, stubborn
•Control, domination and suppression
•Destructiveness, destroys for the love of it
•Forces personal values on others

---

* Michael Robbins. *Tapestry of The Gods.*

RA(Y) 2
THE RA(Y) OF LOVE-WISDOM
Some Strengths Characteristic of Those Upon The Second RA(Y)*
• Loving, wise, understanding, teaching, healing type
•Unconditionally loving, magnetic, attractive love
•Power to heal and understand through Love
•Power to teach and illumine
•Wisdom, wise counselor
•Patience, empathy, sympathy, compassion, understanding
•Exquisitely sensitive, receptive, impressionability
•Inclusiveness, cohesiveness
•Love of study, pure knowledge, desire for absolute truth
•Power to heal, redeem and salvage
•Calmness, peacefulness, serene, composed, tact
•Tolerant, patient, tactful
•Heart qualities, faithfulness
•Clear perception, understanding, intelligence, intuitive

Some Weaknesses Characteristic of Those Upon the Second RA(Y)
•Non assertive, lack of energy
•Inferiority complex, self pity, poor self esteem
•Love of being loved, binds others through a need to be loved
•Wanting personal popularity, longing for security
•Fearfulness, emotionally indiscriminate
•Unable to say 'no', limit set,
• Oversensitivity, vulnerable, overabsorbent, impressionable
•Fearing anger, rejection, disapproval of others
•Overattachment, overprotectivesness, overguarding
{Mental types}
•Cold and indifferent
•Over absorbed in study
•Scorns mental limitation in others

---

* Michael Robbins. *Tapestry of The Gods.*

RA(Y) 3
THE RA(Y) OF ACTIVE INTELLIGENCE
Some Strengths Characteristic of Those Upon The Third RA(Y)*

• Active, intelligent, strategist, business planning type
• Capacity for wide ranging abstract thinking
• Acute, powerful intellect
• Ability to plan, strategise, theorise, speculate
• Understands relativity
•Power to recognize and think within the blueprint of the Divine Plan
•Power to explain complexly woven patterns and trends
• Power to manipulate
• Capacity for rigorous analysis, reasoning and complex thought
• Great mental agility, fertility, creativity
• Skillful communicator, power to put thought into words, facility with language
• Great activity and adaptability
•Executive/business skill, economical ability, philanthropic
• Facility at understanding and handling money

Some Weaknesses Characteristic of Those Upon the Third RA(Y)

• Superficial thought, intellectual pride, criticism
• Vague, confused, absent minded, overly-complex thought and expression of thought, perplexity, impractical ideas, 'gab, but no gift'
• Excessive thought without practical action, scattered reasoning
• Inaccurate, careless with detail
• Devious, untruthful, deceitful, deceptive words, opportunism
• Manipulativeness, calculatedness, scheming
• Chameleon-like overadaptability
•Amoral materialism
•Hyperactivity, restlessness, wasted motion and rush
•Disorder and chaos
•Tendency to be "spread too thin", scatter
•Constant preoccupation and 'busyness'

---

* Michael Robbins. *Tapestry of The Gods.*

RA(Y) 4
THE RA(Y) OF HARMONY THROUGH CONFLICT
Some Strengths Characteristic of Those Upon The Fourth RA(Y)*
• Artistic type
•Facility for bringing harmony out of conflict
• Capacity to grow spiritually and psychologically through constant struggle
•Capacity to reconcile, compromise, mediate and bridge opposites
•Facility for achieving 'at-onement'
•Love of beauty and the capacity to create and express it
•Refinement of artistic and aesthetic tastes and sensibilities
•Strong imagination, intuition
•Abundant creativity, love of colour, drama, literary ability, musicality
•Ability to entertain, amuse, delight
•Spontaneity and improvisation
•Fighting spirit
•Ability to make peace

Some Weaknesses Characteristic of Those Upon The Fourth RA(Y)
•Embroiled in constant inner/outer conflict
•Lack of confidence and composure
•Worry, agitation, moodiness, self absorbed in suffering
•Exaggeration, overly dramatic expression
•Tempermentalism, impracticality and improvidence
•Overeager for compromise
•Unstable activity patterns, spasmodic action, ups & downs, highs & lows swings to extremes
•Confused combativeness, fights for sake of fighting
•Moral cowardice, indecisive
•Ambivalence, indecisiveness and vacillation
•Overeagerness for compromise
•Unregulated passions, unpredictable, tempermental
•Inertia, indolence, procrastination, unreliable

---

* Michael Robbins. *Tapestry of The Gods.*

RA(Y) 5
THE RA(Y) OF CONCRETE KNOWLEDGE AND SCIENCE
Some Strengths Characteristic of Those Upon The Fifth RA(Y) *
•Scientific type
•Capacity to think and act scientifically, mathematically
•Keen, focused intellect yielding the power to know
•Power to define
•Power to create thoughforms
•Facility for mathematical calculation
•Highly developed power of analysis and discrimination
•Detached objectivity
•Accuracy and precision in thought and action
•Acquisition of knowledge and the mastery of factual detail
•Power to discover through observation, research, investigation
•Power to verify through experimentation, the discrimination of truth from error
•Technical and mechanical ability and expertise
•Practical inventiveness
•Determines cause and effect relationship
•Lucidity of explanation
•Specialization, Master a field of knowledge, expertise

Some Weaknesses Characteristic of Those Upon The Fifth RA(Y)
•Excessive mentalism, rigid and set thought patterns
•Overanalysis, over-specialization, over detailed, ultra-rationalism, unrelieved linearity
•Excessive doubt, skepticism, irreverence, lack of intuitive sensitivity
•Denies validity of anything which cannot be weighed or measured
•Prejudiced, harsh criticism, narrowness, intellectual pride
•Seeks to control through knowledge
•Lack of emotional responsiveness and magnetism, social awkwardness

---

* Michael Robbins. *Tapestry of The Gods.*

RA(Y) 6
THE RA(Y) OF DEVOTION AND ABSTRACT IDEALISM
Some Strengths Characteristic of Those Upon The Sixth RA(Y)*

•Visionary, idealism, devotional type
•Transcendent idealism, power of abstraction
•Intense devotion, aspiration, dedication, reverence
•Self sacrificial ardor
•Unshakable faith and undimmed optimism
•One-pointedness; single mindedness
•Utter loyalty and adherence
•Earnestness, sincerity, profound humility
•Receptivity to spiritual guidance
•Unflagging persistence
•Power to arouse, inspire and persuade
•Ability to achieve ecstasy and rapture
•Purity, goodness, sainthood, mysticism, religious instincts
•Live and die for a cause, intense personal feeling
•Love

Some Weaknesses Characteristic of Those Upon The Sixth RA(Y)

•Rigid idealism, narrow mindedness, exclusive vision, bigotry
•Blind faith, blinded by truth, idealistic impracticality
•Unreasoning devotion, ill-considered loyalty
•Excess, extremism, hyperintensity, emotionalism, overdoing
•Fanaticism and militarism
•Selfish and jealous love, dependency, overleaning on others
•Unwise susceptibility to guidance
•Superstition and gullibility, lack of realism
•Self abasement, masochism, the martyr-complex
•Frenzied follower, fanatic leader
•Seeing things as either perfect or intolerable
•Unnatural suppression of the instinctual nature

---

* Michael Robbins. *Tapestry of The Gods.*

KaAbBa Building The Lighted Temple
The Spiritual B(ARK)

RA(Y) 7
THE RA(Y) OF CEREMONIAL RITUAL, ORDER AND MAGIC
Some Strengths Characteristic of Those Upon The Seventh RA(Y)*
•Organizational type
•Power to manifest and to work upon the material plane
•Power to plan, organise, create order, bring order out of chaos
•Ritualism and ceremonialism
•Keen sense of rhythm, timing
•Power to perfect form
•Power to manage detail
•Power to coordinate groups
•Power to understand and implement the law, attention to rule and precedent
•Power to build, renovate, transform, and synthesize
•Power as a magician
•Power to work with the devas and elemental forces
•Skill in business, practicality
•Designer of beautiful forms
•Extreme care in details, doing things decently and in order

Some Weaknesses Characteristic of Those Upon The Seventh RA(Y)
•Rigid orderliness, formalism, crystallization
•Overconcern with rules, regulations and the 'dead letter' of the law
•Rigid routines and subservience to habit, formalism
•Meaningless ritualism, pretentious ceremonialism
•Materialistic, earthboundedness
•Intolerance of individuality, lack of originality
•Excessive conformity (or nonconformity), intolerance of anything different
•Excessive perfectionism
•Bigotry, sectarianism
•Superficial judgment based upon appearances
•Addiction to occult phenomena, spiritualism, perversion of the magical process,
Sex-magic

---

* Michael Robbins. *Tapestry of The Gods.*

The Ausarianization of Consciousness Series 1
Metaphysical Keys To the Tree of Life & Oracle Keys to Dis-spelling Illusion
The Spiritual Journey in Unfolding Consciousness

272

The Judgment Scene Hall of Amenta part 1
Psychostasia:
The Judgment of the Heart of Ani
From the Funerary papyrus of Ani

Sia & Hu   Hathor   Heru   Het-Heru   Nut   Geb   Tefnut   Shu   Ausar   Ra
& Auset

Ani and wife Ammitt	Meskhenet	Shai	Anubis	Tehuti
Devour of	Renenutet	Ani's Soul	testing tongue	recording
	Goddess of Birth	Ani's embryo	of balance	result of
Unjustified	Goddess of Harvest	Luck or Destiny		weighing

KaAbBa   Building The Lighted Temple
The Spiritual B(ARK)

The Judgment Scene Hall of Amenta part 2
Psychostasia:
The Judgment of the Heart of Ani
From the Funerary papyrus of Ani

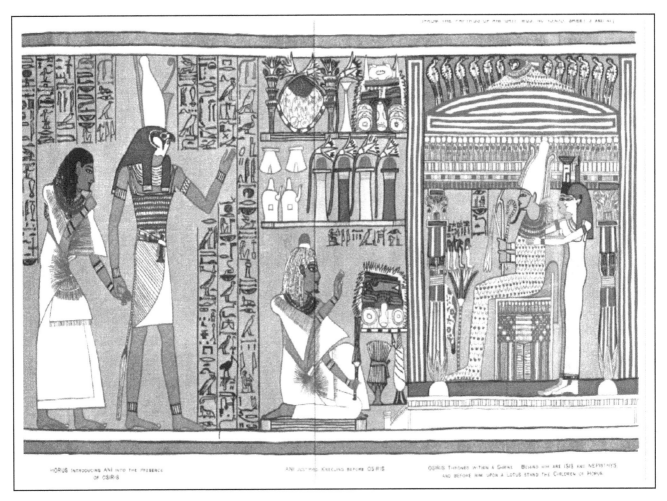

Heru Leading Ani   Heru Ani Justified   Ausar with Auset & Het-Heru behind & 4 children
Before presence of Ausar   Kneeling before Ausar   of Heru before HIM on Lotus stand.

Vignette: E. A. Wallis Budge. Prt Em Hru. (Egyptian Book of the Dead), p. 255-257.

"Scene of the weighing of the Heart of the Dead. Ani and his wife enter the Hall of Double Law or Truth, wherein the heart, emblematical of the conscience, is to be weighed in the balance against the feather, emblematical of law. Above, twelve gods, each holding a scepter, are seated upon thrones before a table of offerings of fruit, followers, etc. Their names are: - Harmachis, "the great god within his boat"; Tmu; Shu; Tefnut, "lady of heaven"; Seb; Nut, "lady of Heaven"; Auset; Het-Heru; Heru, "the great god"; Hathor, "lady of Amenta"; Hu; and Sa.

Upon the beam of the scales sits the dog-headed ape which was associated with Tehuti. The god Anubis, jackal-headed, tests the tongue of the balance, the suspending bracket of which is in the form of the feather. The inscription above the head of Anubis reads: -"He who is in the tomb saith, 'I pray thee, O weigher of righteousness, to guide the balance that it may be stablished." On the left of the balance, facing Anubis, stands Ani's "Luck" or "Destiny", Shai, and above is the object called mesxen, which has been described as "a cubit with human head", and which is supposed to be connected with the place of birth. Behind these stand the goddesses Meskhenet and Renenet: Meskhenet presiding over the birth-chamber, and Renenet probably superintending the rearing of children. The name of this goddess is probably connected with the word renen, "to suckle". (M. Pierret identifies her with the goddess of that name who presided over harvests, and is described as the "lady of the offerings of all the gods" having a snake's head, which in some instances is surmounted by the disk, horns and feathers of the goddess Hathor.)

Behind the meskhen is the soul of Ani in the form of a human-headed bird standing on a pylon. On the right of the balance, behind Anubis, stands Tehuti, the scribe of the gods, with his reed-pen and palette containing black and red ink, with which to record the result of the trial. Behind Tehuti stands the female monster Amam, the "Devourer", or Ammit "the eater of the Dead".

A Hymn To Heru

From the Metu Neter text The Death of Heru
"Heru is the savior who was brought to birth,
as light in heaven and sustenance on earth.
Heru in spirit, verily Divine,
who came to turn the water into wine.
Heru who gave his life, and sowed the seed
for men to make the bread of life indeed.
Heru, the comforter, who did descend
 in human fashion as the heavenly friend.
Heru, the word, the founder in youth,
Heru, the fulfiller of the word made truth.
Heru, the Lord and leader in the fight
against the dark powers of the night.
Heru, the sufferer with cross bowed down,
who rose at Easter with his double crown.
Heru the pioneer, who paved the way
of resurrection to the eternal day
Heru triumphant with battle done,
Lord of two worlds, united and made one."•

• Budge. *Prt Em Hru.* (*Egyptian Book of The Dead*).

The Ausarianization of Consciousness Series 1
Metaphysical Keys To the Tree of Life & Oracle Keys to Dis-spelling Illusion
The Spiritual Journey in Unfolding Consciousness

276

Prt Em Hru p. 273

(*Egyptian Book Of The Dead*, E. A. Wallis Budge)
*Modified as first person speaking
fill in your Ren (Name) as you recite

O ye who make perfected souls to enter into the Hall of Heru, may ye cause the perfected soul of Heru _____(fill in your name) victorious {in the Hall of Double Truth}, to enter with you into the house of Heru. May I hear as ye hear; may I see as ye see; may I stand as ye stand; may I sit as ye sit!

O ye who give bread and ale to perfected souls in the Hall of Heru, give ye bread and ale at the two seasons to the soul of Heru_____(fill in your name) who is victorious before all the gods of Abtu, and who is victorious with you.

O ye who open the way and lay open the paths to perfected souls in the Hall of Heru, open ye the way and lay open the paths to the soul of Heru_____(fill in your name) (offerings), {who is triumphant} with you.

May I enter in with a bold heart and may I come forth in peace from the house of Heru. May I not be rejected, may I not be turned back, may I enter in {as I} pleaseth, may I come forth {as I} desireth, and may I be victorious.

May my bidding be done in the house of Heru; may I walk, and may I speak with you, and may I be a glorified soul along with you. I hath not been found wanting there, and the Balance is rid of {my} trial.

Chapter 29
The Chapter of The Heart Not Being Carried Away In The Underworld
p. 313 Papyrus of Ani. *Prt Em Hru*   (*Egyptian Book Of The Dead*, E. A. Wallis Budge)

My heart is with me, and it shall never come to pass that it shall be carried away. I am the lord of hearts, the slayer of the heart. I live in right and in truth, and I have my being therein. I am Heru, a pure heart within a pure body. I live by my word, and my heart doth live. Let not my heart be taken away, let it not be wounded, and may no wounds or gashes be dealt upon me because it hath been taken away from me. May I exist in the body of my father Seb, and in the body of my mother. I have not done evil against the gods; I have not sinned with boasting."

Metaphysical Key To:
Kemetic Neteru and Yoruba Orishas

KEMETIC NETERU   YORUBA ORISHAS

KEMETIC NETERU	YORUBA ORISHAS
AMEN	OLODUMARE
AUSAR	OBATALA
TEHUTI	ORUNMILLA
SEKER	BABALU AYE
MAAT	AJE CHAGULLIA
HERUKHUTI	OGUN
HERU	SHANGO
HET-HERU	OSHUN
SEBEK	ELEGBA
AUSET	YEMAYA

KaAbBa Building The Lighted Temple
The Spiritual B(ARK)

Prayer of Protection
I clothe myself in a robe of Light
Composed of the Love, Wisdom and Power of God.
Not only for my protection
but so that those who see it and come in contact with it
they too are drawn to God and healed.
Forbidden now is the drawing upon my own limited essence
for the Father (Mother) within me doeth the work
Forbidden now is the drawing upon my own limited essence.
(author unknown)

As you do this prayer really see yourself surrounded in Light. This Light (composed of the love, wisdom and power of God) extends just beyond the physical body. As you come into the presence of others or as others come into your presence this Light goes before you and makes intercession for you. Even if someone intended you 'ill' these harmful energies are neutralized by this intervening Light. At the same time, others will see your radiating Light and be reminded of their own Divinity within. Thus, they too are drawn to God and healed. Your practice of protection has a dual force, protecting and uplifting you and others.

This Light also clarifies 'spaces' you enter and protects you from negative thoughtforms that may be present even when 'unoccupied' by someone. When you say 'forbidden is the drawing upon my own limited essence, you recognize that even though you do everything in your power to protect yourself and 'look both ways', you can't even get across the street without Divine intervention. Witness how many adults (not just children) are struck by cars in this single act. It is important to make every effort to 'protect' ourselves (look both ways, lock our doors, etc). In other words, you do what is humanly possible to stay out of harms way. At the same time you do not rely on the limited self alone which is finite, but rely instead upon an *Infinite Source*. Some people are 'foolish' going out in the 'bad weather of negative energies' with no thought, preparation or protection. On the other hand some people are wasteful of their energy and violate The Law of Economy. They are constantly preoccupied, engaging in self protective thought and behavior almost to the point of paranoia. Their fear and lack of time makes them of little use in the service of humanity. Be in accord with the Law of Economy. Do your protective work, expending some thoughtfulness to guard and clear your aura - then-forget about it, allowing the power of the Divine to do the rest. As your practice advances:
1. You will draw a circle of Light around you using your 1st eye
2. You will *know* this Light radiates from within you and already radiates all around you

The Ausarianization of Consciousness Series 1
Metaphysical Keys To the Tree of Life & Oracle Keys to Dis-spelling Illusion
The Spiritual Journey in Unfolding Consciousness

280

MASTERY

"I, at last, have reached the Goal
And solved the mystery of my Soul;
I am that to which I prayed.
That to which I looked for aid;
I am that which I did seek,
I am my own mountain peak;

I upon creation look
As a leaf in my own book;
For I THE ONE, "the many" make,
Of substance which from me I take;
For all is me, there are no two;
Creation is myself, all through;

What I grant unto myself,
I take down from my own shelf,
And give to me-The ONLY ONE-
For I'M the Father and the Son.
When I want, I do but see,
My wishes coming forth in me;
For I'm the Knower, and the Known,
Ruler, Subject, and The Throne;
The "Three in One" is what I am,
Hell itself is but my dam,

Which I did put in my own stream,
When in a nightmare I did dream
"That I was not, THE ONLY ONE,"
Thus by me was pain begun,
Which ran its course till I awoke,
And found that I with me did joke,
So now that I do stand awake,
I, my throne, do wisely take,
And rule my kingdom which is me,
A Master through Eternity."

Retsame

Group Alignment

Upon Entering The Great Inner Council Chamber Hall
Focus your attention within the 1st eye, (between the eyebrows –
Mer/Ajna energy center).

Holding your hands open in a posture of invocation, in-gather the Ra(y)s
of the Sun- 'RA' feeling the Livingness and Luminous Essence of this
Solar Neter/Deity as you do so:
Chant the Hekau RA rolling out the   Rrrrrrraaaaaaaaa sound.

Anoint your Head and Face	Silently or Audibly Affirm	'BA'
In-gather again		
Anoint your Heart	Silently or Audibly Affirm	'AB'
In-gather again		
Anoint your Hands		
In-gather again		
Anoint your Feet	Silently or Audibly Affirm	'KA'

As you enter through the Portal of the Inner Council Chamber Hall
silently or audibly affirm:
'Together and as One with my Group Brothers and Sisters May My
Head, Heart, Hands and Feet Work in Accord with Divine Will and
Purpose Manifesting The Divine Plan.'

Hold this awareness throughout our Group Meditations, Seminar,
Meetings, etc.

Additional Preparation, Purification and Alignment when
Spiritually indicated/desired
Use Sage Smudging - Fire/Earth elements
Use Blessed Water to Aura Cleanse - Water/Air elements

Group Salutation

Ausarian Arm Crossing
Right hand over Right shoulder in lashing action
Silently/Audibly affirm:
'Ba'
'I have disciplined myself'
'I am in accord with Divine Will'

Ausarian Arm Crossing
Left hand over Left shoulder in carrying the Crook action
Left hand holding Crook making digging, climbing action in the Earth
Silently/Audibly affirm:
'Khu'
'I behold the Divinely intended design' 'I carry my treasure/load, I make
offering, I shepherd, I travel the steep ways of Descent & Ascent'

Ausarian Arm Crossing
Right and Left hands holding grasp of Rod of Power action
Silently/Audibly affirm:
'Sekhem'
'I hold the sceptre of Power wisely used to fulfill the Divinely intended
design and manifesting the Divine Plan'

Arms in Ka Posture
Silently/Audibly affirm:
'Ka'
'My Approximating Ka is/as Spirit Ka -The Image and Likeness of
God'
       'I am Ka-Ra-Acter, 'I am Ka-erect-er'

Palms facing forward
'I reflect forth all the Godliness that I am to you my group Brothers & Sisters'
Right closed fist (gavel) striking on top of left closed fist (twice) –sealing
action (*the lub-dub of the heart*)
Silently/Audibly affirm:
Ab
And so it is in (the beat of) my heart

KaAbBa   Building The Lighted Temple
The Spiritual B(ARK)

Ausar in his closed shrine, accompanied by Auset and his four grandsons. From the Papyrus of Ani.

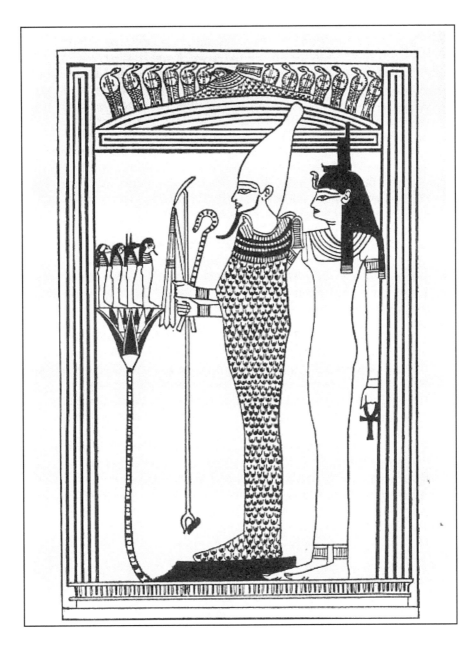

Select Bibliography & Suggested Reading List

Adler, Vera Stanley. *The Initiation of The World.* York Beach, ME: Samuel Weiser, 1972.

African World History Project. Los Angeles, CA: Association for the Study of Classical African Civilizations, 2002.

Amen, Ra Un Nefer. *Metu Neter, V.I & II.* Bronx, NY: Khamit Corp., 1990.

Arquelles, Jose.*The Mayan Factor.* Santa Fe, New Mexico: Bear & Company, 1987.

Arquelles, Jose.*The Surfers of the Zuvuya.* Santa Fe, New Mexico: Bear & Company, 1989.

Ashby, Dr. Muata. *The Ausarian Resurrection.* Miami, FL: Cruzian Mystic Books, 1995.

Barborka, Geofrey. *The Divine Plan.* London, England: Theosophical Publishing House,1964.

Ben-Jochannan,Yosef. *Black Man of The Nile and His Family.* Baltimore, MD: Black Classic Press,1989.

Blavatsky, H.P. (Scribe). *Isis Unveiled, V.I & II.* Pasadena, CA: Theosophical University Press, 1988.

Blavatsky, H.P. (Scribe). *Secret Doctrine, V.I & II.* Theosophical University Press, 1988.

Blavatsky, H.P. *Theosophical Glossary.* Los Angeles, CA: Theosophy Company, 1990.

Bocock Robert. *Freud and Modern Society.* New York, NY: Holmes & Meier, 1978.

Browder, Anthony. *Nile Valley Civilization.* Washington, DC: Institute of Karmic Guidance, 1992.

Budge, E. A. Wallis. *Amulets and Superstitions.* New York, NY: Dover Publications, 1978.

Budge, E. A. Wallis *Prt Em Hru. The Book of Coming Forth By Day.* (Egyptian Book of the Dead). New York, NY: Dover Publications, 1967.

Budge, E. A. Wallis. *Osiris: The Egyptian Religion of Resurrection.* New Hyde Park, NY: University Books, 1961.

Budge, E. A. Wallis. *An Egyptian Hieroglyphic Dictionary, V.I & II.* New York, NY: Dover Publications, 1978.

Budge, E. A. Wallis. *The God of The Egyptians, V.I & II.* New York, NY: Dover Publications, 1969.

Burgoyne, Thomas. *The Light of Egypt. The Science of the Soul and the Stars. V.I & II.* Santa Fe, NM: Sun Publishing, 1980.

Churchward, Albert. *Signs and Symbols of Primordial Man.* Brooklyn, NY: A & B Books, 1903.

Churchward, Albert. *Origin and Evolution of the Human Race.* London: George Allen & Unwin LTD. 1921.

Churchward, Albert. *Origin and Evolution of Primitive Man.* London: George Allen & Company, 1912.

Churchward, Albert. *The Arcana of Freemasonry.* London: George Allen & Unwin LTD, 1922.

De Lubicz, Isha Schwaller. *Her-Bak: Egyptian Initiate.* Rochester, VT: Inner Traditions International, 1967.

De Lubicz, Isha Schwaller. *The Opening of The Way.* New York, NY: Inner Traditions International,1981.

Diop, Cheikh Anta. *African Origin of Civilization: Myth or Reality.* Chicago, IL: Lawrence Hill Books, 1974.

KaAbBa Building The Lighted Temple
The Spiritual B(ARK)

Diop, Cheikh Anta. *Civilization or Barbarism.* Brooklyn, NY: Lawrence Hill Books, 1991.

Hall, Manly P. *Freemasonry of the Ancient Egyptians.* Los Angeles, CA: Philosophical Research Society, 1965.

Heindel, Max. *The Rosicrucian Cosmo-Conception.* Oceanside, CA: Rosicrucian Fellowship, 1988.

Hassan-El, Kashif Malik. The Willie Lynch Letter and The Making of a Slave. Chicago: Lushena Books. 1712, 1999.

Hurtak. J. J. The Book of Knowledge: The Keys of Enoch. Los Gatos, CA: Academy for Future Science, 1973.

Jackon, John. *Introduction to African Civilizations.* Secausus, NJ: Citadel Press, 1970.

Jackon, John. *Man, God and Civilization.* Secausus, NJ: Citadel Press, 1972.

James, George, G. M.. *Stolen Legacy.* San Francisco CA: Julian Richardson Assoc.1954, 1985.

Karenga,. Dr. Malauana. *The 7 Principles of Kwanzaa.* Los Angeles, CA: University of Sankore Press, 1988.

Kuhn, Alvin Boyd. *The Lost Light.* Henry Holt & Company,1931.

Lawlor, Robert. *Voices of The First Day.* Rochester, Vermont: Inner Traditions International, Ltd., 1991.

Ligon, A. Black Knostic Study Teachings of Dr. Ligon. (Private Group Study).

LEVI. *Aquarian Gospel of Jesus The Christ.* Marina Del Rey, CA: DeVorss & Co, 1982.

Mackenzie, Donald.*Egyptian Myths and Legends.* Avenel, NJ: Random House Value, 1980.

Massey, Gerald. *Ancient Egypt, The Light of The World V.I & II.* Baltimore, MD: Black Classic Press, 1992.

Massey, Gerald. *A Book of the Beginnings. V.I & II.* Secaucus, NJ: University Books, 1974.

Mead, G.R.S. *Thrice Greatest Hermes.* York Beach, ME: Samuel Weiser, 2001.

Martin, Tony. *Marcus Garvey.* Dover, MA: The Majority Press, 1986.

National Council For Geocosmic Research, 93rd edition.

Parfitt, Will. *The Living Qabalah.* Longmead: Element Books, 1988.

Ponce, Charles. *Kabbalah.* Wheaton, IL: The Theosophical Publishing House, 1973.

Regardie, Israel. *The Tree of Life.* York Beach, ME: Samuel Weiser, 1972.

Robbins, Michael. *Infinitizing of Selfhood.* Mariposa, CA: University of The Seven Rays, 1997.

Robbins, Michael.*Tapestry of the Gods. V.I & II.* Jersey City Heights, NJ: University of The Seven Rays, 1988.

Satguru Sivaya Subramuniyaswami. *Lemurian Scrolls.* India: Himalayan Academy, 1998.

Three Initiates. *The Kybalion, Hermetic Philosophy* Chicago, IL: Yogi Publication Society, 1940.

Tyberb, Judith. *Sanskrit Keys to the Wisdom Religion.* San Diego, CA: Point Loma, 1976.

Tibetan (scribe, A. Bailey). Twenty-Four Books of Esoteric Philosophy, CD-ROM, New York: Lucis Publishing Company, 1998.

Tibetan (scribe, A. Bailey). *Cosmic Fire. Esoteric Astrology. Esoteric Psychology, V.I & II. Rays And Initiations. Initiations Human and Solar.* See 24 Books as reference source.

Westcott , William Wynn. *Collectanea Hermetica.* York Beach, ME: Samuel Weiser, 1998.

Williams, Chacellor. *The Destruction of Black Civilization.* Chicago, IL: Third World Press, 1987.

CPSIA information can be obtained
at www.ICGtesting.com
Printed in the USA
BVHW07s2054270618
520208BV00011B/145/P